PETER NORBECK

Peter Norbeck

PRAIRIE STATESMAN

by GILBERT COURTLAND FITE

With an Afterword by R. ALTON LEE

SOUTH DAKOTA STATE HISTORICAL SOCIETY PRESS

Pierre, South Dakota

New material © 2005
South Dakota State Historical Society Press
©1948 University of Missouri, Columbia.
First published as Volume 22, no. 2,
The University of Missouri Studies.

This publication is funded, in part, by the Mark Meierhenry family.

Library of Congress Cataloging-in-Publication data
Fite, Gilbert Courtland, 1918–
Peter Norbeck, prairie statesman / by Gilbert Courtland Fite ;
with an afterword by R. Alton Lee.
p. cm.
"First published as vol. 22, no. 2,
The University of Missouri Studies"—T.p. verso.
Originally published: Columbia : Univ. of Missouri, 1948.
Includes bibliographic references and index.
ISBN 0-9749195-0-0
1. Norbeck, Peter, 1870–1936. 2. Legislators—United States—
Biography. 3. United States. Congress. Senate—
Biography. 4. Governors—South Dakota—Biography. 5. South Dakota –
Politics and government. 6. Agriculture and politics—
South Dakota—History—20th century. 7. Businessmen—
South Dakota—Biography. I. Title.
E748.N63F58 2005   978.3'031'092—dc22
[B]   2005042578

Printed in the United States of America

09 08 07 06 05   5 4 3 2 1

FRONTISPIECE: Peter Norbeck, 1921. *Karl Wegner Collection*

For my father and mother

who, with thousands of other

South Dakotans,

farmed and voted for

Peter Norbeck.

CONTENTS

PREFACE

To many South Dakotans the career and personality of Peter Norbeck tower above that of any citizen in the state's history. From 1908 until his death in 1936 Norbeck was continually favored with the highest offices South Dakota could offer. He climbed the political ladder in the traditional manner, being first elected state senator, then lieutenant governor, governor, and United States senator.

Soon after the turn of the century, as he was making a comfortable fortune drilling artesian wells, he joined the progressive Republicans. The progressivism of Theodore Roosevelt became his creed, and to this he was always intensely devoted. During the decade following the first World War, when progressivism was at a low ebb in the Republican party, Norbeck was a constant and persistent worker for the liberalism of his "idol and ideal," Theodore Roosevelt. And when his party definitely rejected progressivism in the 1930s, he supported another liberal, Franklin D. Roosevelt.

Norbeck became the champion of the farmers and his career reflected the agricultural discontent so prevalent in the North-Central states after 1915. When his party bungled the farm problem during the 1920s, he, as United States senator, became an accredited voice of protest, a spokesman of popular rebellion against existing economic conditions in his section. Although he was chiefly concerned with agricultural problems during his long and active political career, he was a man of varied interests.

The purpose of this book is to trace Norbeck's career as it reflected significant trends in recent American history. His public life mirrored such important currents as progressivism, rural unrest and revolt, and isolationism. But perhaps most important of all was his persistent advocacy of extending the powers of state and national governments.

This biography has been made possible through the splendid cooperation of Mrs. Peter Norbeck, Harold Norbeck, the senator's son, and all members of the Norbeck family. Harold Norbeck placed unreservedly at my disposal all of the files containing his father's correspondence.

I am also under obligation to Chester C. Davis, Mrs. Vera Way Marghab, and C. M. C. Woodland for making available materials otherwise unobtainable. To the University of Oklahoma Faculty Research Committee, I am indebted for financial aid.

The following people have given me valuable assistance: Professors William L. Bradshaw, W. Francis English, and the late Jonas Viles, all of the University of Missouri. Carl Coke Rister, my friend and colleague at the University of Oklahoma, also has lent valuable aid.

Most of all I am indebted to Professors Elmer Ellis and Lewis E. Atherton of the University of Missouri, and Professor Herbert S. Schell of the University of South Dakota, for the helpfulness of their broad scholarship and stimulating criticism.

Gilbert C. Fite
Norman, Okla. 1948

INTRODUCTION

Although *Peter Norbeck: Prairie Statesman*, first published in 1948, has been out of print for many years, the impact of Peter Norbeck's compelling ideas and accomplishments has been ongoing in the history of South Dakota. Norbeck's career covered the years from the Progressive Era led by Theodore Roosevelt to the middle of the Great Depression and the administration of another Roosevelt, Franklin Delano. During a span of twenty-eight years, Norbeck held public elective office and labored hard to achieve benefits for the common people. Indeed, for many South Dakotans, the personality and career of Norbeck continue to tower above those of others in the state's history. Ted Hustead, who established Wall Drug Store, once remarked, "I can't think of anyone who matches Governor Norbeck in the impact one individual can have on a state."

Of Swedish-Norwegian heritage, Peter Norbeck was born on 27 August 1870 on his parents' farm in Clay County. After sporadically attending a country school when he was not needed at home, he became a student at the University of Dakota in Vermillion for several short terms. In 1892, he began to drill water wells and soon had a thriving business. He entered politics in 1908 and was elected to the state senate, where he joined with other progressive Republicans and followed the ideals of his political idol, Theodore Roosevelt. Norbeck later served as lieutenant governor, governor, and United States senator, holding political office from 1909 until his death in 1936. He never abandoned the progressive ideals that he developed early in his political career.

Like Thomas Jefferson, Norbeck had a strong strain of agrarianism. He supported legislation that would, in his estimation, lead to a prosperous farm sector and a healthy national economy. Consequently, he became a vigorous and outspoken champion of agriculture and the needs of farmers. In the true progressivism of the time, he believed in extending the powers and services of the state and federal governments to solve economic and other problems. This philosophy was best reflected during his term as governor (1917–1921), when he pushed through legislation that provided for state-owned-and-operated agencies that he believed would aid farmers and other rural residents. These enterprises included a coal mine, hail insurance, a cement plant, and a rural-credits law. In his 1921 message to the legislative session as retiring governor, Norbeck called the rural-credits program, which loaned money directly to farmers at low interest rates, "a great forward step." Although the program was a dismal failure through which the state suffered huge financial losses, it and other failed state enterprises, as well as the successful state cement plant, showed Norbeck's belief in extending the powers of government to serve the people.

As a United States senator in the 1920s, when the conservatives in the Republican party gained control, Norbeck continued to demand a progressive program for farmers that involved direct federal action to raise agricultural prices. In 1932, he campaigned under a slogan that urged South Dakotans to vote for Norbeck and Franklin D. Roosevelt. After election, the senator supported most of Roosevelt's New Deal initiatives.

Beyond his concern for the welfare of agriculture and farmers, Norbeck was a strong and effective advocate of conservation of the state and nation's natural resources, another testimony to his support of what he called Theodore Roosevelt progressivism. The father of Custer State Park, Norbeck worked to get the federal government to preserve other areas in the Black Hills and elsewhere, including Grand Teton National Park. He was also primarily responsible for passage of the Migratory Bird Act of 1929.

Perhaps Norbeck's most lasting achievement was the funding he secured from a depression-era Congress to further the carving of Mount Rushmore. The brilliance of Gutzon Borglum's conception and design, the hard work of mountain carvers, the financial management talents of John Boland, and the help of others would not have been enough to finish the project without the funds that Senator Norbeck wrangled from a skeptical Congress.

While I earlier recognized the people who were so helpful to me in writing my biography of Norbeck, I want to again acknowledge the assistance that Harold Norbeck, the senator's son, gave me. He placed unreservedly at my disposal all of his father's files and correspondence. Without those records, this book could not have been written. The Norbeck collection is now deposited at the archives in the I. D. Weeks Library at the University of South Dakota in Vermillion. I am grateful to Karl Wegner, Norbeck's grandson, for providing a number of family photographs that are included in this book. I also want to express my gratitude to the South Dakota State Historical Society Press and its staff, Nancy Tystad Koupal and Patti Edman, for their help and support. My deepest appreciation goes to my wife, June, who has always been my best supporter and chief counsel.

Gilbert C. Fite
July 2004

CHAPTER I

DAKOTA PIONEER

In April, 1868, a few miles west of the little village of Sioux City, Iowa, a small band of Scandinavian immigrants camped on the banks of the Big Sioux a short distance north of its confluence with the muddy Missouri. A week earlier they had left LaCrosse, Wisconsin, in hopes of finding free and fertile land in Dakota Territory. Their desires seemed close to realization for as far as the eye could see in a northwesterly direction lay the flat rich bottom land, most of which was yet unturned by the homesteader's plow. The leader of these land hungry pioneers was Goran Person Kjostad, known in America as George Norbeck.[1]

George Norbeck had been born in the poor mountainous province of Jemtland, Sweden, in 1836. Because of economic difficulties, however, he left home at the age of eighteen and went to Norway where the prospects for personal gain appeared brighter. He soon settled in Trondheim, finding employment as a carpenter, painter, fisherman and part-time preacher. In 1859 he was converted in a revival meeting sponsored by the Haugeans, a pietist faction in the Lutheran church, and following this experience he spent much time preaching and doing missionary work.[2] While his education was limited to the "three R's," he had a great desire to spread the Christian gospel.

Although he found it easier to make a living in Trondheim than in his native Sweden, Norbeck did not prosper. Like thousands of his compatriots, he longed for greater economic opportunities and seriously considered emigrating to America. A substantial number of Norwegians arrived on American shores even before the Civil War but the number was indeed small when compared to those coming after 1865.[3] The possibility of economic betterment, political discontent of the freeholder class, religious dissatisfaction, and enthusiastic letters from friends already in America were all contributing factors to Norwegian emigration.[4]

The prospect of obtaining free land in the United States was the dominating motive behind Norbeck's decision to emigrate. He was essentially a man of the soil to whom the Homestead Act naturally made a strong appeal. Therefore in the summer of 1866, he and a number of friends left for America.

---

1 John Langbak, *Recollections of Former Times.* Langbak's *Recollections* were partially reprinted in a number of South Dakota newspapers in 1929. The writer used the account in the Platte *Enterprise,* November 29, 1929.

2 Rev. George Norbeck, *Recollections.* These were published as an appendix in the small book by his sons, Peter and George, *The Norbecks of South Dakota* (Privately printed, 1938), p. 86.

3 Theodore C. Blegen, *Norwegian Migration to America, 1825-60* (Northfield, 1931). Carlton C. Qualey, *Norwegian Settlement in the United States* (Northfield, 1938), p. 5.

4 Qualey, *Norwegian Settlement,* p. 8.

After an uneventful voyage they arrived in Milwaukee on July 19 in sweltering heat that made the newcomers long for the comfort of Norway's cool fjords.[5]

Norbeck soon learned that living in a pioneer country was not easy. At the Prairie Spring settlement in Wisconsin, however, he found employment in the wheat fields and later worked as a painter and carpenter. Although these tasks brought him only a limited income, he wrote to friends in Norway that "it would be easier to make a living in America than in Norway," and urged them to make the trip.[6] The following year a number of his acquaintances from around Trondheim came to Wisconsin. Neither Norbeck nor his friends intended to remain day laborers in a country with an abundance of free land, so early in 1868 they inquired about homesteads.

Reports of conditions in Dakota Territory, created in 1861, were available to Norbeck and his friends, since the Norwegian-American press drew attention to that area by publishing letters received from settlers around Vermillion in southeast Dakota.[7] The prospect of obtaining good land there appeared bright.

Norbeck later recalled that since childhood he had desired to own a small farm in his native Jemtland. But he added: "when I saw the large, waving wheat fields [in Wisconsin] I decided that if I should have a farm it should be in America."[8] It was this desire that prompted Norbeck and John Langbak, accompanied by six others, to leave Wisconsin for Dakota Territory in the spring of 1868. The party traveled to Dubuque, Cedar Rapids, and then to Sioux City.[9]

Having crossed the Big Sioux into Dakota, the group pushed northwest on foot over the Missouri river bottom, much of which was covered with water from the heavy spring rains. Only a few sod houses, dug-outs, and frame shacks could be seen but the settlers were busy plowing and planting, and erecting new buildings, and scores of other homesteaders were arriving daily. For about two weeks the men explored the possible locations on which they could file homestead entries. Norbeck finally chose 160 acres of level treeless prairie about eight miles northeast of Vermillion in Clay county.[10]

The exact number of Norwegian and Swedish immigrants in Dakota in 1868 is not known, but in 1870 there were 1559 in a total population of 14,181. Approximately one third of the residents of Clay county had immigrated from the Scandinavian countries.[11] Norbeck, however, was the only person of Swedish ancestry in his immediate neighborhood.[12]

5   Norbeck, *Recollections*, p. 90.
6   Langbak, *Recollections*.
7   Qualey, *Norwegian Settlement*, p. 138.
8   Norbeck, *Recollections,* pp. 92-3.
9   Langbak, *Recollections*.
10   Records of the United States District Land Office, Pierre, South Dakota.
11   *Ninth Census of the United States, 1870,* vol. I, *Population and Social Statistics,* p. 348.
12   August Peterson to Author, September 21, 1944.

Presently Norbeck had exhausted his funds and sought employment so that he could break his land and sow a crop. With a number of friends he went to Sioux City and Omaha where he obtained work, thus adding to his meager amount of cash.[13] This was a fairly common practice among the immigrants of the Middle Border.

But he devoted only part of his time to material pursuits. At every opportunity this earnest apostle preached to the lonely pioneers, both in private homes and in makeshift meeting houses; and shouts of praise and psalms of thanksgiving filled many a meeting place. The fact that he was not ordained made little difference to people hungry for spiritual sustenance and lonely for human companionship. He helped establish the first Lutheran church in Vermillion in 1873.[14] Ordinarily he preached in the Norwegian tongue, but he could also speak and write English. During his stay in Wisconsin, he had attended a country school for two short winter terms.[15]

During the early part of 1869 he continued to labor at various jobs in the vicinity of Sioux City. One of his neighbors broke his land in preparation for the planting season of 1870. While he was in Sioux City, he met Karen Larsen, who had migrated from Trondheim two years earlier. It is believed that Norbeck met her at one of the frequent prayer meetings. On November 4, after a brief courtship, Karen and George were married.[16]

The young couple left immediately by team and wagon for their new home in Clay county. Theirs was indeed a pioneer dwelling. The previous fall Norbeck had dug a cellar and had started to build a frame house over it but this was not finished. The bride and groom moved their few belongings to the cellar where they spent the first year of their married life. It was in this crude abode on August 27, 1870, that their first son, Peter, was born.

Dakota Territory was now booming because of wet years and the coming of a railroad.[17] Pioneer life still held many hardships as the Norbecks and others learned, but in comparison with the middle 1860's conditions were relatively good. Severe drouths which had afflicted this region during the middle sixties had temporarily ceased, the grasshopper plagues had subsided, and the Indian troubles were over. The Dakota Southern railroad was built westward from Sioux City in 1872 into Union, Clay, and Yankton counties, reaching the little village of Yankton early in 1873. With improved marketing conditions and better transportation facilities thousands of immigrants poured into the area and counties north and west of Clay were rapidly populated, to a large extent by Scandinavians.[18]

Peter's boyhood was much like that of other pioneer Scandinavian boys

13 Norbeck, *Recollections*, p. 94.
14 A. T. Andreas, *Historical Atlas of Dakota* (Chicago, 1884), p. 134.
15 Peter and George Norbeck, *The Norbecks of South Dakota*, p. 27.
16 Norbeck family records, Platte, South Dakota.
17 Stephen S. Visher, *The Geography of South Dakota*, State Geological Survey Bulletin, No. 8, (Vermillion, 1918), p. 161.
18 Herbert S. Schell, Unpublished Manuscript (Vermillion, South Dakota).

portrayed so well in Rölvaag's novels, especially *Peder Victorious*.[19] He was kept busy twisting hay for fagots, herding and milking cows, helping care for his younger brothers and sisters, and working at many other tasks.

On this frontier godliness and hard work were regarded as essential virtues. Perhaps Peter had to work a little harder and assume more responsibility than the average boy of his age. If so, it was because he was the oldest of six children and because his father was away from home much of the time on his "missionary journeys." And these trips occurred more and more frequently as Peter grew older. Rev. George Norbeck helped organize numerous Christian societies, visited remote settlers in other Dakota counties, and even traveled to surrounding states. Sometimes Peter accompanied him, but usually he stayed at home and helped sow and harvest the crops of wheat, corn, and barley. In addition, the Norbecks had a small herd of livestock and the combination of stockraising and farming produced an adequate income for the family when judged by pioneer standards.

Self-sufficiency characterized the household. Barley was roasted and ground for "coffee"; mush was a winter evening staple, a dish that young Peter heartily detested. Occasionally supper consisted only of a large bowl of bread and milk placed in the center of the table from which everyone helped himself. Mrs. Norbeck made the children's clothes, some of them from the wool produced on the farm.

Since Peter was needed badly at home, he had little opportunity to attend school. He did manage, however, to spend about three months each winter in the Prairie Center school, a dilapidated and over-crowded structure a mile and a half from his home. There are no records of this school prior to 1884, but in that year he was enrolled. As was the case in most frontier schools, the curriculum was devoted mostly to the "three R's." With fifty-two children crammed in the small schoolhouse conditions were not conducive to learning. The teacher complained to the County Superintendent that attendance was very irregular and that only the best students could make any progress under such conditions. Peter was one of the worst offenders in this respect and was absent forty out of a total of 110 days.[20]

Nonetheless, his father and mother did not neglect him. From them he learned his most significant lessons. As might be expected of a minister's son, he was required to memorize long passages from the Old and New Testaments. Prayer and Bible reading were a daily feature, and often in the evenings Mrs. Norbeck would read to the sleepy children portions of *Pilgrim's Progress* or *Uncle Tom's Cabin*.[21] The only newspaper found in the Norbeck home during those early years was the *Skandinaven*. Best of all, Peter liked to hear his mother tell of Norway's beauties and relate the folklore and early history of the North Countries. Religious training by de-

19 Some people believed that Rölvaag may have received some ideas for his writings from Norbeck's early career, but Norbeck denied this.
20 Teacher's Report, Prairie Center School, District 27, Clay County, 1884-5.
21 Peter and George Norbeck, *The Norbecks of South Dakota*, p. 60.

voted parents, steeped in puritanical practices, was an important element in Peter's early life.

In the summer of 1885 George Norbeck received a "call" to preach for the Franckes congregation in Charles Mix county, 130 miles to the west.[22] Other members of the family were reluctant to leave a well established community and comfortable home to go to an area where pioneer hardships must be faced again. But in April of the next year Rev. and Mrs. Norbeck and the six children, with heavily loaded wagons, began their trek westward.

When they arrived at their new home Peter was almost sixteen. He was a strong robust lad and much of the responsibility for establishing a new home devolved upon him. His first task was to haul lumber for a new house from White Lake, the nearest railroad town about thirty miles away. In usual frontier fashion the neighbors came in and helped build.[23]

Most Charles Mix county boys did not attend school beyond the eighth grade and many did not even complete that. Peter, however, had an intense desire to obtain additional schooling and even as a younger boy he read as much as time and the limited Norbeck library would permit. He read the Bible assiduously along with other religious literature, and, of course, always the *Skandinaven*. E. L. Senn, pioneer school teacher who boarded at the Norbeck home, recalls Peter's eagerness to learn. "Many were the nights," said Senn, "he kept me awake in bed answering his questions."[24] With unconcealed enthusiasm he listened to his father tell about his experiences in the territorial legislature where he served in 1873. But Peter had little reason to expect that he would ever obtain much formal schooling. His lot was that of milking cows, plowing, harvesting, and doing a multitude of other tasks required of a farm boy.

His desire to obtain more education was partially realized, however, when in the fall of 1887 the family somehow managed to save twenty-five dollars to help him attend a term at the University of Dakota near the old family home in Vermillion. In December he left for Vermillion accompanied by a boyhood friend, Hans Gjolme. Upon arrival the two boys obtained board and lodging at a rooming house known as the "Farmers' Home," for which they paid two dollars and fifty cents a week.[25]

It was gross exaggeration to apply the term University to the Dakota school. Having been in operation only five years when Peter and Hans arrived, it was a typical frontier institution. A faculty of twenty-two members expounded the academic offerings to approximately 300 students, only forty of whom were on the collegiate level. The physical plant consisted of one main building and two dormitories. The library had only 1600 volumes and did not contain a single complete set of general encyclopedias![26] Social

22 Norbeck, *Recollections,* p. 98.
23 Peter and George Norbeck, *The Norbecks of South Dakota,* p. 72.
24 E. L. Senn to Author, November 23, 1944.
25 Hans K. Gjolme, in interview with Author, August 18, 1944.
26 *Report to the President of the University of South Dakota,* 1889, p. 26.

life was limited largely to the literary societies and Christian associations. Each morning students were expected to attend chapel services where "brief and simple religious exercises" were held. By act of the legislature no intoxicating liquors could be sold and "no billiard saloons or other questionable resorts" were permitted within three miles of the University grounds.[27]

Peter was among the "Students not in Regular Courses." There is no record to indicate what he studied but it is known that he pursued a physiology course taught by the venerable Lewis Akeley, a subject which the Dean recalls as being very difficult for students on the secondary level.[28] He took active part in classroom discussions and showed special interest in political and economic topics. Peter did not participate in athletics or other extra-curricular activities, and he showed no interest in girls. About the campus he was recognized as a hard worker and attentive student. His mind was thorough rather than facile and his retentive memory held most of the significant facts. In addition to his class work, Peter did odd jobs in and around Vermillion to supplement his meager store of cash.[29]

In the spring of 1888 the two boys returned home and Peter again resumed farming. But after attending the University farm life seemed even less interesting than before. Its isolation and limited opportunities seemed to oppress and hem him in. In the winter of 1889 he returned to Vermillion for a second term and registered for the first year normal course with the intention of preparing to teach school.[30] Little is known about Peter's activities during this session. Neither the incomplete University nor county records reveal whether he received a teacher's certificate. He returned to the farm at the close of the term.

It was partly luck and partly native ability and ambition that gave young Norbeck his first opportunity to do something other than till the soil. The problem of securing an adequate water supply was one of the most serious difficulties confronting pioneers on the Great Plains. West of the ninety-eighth meridian a marked deficiency in rainfall existed, not only endangering growing crops but often proving insufficient even for human and livestock consumption. The shallow wells so common farther east, while by no means non-existent, were relatively few, and the under-ground supply of water was often as much as 300 feet below the surface.[31]

Fortunately, however, an extensive artesian water basin under-laid part of Dakota, the heart of which extended along the James river valley and west to the Missouri. If this could be utilized the water problem for hundreds of farmers would be largely solved. Even windmills, which had been introduced on the Great Plains as a source of power, would be unnecessary because in many places there was sufficient internal pressure to force the water above

27 *Catalogue,* University of Dakota, 1887-8.
28 Dean Lewis Akeley, in interview with Author, August 18, 1944.
29 Hans K. Gjolme, in interview with Author, August 18, 1944.
30 *Catalogue,* University of Dakota, 1888-9.
31 Walter P. Webb, *The Great Plains* (New York, 1931), p. 319 ff.

ground. The provision of cheap and efficient wells was the chief problem in the areas where large quantities of artesian water existed.

The first such well in Dakota Territory was drilled at Yankton in 1881. It was 615 feet deep and cost $2,800.[32] The following year another was drilled at Aberdeen to the depth of 1,060 feet. The success of these and other wells inaugurated a general well-drilling movement which eventually furnished an abundant water supply for thousands of Dakota farmers.

The first artesian wells were very expensive, and few, if any, individual farmers could afford one. In the 1880's and early 1890's the average price for a four to six inch well was $3,000 to $5,000. A few ranchers had them but municipalities were the best patrons of the early well-drillers.[33]

The Norbecks lived in a community where the water problem was serious. The average rainfall was about twenty-one inches, but in many years the amount was much less and insufficient to assure crop production. A critical situation was created when many of the surface wells went dry during the drouths of the late eighties and early nineties. Conditions became so bad in Norbeck's immediate neighborhood that Darlington township took advantage of a legislative act permitting townships to issue bonds up to $20,000 for the purpose of drilling township wells. At a cost of about $4,000 a deep artesian well for common use was drilled in the center of the township.[34]

Many of the wells drilled during that period were used for irrigation purposes, but this method of irrigation proved generally inadequate in spite of success in limited areas. In order to make the expensive drilling machinery available to farmers, counties, in some instances, purchased equipment for the purpose of providing cheap wells. In 1890, for example, Brule county bought three machines at $850 each, but all proved deficient.[35] As yet no one was prepared to do such work at a price which the average farmer could afford.

Here was Peter Norbeck's opportunity. In the summer of 1892 the Reverend Norbeck purchased an old well-drilling machine while visiting friends in Clay county. Farmers there were drilling deep wells and he hoped he might do the same on his Charles Mix county farm. He certainly did not see the well-drilling potentialities that his son realized so soon afterward, but being a practical man he made the purchase and returned home.[36] The outfit was a crude affair which his neighbors probably viewed with considerable skepticism, especially when it was compared to the rigs and machines owned by the large well-drilling firms.

32 Edwin P. Nettleton, *Artesian and Underflow Investigation,* 52 Cong., 1 Sess., Sen Ex. Doc., 41, Pt. 2, p. 65.
33 *Ibid.,* p. 41.
34 E. Frank Peterson, *History of Charles Mix County* (Geddes, South Dakota, 1905), p. 118.
35 Herbert S. Schell, "Drought and Agriculture in Eastern South Dakota During the Eighteen Nineties," *Agricultural History,* 5:162-80 (October, 1931).
36 Enoch Norbeck, in interview with Author, July 11, 1944.

The machine operated on what is known as the jetting principle. The bit was fastened to the end of a drill rod or drill string of hollow wrought iron pipe. Mud pumped down inside the drill string returned to the surface in the hole outside carrying up the cuttings of the drill and also plastering the sides of the hole to prevent caving. The machine dropped the drill rod and operated the pump. As it lifted the drill rod and let it drop, the pump forced water through the hollow pipe and this in turn forced the drillings from the well. The power was furnished by a single horse walking in a circle, although the large rigs used steam power.

Since Norbeck had no intention of operating his newly acquired outfit, he turned it over to his son, Peter. To Peter's father, the search for "a well of water springing up into everlasting life" was more important than tapping one of the richest artesian basins in the country. Peter, on the other hand, displayed an early interest in well-drilling that was sustained throughout his life.

Young Norbeck was not entirely ignorant of well machines and his previous interest in them may partially account for his father's purchase of one. Peter had studied publications distributed by the manufacturers of well-drilling equipment and had observed some rigs in operation. Thus, when he began to remodel the machine, it was not without some previous knowledge. The old outfit was in such a dilapidated condition, however, that it required an almost complete rebuilding to put it in working order. Several parts were missing and had to be supplied from junk piles. In the meantime Peter had interested his cousin, Peter Erickson, in his project and together the young men repaired the machine.

During the hot, dry summer months of 1892 they fixed worn parts and made new ones until the machine appeared ready for the task ahead. With enthusiasm and high hopes of success Peter and his cousin began drilling, but the days stretched into weeks, and finally, after reaching what they considered tremendous depths—between 200 and 300 feet—they abandoned the well. Although they were discouraged, they made a second attempt on a neighbor's farm. And again they drilled a dry hole!

Norbeck's failure to obtain water probably convinced him of the truth of an old story related by Willard D. Johnson, famed geologist. On one of his trips to southwestern Kansas, near the abandoned town of Springfield, Johnson encountered a farmer hauling water from the Cimarron river five miles away. The geologist suggested that water might readily be had by boring, to which the farmer replied: "It is about as far down as it is across."

Although Peter found the subsoil dry in 1892, it was definitely "wet" in another sense. South Dakota was legally "dry," but the law enforcing "wets" were lax and saloons ran wide open. The prohibitionist elements in many localities formed law enforcement leagues to supplement inactive and dilatory officials. Peter, now twenty-two years old, was elected township constable, his first political office. A tough and hardened 220 pound physique was his chief asset as a candidate.

With a dispatch completely unfamiliar to illicit interests in most counties, Peter promptly placed one of the most notorious violators, a Castalia saloon owner, under arrest. But his efforts to enforce the law proved futile. When the saloon keeper was arraigned before a Platte justice, a former Kentuckian who believed the best way to "do away with liquor" was to drink it, he was freed. This ended Peter's activities as a prohibition agent. But it left him with a strong desire to bring about genuine prohibition in South Dakota. On occasions he might take a drink, but he believed in legal prohibition vigorously enforced.[37]

Discouraged over the outcome of his well-drilling attempts, Peter was now uncertain as to what course he should follow. He decided, however, to return to the University. On January 4, 1893, he registered for the winter quarter in what was then known as the sub-freshman department. He studied language and composition, civics, and elementary algebra. During this term he showed a greater interest in some of the popular economic and political questions of the day. There was nothing to show during this period, however, that he might have become infected by rampant Populism. At the end of the term he received grades of B in English, B in Civics, and C in Algebra, indicating that he did a little better than average work.[38] This ended his formal education.

Even though he was intensely interested in his University work, he could not dismiss the well machine from his mind. Having completed the school term, he returned home and in the fall and winter of 1893 and 1894 he and Erickson again made unsuccessful attempts at well-drilling. Following these vain endeavors, Norbeck was ready to return to farming. That fall he hauled wheat twenty-three miles to the railroad and sold it for forty cents a bushel. His hogs brought only three cents a pound and good cows sold for ten to fifteen dollars a head.[39] The Panic of 1893 was horribly real to him. He detested farm life, yet depression farming was more remunerative and less strenuous than drilling dry holes in the ground.

37   E. L. Senn, "Half A Century on Midwest Frontiers," Unpublished Manuscript, Deadwood, South Dakota.
38   Records of the Registrar, University of South Dakota, 1893.
39   Norbeck to C. W. Deer, December 19, 1921. Norbeck MS.

CHAPTER II

THE WELL-DRILLER

As a hot sun burned and shriveled his crops in the summer of 1894, Norbeck's thoughts returned to well-drilling. He felt that his earlier failures to reach water came from not drilling deep enough. His rig drilled a small hole but did not have sufficient power to make the jetting process work at 700 or 800 feet below the surface. His main problem then was to equip his machine with additional power.

He finally decided to incorporate a personally devised gear which would furnish greater force on the drill rod. Then he built a special hoist and eliminated lost motion in other parts of the machine. The United States Patent Office records do not show that his contrivances were ever patented, but they were later used on all his outfits. He had made no great mechanical changes, but had simply perfected principles already in use.

After making these improvements, he and Erickson took the equipment to a distant community. On a farm about ten miles north and one mile west of Mount Vernon in Davison county Norbeck completed his first successful well, the first in a total of over 10,000. It was 420 feet deep and had a two-inch flowing stream.[1] Success at last! As the water spouted forth, anxiety rolled away like fog under a hot July sun.

Other settlers soon heard of his new well and asked him to drill for them. There is no record indicating the number of wells Norbeck drilled in 1894 and 1895 but the next year he reported the completion of ten to the United States Geological Survey.[2]

While there was plenty of demand for wells, the payment was often uncertain, both as to amount and kind. During the first years, he seldom received cash for his services, often accepting almost anything that a farmer had to offer.[3] In spite of this, Norbeck prospered because practically all of his income represented profit. His original investment was small and he furnished most of his own labor by working fourteen to fifteen hours a day. Hard work, a desire to succeed, a certain amount of mechanical ability, and the application of good common sense were largely responsible for his first triumph. This same formula was followed during most of his business career.

After drilling intermittently for two seasons in Davison county, Norbeck returned home in December, 1896. Now on the home place where he and Erickson had failed two years earlier, he drilled a strong flowing 830 foot well.[4]

1 Unnamed newspaper, Norbeck MS.
2 Nelson H. Darton, "New Developments in Well Boring and Irrigation in Eastern South Dakota," *Eighteenth Annual Report of the United States Geological Survey*, Pt. IV, p. 574.
3 Enoch Norbeck, in interview with Author, July 11, 1944. From 1900 to 1945 Enoch Norbeck operated an independent well-drilling firm at Platte.
4 *Ibid.*

This brought "Pete," as everyone called him, a great deal of favorable publicity, and contrary to the Biblical maxim, he was not without honor in his own country. He immediately began receiving requests for wells in Charles Mix and surrounding counties. Never again would he consider returning to the farm. A quiet rural life could not compare with the thrill of bringing in a well which sometimes spouted water one hundred feet in the air.

The year 1896 was an eventful one for Norbeck as well as the nation. For him it meant the completion of almost two years of successful business. The nation witnessed the culmination of the agrarian struggle led by William J. Bryan, against the growing industrialism, fostered by Mark Hanna and William McKinley. Too busy drilling wells, Norbeck took only a perfunctory interest in the presidential election. Bryan carried South Dakota by a very narrow margin, but the young well-driller voted for McKinley. Like many other immigrants of the Middle Border, Peter's father was a staunch Republican. He had not only served in the territorial, but also in the first state legislature. To him the Grand Old Party was the only decent and reliable organization to run the country, a feeling shared by other members of his family. Peter later recalled that while he believed Bryan was a good citizen and did more good than harm, people did not elect him president because they lacked confidence in his judgment and felt his leadership was unsafe.[5]

Business was good. Requests for wells came in ever increasing numbers and this meant more hard work and expansion. In some respects, but in a much smaller way, Norbeck might be compared to Henry Ford. He had something the people wanted, offered it at an opportune time, and charged a price for his product which was within reach of the average Dakota farmer. He drilled wells for about one-fourth the amount charged by most of the out-of-state firms which had previously dominated the field. The average farm well cost from $300 to $500, depending upon the size, depth, and difficulty in drilling. So by setting a price which many could afford he created an unusual demand. In addition, he guaranteed his workmanship. If a Norbeck well proved faulty he promptly drilled another without charge. This policy was very popular.

The cheap, durable well developed by Norbeck had considerable influence on South Dakota's agricultural development. Many farmers, as well as townspeople, had begun to doubt the wisdom of expending large sums on artesian wells. Even though they were expensive, it was common for them to fail after a short period of operation.[6] The situation was entirely changed, however, with the development of the small bore well, adequately cased, which would continue to flow over a long period of years. The smaller

5 Norbeck to Selma Norbeck, February 15, 1926. Norbeck MS.
6 Nelson H. Darton, "Preliminary Report on Artesian Water of a Portion of the Dakotas," *Seventeenth Annual Report of the United States Geological Survey,* Pt. II, p. 691.

well was also more desirable because less water was wasted. Water now could be obtained in areas which otherwise could hardly have been inhabited because of an inadequate water supply.

Since lack of water constituted a retarding factor in the settlement of some portions of South Dakota, the cheap artesian well probably hastened settlement to some degree in limited areas.[7] A much more marked effect, however, was the influence on the price of land. There was a much greater demand for farms which had artesian wells and farmers were willing to pay substantially more for them. In 1905 the United States Department of Agriculture reported that the rise in land values in Edmunds county, South Dakota, "is said to be mostly due to the artesian wells which are now guaranteed to be flowing for $300 to $500."[8] For this development, Norbeck was more responsible than any other single person.

While he was drilling in Davison county, Peter became acquainted with Charles and Oscar Nicholson. They showed a great interest in well-drilling and in 1898 he took them into his business. At the same time they bought a second well rig and put it in operation.

But misfortune soon overtook the growing young partnership. One of South Dakota's frequent prairie fires swept the area west of Geddes, and burned his outfit.[9] This created a serious problem, but it proved to be a blessing in disguise. Ideas for mechanical improvements had been crystalizing in his mind for several months and he felt that now was the time to have a well machine built to his own specifications. After making the necessary financial arrangements he left for Aurora, Illinois, the home of the American Well Works.

Pete was too busy and anxious about the plans for his new machine to pay much attention to the news that Colonel Roosevelt and the Rough Riders were storming San Juan and Kettle Hills near Santiago, Cuba. There is nothing to indicate that he ever considered volunteering for war service in 1898. Roosevelt, the Rough Rider, had little appeal for the Charles Mix county farm youth. It was Roosevelt, the politician, who became his idol.

Pete was then twenty-eight. He was a big man, six feet tall, weighing about 225 pounds. His shoulders were broad and powerful. His thick neck supported a large head with a heavy mop of wavy brown hair and a heavy reddish, not too well kept, mustache covered his upper lip. His feet and hands were large but not ill-proportioned. His reddish complexion might well have given the impression of perpetual embarrassment, and his rustic features were accentuated by a very pronounced Norwegian accent.

In spite of a gawky appearance, Norbeck possessed some engaging traits. A warm smile, a hearty greeting, and firm handshake identified him with the democratic West, and helped him make friends quickly and easily. Be-

7 Visher, *The Geography of South Dakota*, p. 19.
8 *Yearbook of Agriculture*, 1905, p. 526.
9 Enoch Norbeck, in interview with Author, July 11, 1944.

cause of his apparent sincerity and integrity, he gained the confidence of most of those whom he met. Besides creating an impression of solidity and dependability, he possessed a native shrewdness that commanded attention.

It was not conceit or presumptuousness that gave Norbeck complete confidence in his own abilities. He believed that through hard work and full utilization of one's capacities most ordinary problems could be solved. In some ways he may have seemed over-confident and slightly audacious to his less adventurous neighbors. But he never doubted that he could direct the construction of a much better well-drilling machine than any he had thus far used. Here was a bold, aggressive, and ambitious young man.

Upon his arrival at the American Well Works, Norbeck asked to see President Matthew T. Chapman and was ushered into the president's office.[10] An apparently green country youth, dressed in an eleven dollar suit, and with a pronounced Norwegian accent, probably did not immediately inspire confidence. But Norbeck presented his plans for a new artesian well-drilling machine with boldness and self-assurance.

The American Well Works' records reveal that the new machine was completed in the spring of 1899. The company files refer to it as a "Special Well Machine made from Sketch and Instructions." Without the gasoline motor, the outfit cost $270, of which $200 was paid in cash.[11]

The principle of his new machine proved to be but little different from the one constructed on his farm, although it possessed more strength and power and was specifically designed to drill a small bore well. The effect of these improvements may be seen from the fact that in the 1890's other jetting processes for two-inch wells were limited to about 800 feet, but Norbeck was soon drilling to a depth of 1700 or 1800 feet.[12]

For drilling two and three inch artesian wells, this machine was probably the best in the Midwest. By the fall of 1899 his gasoline-powered outfit was reported to have broken all records by drilling a well nearly 800 feet deep in the unprecedented time of four days.[13] This revolutionized artesian well-drilling in the Dakotas. Norbeck's ambition to provide a well within reach of the ordinary Dakota farmer had been achieved.

The Norbeck and Nicholson partnership now became one of the most successful and substantial local business enterprises in the south-central section of the state. After the success of his new machine he remodeled others on the same plan, thus making possible the acceptance of more contracts. The firm drilled over fifty wells in Charles Mix and Brule counties during the latter part of 1899, but as prospects appeared better farther north, Pete and Charles Nicholson moved their machines into Hughes and Sully

10 Norbeck to American Well Works, July 29, 1921. Norbeck MS.
11 M. W. Greene, Traffic Manager of the American Well Works, to Author, August 24, 1944.
12 Norbeck to W. R. Ronald, February 25, 1935. Norbeck MS.
13 Yankton *Press and Dakotan*, April 24, 1896.

counties in 1900. (Oscar Nicholson was no longer a member of the partnership.)

During the five years preceding 1899, Norbeck had devoted himself almost wholly to business. Social life, particularly as it related to girls, had not interested him in the least. But now he sought the society of demure and attractive Lydia Anderson, one of his sister's neighborhood girl friends. Peter had always liked Lydia in a friendly sort of way, but he was bashful around girls. Probably, too, he felt that there was little about him that was outwardly attractive. He showed extreme carelessness about his dress. A necktie was a complete novelty and he shied from white shirts and pressed trousers.

It was not until two other young men in the community began to show Lydia serious attention that Peter was stirred to action. Then with even more cleverness than he had employed against competing well-drillers, he soon out-distanced her other suitors.

On June 7, 1900, they were married at the home of Lydia's sister in Sioux City. It was a simple ceremony, but the occasion demanded that Peter appear at his best. Since he was attired in a well tailored black suit, new black dress shoes, and a gleaming white shirt topped by a scottish plaid silk cravat, few would have recognized him as Pete Norbeck, the well-driller.

Following a wedding trip to Niagara Falls Norbeck and his wife returned to South Dakota and began housekeeping on Peter's homestead.[14] There, life was lonesome for the new bride since she was left alone much of the time. While Norbeck always supplied her with an abundance of material things, he was less thoughtful in showing her the attention and affection that a bride had every right to expect. Probably few men were more devoted to their wives, but often he would be gone two or three weeks at a time on business trips. Sometimes two weeks would pass without Lydia receiving a single letter from him. Writing in his almost illegible hand was too great a trial. It was not until he could employ a secretary that he became a better correspondent.

Norbeck now devoted even more of his boundless energy to business. He purchased competing companies, buying out men who were tired of the well-drilling business, and causing others to leave the field because they could not match his services and prices.[15] P. J. Stacy, an Aberdeen driller was only one of those who felt the death sting of Norbeck's competition. In 1900 he wrote to Norbeck concerning bids on a well for the little village of Mellette, saying: "I have come to the conclusion [because] of the extreme lowness of your bid that you did not understand what they wanted." And in an apparent effort to frighten Norbeck, he said that the town had no

14 Norbeck had filed a homestead entry in 1898.
15 Fred Sletvold to Author, November 15, 1944. Sletvold became manager of Norbeck's North Dakota Company.

money with which to pay for a well. He explained that he could drill wells as cheaply as anyone, but that he had always bid on the profit side.[16]

Here was a man obviously unable to meet Norbeck's sharp competition. Only two months later the Mellette well was completed. "The town is feeling good," wrote Nicholson, "says we are the best well-drillers in the state."[17] Nicholson's Mellette report was echoed from other parts of the state. By 1901 he and Norbeck had fifteen drilling outfits in operation, spelling doom for a number of competing firms.

In the same year they decided to establish their permanent base of operations farther north, in the heart of the artesian basin. Late that summer most of the machines and drilling equipment were moved to Redfield in Spink county. Next they decided to incorporate their business. The charter was granted on September 26, 1901, permitting a capital stock of $60,000. As president of the company, Norbeck owned a majority of the stock and it was evident from the stock's distribution that he did not intend to have his control threatened, not even if the other stockholders pooled their entire voting strength.[18] Charles Nicholson was vice-president and later still he became treasurer.

Norbeck was now thirty-one. For six years he had been pushing forward in business slowly and cautiously. These years saw a diffident, quiet, unworldly farm boy emerge into a vigorous, active, and confident business man. His pride in his business and his reputation found expression in a new ten room house, quite beyond the means of all but a few residents of Redfield. That year demands for wells proved so heavy that he was ordinarily from two to four months behind in his contracts. He was full of hope and faith, and perhaps just a little cocky. He believed that if a man really wanted to get somewhere in life, he could.

The inventory of November 1, 1903, taken just a little more than two years after incorporation, reveals the company's rapid development. The firm's appraisal was $74,001.81. This was a substantial growth in five years, since the assets at the earlier date consisted of one good well rig and a second about ready to be junked. Conditions had been favorable, however, and Norbeck did not muff his opportunities. Although Nicholson was a good business man, especially when it came to soliciting patronage, Norbeck was always the driving force behind the company. By 1903 his personal assets were listed at $43,920.75 and property amounting to over $12,000 was held by Mrs. Norbeck.[19]

By 1905 Norbeck had twenty-five artesian well rigs in operation in South Dakota alone. He labored long hours in his Redfield office at the job of directing an organization which now covered the Dakotas, and one

16 P. J. Stacy to Norbeck, December 10, 1900. Norbeck MS.
17 Oscar Nicholson to Norbeck, February 9, 1901. Norbeck MS.
18 Record of Incorporation filed in the office of the South Dakota Secretary of State, Pierre.
19 Norbeck and Nicholson, Annual Statement, 1904. Norbeck MS.

which operated in parts of Nebraska, Iowa, Minnesota, Wyoming, and Montana. It was not uncommon for him to remain at his office until eleven or twelve o'clock at night.[20]

Although Norbeck and Nicholson had originally drilled mostly in South Dakota, in 1905 they formed the North Dakota Artesian Well Company of Oakes with an authorized capital stock of $40,000. Norbeck owned and controlled the dominant interest as was his custom in his business affairs. As president, he advertised his old policy that every well was guaranteed and that it could be drilled to any depth and size. Between 1905 and 1909 this company alone drilled 710 wells.[21]

The formation of the North Dakota company gave him control over a substantial amount of the drilling business in the Dakotas. With the control of more than forty well-drilling machines, Norbeck tapped the artesian basin at a rate thought impossible ten years before. Outfits outside the Norbeck organization found it increasingly difficult, if not impossible, to meet his competition. There was a certain ruthlessness about him, so characteristic of the business world at that time, and he did not hesitate to drill wells at a loss in order to cause competitors to sell out to him or to meet with disaster.[22]

When the books were balanced on November 1, 1905, Norbeck estimated the total assets of his company at $145,888.67, double the figure for 1903.[23] But, in spite of this, he lamented to his wife that the current year produced only thirty-five per cent profit on his investment!

Well-drilling, however, was never without its problems, and collecting accounts from financially distressed farmers was an ever-present one. No longer was it necessary for him to accept anything the farmer had to offer in payment. While his accounts indicate that he usually extended generous credit, a law suit to collect a bill was not uncommon.[24] And on at least one occasion, he was indicted for having employed men more than the legal eight hours while fulfilling a government contract. Although the court cleared Norbeck and Nicholson on this charge,[25] the average work day for their employees was twelve hours on most jobs. Such events as these, however, only added to the challenge of his business. Actually, labor difficulties were of only minor consequence.

In fact, part of Norbeck's success came from the loyalty of his employees, numbering between fifty and 100, most of whom worked for twenty-five to forty dollars a month. He often hired newly arrived immigrants from Norway and Sweden who looked upon employment at thirty dollars a month, and board and room, as generous. Norbeck warned his foremen to avoid

20 Norbeck to Mrs. Norbeck, December 4, 1905. Norbeck MS.
21 North Dakota Artesian Well Company, Statement to the Stockholders, December 5, 1907. Fred Sletvold to Author, November 15, 1944.
22 Sterling Norbeck to Author, June 18, 1944.
23 Norbeck and Nicholson, Annual Statement, 1907. Norbeck MS.
24 Norbeck to George Winston, April 12, 1909. Norbeck MS.
25 Fargo *Forum and Daily News*, July 13, 1910. Clipping in Norbeck MS.

quarreling with the men and urged them to create good will. "Make them feel cheap and not mad," was his advice. But when the occasion required, he ignored his own counsel and with a violent blast of heavily accented profanity, he would deal with shirking workers.

Around Christmas the "gang" often came to Redfield to "settle up" and for the "annual carousal." Norbeck would write the checks and then the drillers would be off to the nearest saloon. He usually took a social drink with them and went home, but his "boys," many of them less temperate, would keep the sleepy residents awake with their antics far into the early morning hours.[26]

Life was not all well-drilling for Norbeck in those first years of the new century. Prior to 1906 he had no time for study, but about that time he began reading rather extensively in history, philosophy, religion, science, and many special works on the history and folklore of the Scandinavian countries. He began accumulating a library of "heavy" reading, especially for a man of limited schooling. He scarcely ever read a novel or so-called light literature, and during the period when the children were small, he invariably bought books much too advanced for their ages. Men with more formal education were usually surprised at his broad knowledge. Most of all he enjoyed reading the sagas of the Norsemen. He was proud of his heritage and the accounts of his forebears thrilled him. He read slowly but thoroughly and had an uncanny knack of remembering facts.

His interest in religion was deep, but he was not a pious man like his father. He attended church activities irregularly but made substantial gifts, such as to the establishment of Our Saviour's Lutheran Church in Redfield. Mrs. Norbeck, unusually devoted to the church, was sometimes disappointed because her husband was not as interested as she.

In 1905 he had the interesting experience of making the first automobile trip from the Missouri river to the Black Hills. With two friends, Ole Iverson and Oscar Nicholson, he drove a single cylinder, nine-horse power Cadillac across approximately 150 miles of gumbo prairie. Starting at Fort Pierre, a departing point for many stage coaches of earlier days, he steered the chugging "one-lunger" over the unmarked trails.[27] While in the Black Hills, Norbeck became interested in establishing a state game park in Custer county in order to preserve South Dakota's native game, such as the buffalo and antelope, which was rapidly becoming extinct. He believed that the southern part of the Hills with their rolling uplands and rugged mountains would be ideal for a game preserve. He was not a sportsman, and, although he belonged to the Redfield gun club and owned a fine shotgun, he made very little use of it.[28]

He soon became one of the state's most conspicious champions of wild-

26 R. J. Hutchings to Mrs. Peter Norbeck, December 9, 1905. Norbeck MS.
27 Rapid City *Daily Journal,* September 26, 1924.
28 Norbeck to B. A. Williams, February 19, 1925. Norbeck MS.

life conservation. He and other Redfield business men imported some of the first pheasants into the state in 1910.[29]

Early in 1906 Norbeck and Nicholson took another trip, this time to the West Coast and Alaska. Norbeck's conception of Alaska was that of many people in the United States. Envisioning bitter cold, he took an unusually heavy fur coat which caused him some embarrassment when he found that temperatures at Juneau were milder than those at Redfield.[30] Although he did not go farther north than Juneau, he became deeply impressed with the possibility of game preservation in the Territory, a matter with which he later became intimately connected.[31]

Since Norbeck was a man of multiple interests and ambitions, he spent relatively little time with his wife and family. He believed that he had largely done his part when he provided liberally for their needs. Therefore, the task of raising the children, Nellie, Ruth, Harold, and Selma, was left almost entirely to his wife. She was content with this responsibility, since it left her husband free to devote his time and energy to business and other activities.

Prosperity made few changes in Norbeck. He bore affluence soberly and never forgot that his climb to wealth and influence had been by hard work, thrift, and planning. He was in no sense an office-chair well-driller. He knew how to run a well machine better than any of his men and from molten iron he was able to cast almost any part of a well-drill. He often strode unexpectedly into one of his shops and took up the hammer and tongs to beat out a necessary repair part. Whenever a workman was sick or off the job, he would leave his office upstairs and work in the shops below. He believed firmly in hard work which he had learned so well on the Clay and Charles Mix county homesteads.

Since he had forged ahead the hard way, he was suspicious of those who sought another route to success. For instance, in 1905 a Mrs. Herron asked for a loan of $500 to send her son to college. He often received requests of this nature and was usually generous. But he told Mrs. Herron that he would lend only $100. "I really feel as though he could stay out of college a year and earn enough money to finish his education," he explained to Mrs. Norbeck, "or in other words get his the same way as the rest of us have been getting ours."[32]

Norbeck was liberal in expenditures on himself, his family, and his friends. Strict economy in business did not carry over into personal affairs. He liked the good things of life and sought much of what he had missed as a poor boy. When he and Mrs. Norbeck traveled by train they frequently

29 *Annual Report of the South Dakota Game and Fish Department,* 1913, p. 6.

30 Norbeck to unnamed correspondent, February 18, 1906. Norbeck MS.

31 As United States Senator from 1921 to 1936, Norbeck took a leading part in seeking conservation legislation for Alaska.

32 Norbeck to Mrs. Norbeck, December 7, 1905. Norbeck MS.

had a compartment and if they stayed in a large city Norbeck chose the best hotel and would not stay in a second class establishment to save a few dollars. He disliked cheap cars, so he generally bought the more expensive models.

During the first decade of the twentieth century, Norbeck rode along on the seas of prosperity and expansion. He completely dominated his business field, one that had contributed so materially to the development of the Dakotas. Derricks from almost fifty machines, rising like cathedral spires on the Dakota plains, testified to his business success. In 1908 he estimated his company's worth at $206,931.76. With other assets, including 750 acres of land, the total came to well over $300,000.[33] From the ownership of one old well rig to the control of assets of more than $300,000 in ten years was an enviable record, and one not equalled by many other business men in South Dakota.

33 Norbeck and Nicholson, Annual Statement, 1908. Norbeck MS.

CHAPTER III

A WELL-DRILLER ENTERS POLITICS

The years in which Norbeck was busily engaged in establishing and expanding a profitable business coincided with the rise of the progressive movement in American history. Progressivism grew out of unrest and dissatisfaction created by an increasing disparity of wealth, the concentration of business control in the hands of a few financiers, relatively low real wages for labor, and discontent among the farmers, especially in the North-Central states. The concentration of business in the hands of a few, accompanied by the use of economic power to influence, and in many cases, to dominate local, state, and national governments, was becomng a matter of national concern.[1]

These conditions were not new in American life. The Populists had urged strict control of corporations and had advocated the modification of political machinery so that the people might control their government more effectively. But the demands of the so-called radicals like William Peffer, Richard F. Pettigrew, and William Jennings Bryan had gone unheeded.

Soon after the turn of the century muckrakers like Lincoln Steffens and Ida Tarbell scathingly attacked all kinds of graft and corruption in business and government, revealing conditions which awakened a lethargic public to action.[2] A cry arose to wrest city and state governments from the control of big business and to modify the political machinery so that government would be more responsive to public opinion and less amenable to control by special interests. Others demanded humanitarian reforms, while farmers revolted against what they termed big business, represented chiefly by banks, railroads, and grain elevators.

It was in the West and Midwest that the forces of discontent and unrest became articulate and active, and first achieved specific results. In 1902 Oregon, under the leadership of William S. U'Ren, adopted the initiative and referendum, and two years later passed a direct primary law.[3] Soon thereafter in Wisconsin, Governor Robert M. LaFollette brought the railroads under stricter control and forced them to pay heavier taxes. Powerful business interests were driven from influential places in state government; a direct primary law and another regulating lobbying were enacted.[4] Almost simultaneously Governor Joseph W. Folk of Missouri and Albert B. Cummins of Iowa led similar movements. The action of the people in Oregon, Wisconsin, Missouri, and Iowa paralleled the progressive movement in other states.

The enactment of legislation designed to put government more directly

---

1   H. U. Faulkner, *The Quest for Social Justice* (New York, 1937), p. 21 ff.
2   Louis Filler, *Crusaders for American Liberalism* (New York, 1939), p. 55 ff.
3   Fred E. Haynes, *Social Politics in the United States* (New York, 1924),
p. 179.
4   Robert M. LaFollette, *Autobiography* (Madison, 1913), p. 287 ff.

in the hands of the people, to curb the power of special interests and to prevent business from engaging in unfair and monopolistic practices, along with an increasing emphasis on government relief of social and economic distress, illustrate the more important progressive tendencies.

Norbeck was fully aware of these forces which were sweeping the nation. For several years there had been rumblings of discontent in his section. As he had grown to manhood on the Charles Mix county homestead, and as he drilled wells for hundreds of farmers, the sounds were loud and unmistakable. Populist principles which had been received so enthusiastically a decade earlier were still popular.

The principal grievances of the farmers were connected with elevators and grain terminals, railroads, and money-lending agencies. In 1901 an eastern writer noted abuses in wheat grading such as giving a farmer a lower grade than that to which he was actually entitled. In addition, different grades of wheat were mixed for the profit of the elevator, with a consequent loss to the producer, and short weights were common.[5] Farmers were not alone in perceiving these evils. In 1906 the North Dakota Bankers' Association reported that the Minnesota grain terminals were guilty of short weights, unfair gradings, and other dishonest practices.[6]

The farmers bitterly criticized high freight rates and loudly denounced the railroads because of their influence in state legislatures. Speaking to the South Dakota legislature in 1899, Populist Governor Andrew E. Lee said: "The institutions [railroads] have grown so bold and audacious that they appear to believe the state was created for them to plunder."[7] Lee expressed the typical feeling held by many of his rural constituents.

Another problem in the newly developed regions of the Northwest was that of insufficient credit, and of interest rates that often went as high as ten or twelve per cent, and sometimes higher. Norbeck, for instance, received as high as nine per cent on his well-drilling operations.[8]

These conditions created a fertile soil for the growth of progressive principles, especially those designed to regulate big business and to place the government under more popular control. Actually, the progressive movement in South Dakota was little more than the realization of some of the Populist demands by the progressive wing of the Republican party. The similarity between Populism and the progressive movement there is illustrated by the fact that the first piece of legislation recognized as being progressive was enacted under Lee, a Populist. This was a law providing for the

5 Lewis Walker, "Abuses in the Grain Trade of the Northwest," *Annals of the American Academy*, 18:488-90 (November, 1901).

6 Herbert E. Gaston, *The Nonpartisan League* (New York, 1920), p. 73.

7 George M. Smith, *South Dakota, Its History and Its People*, 5 vols. (Chicago, 1915), III, p. 135.

8 Norbeck to J. A. McCartney, January 22, 1903. Norbeck MS.

initiative and referendum, passed in 1898, four years before the Oregon law, and the first in the nation.[9]

Following Lee's two terms as Governor, a conservative Republican, Charles N. Herreid, was elected in 1900. But many Republicans in the state disagreed with Herreid's conservatism and by 1904 a definite movement was under way by a more progressive faction to wrest control of the party machinery from the conservatives. The man largely responsible for inaugurating a real progressive movement in South Dakota was Coe I. Crawford.

Crawford was a native of Iowa. In 1882 he graduated from the University of Iowa Law School and moved to Pierre to establish a practice. In 1892 he was elected attorney-general, and four years later he was a candidate for Congress on the Republican ticket. He was defeated by the fusion of Populists and Democrats and the following year took employment as general counsel in South Dakota for the Northwestern railroad.[10]

In 1904 Crawford resigned his position with the Northwestern and staged a series of meetings in various parts of the state. He advocated a direct primary, direct election of United States senators, and strict regulation of corporations.[11] In general his program was not unlike LaFollette's in Wisconsin and that which progressive leaders in other states were offering.

When he tried to gain control of the state convention in 1904, the conservatives decisively defeated him.[12] A conservative, Samuel H. Elrod, was nominated and elected governor. Although the former railroad attorney was unsuccessful in gaining party control, he had served the progressive cause by drawing the political line between progressives and conservatives. Members of the Republican party must now follow Crawford or remain in the camp of the "Old Guard."

Undaunted, the progressives immediately planned for the election two years hence. In the meantime, they mustered enough strength to initiate a direct primary law, but the legislature, dominated by conservatives, failed to submit it to the people; even though the petitions had twice the required number of signatures.[13]

In spite of a second reverse, the progressives continued active and during 1905 and the early part of 1906, Crawford campaigned throughout the state on behalf of his program. By the time the state Republican convention met in 1906, progressive delegates held a clear majority.[14] As a result, Crawford received the nomination for governor and was elected on a platform praising Theodore Roosevelt and promising to enact laws against railroad

9 Burton E. Tiffany, "The Initiative and Referendum in South Dakota," *South Dakota Historical Collections*, 12:331-66 (1924).
10 *South Dakota Legislative Manual*, 1907, pp. 385-6.
11 Henry L. Speh, "The Progressive Movement in South Dakota, 1902-14," Unpublished Master's Thesis, University of South Dakota, 1936, p. 13.
12 *Ibid.*
13 Tiffany, *The Initiative and Referendum*, p. 360.
14 Speh, "The Progressive Movement in South Dakota," p. 22.

abuses. When the legislature met in January, 1907, the progressives immediately proceeded to carry out their campaign promises. Never before nor afterward did the South Dakota legislature enact so much progressive legislation. Laws were passed regulating lobbying, prohibiting the granting of railroad passes, forbidding corporations to contribute to political campaign funds, requiring the publication of campaign expenditures, authorizing the railroad commission to employ experts to determine the actual value of railroad property, setting the maximum passenger rate at two and one-half cents a mile, and establishing a direct primary law.[15]

Norbeck, the prosperous well-driller, considered these reforms as steps in the right direction. His progressivism did not stem so much from intellectual conviction as from instinct. For a man who had been raised in an atmosphere of conservative Republicanism, and who was rapidly accumulating moderate wealth, Norbeck's progressive alignment may seem like an unnatural relationship. But it must be realized that he was never identified with the moneyed interests in the state. His sympathies, interests, and associations were largely with farmers or people in the small business class whose welfare depended directly upon agricultural prosperity. For that matter, his own financial success closely corresponded with farm prosperity. If lower railroad rates, cheaper interest charges, and government regulation of the grain trade resulted in more prosperous farmers, it also meant more artesian well contracts. It was not selfishness, however, that motivated him to go along with the progressives. He had an inherent sympathy for the common people, especially the farmers, and if beneficial legislation could be passed he favored it. The early hardships of pioneer farm life always remained vivid in his memory.

As a youth, although he had been reared by conservative parents, he was markedly influenced by E. L. Senn, school teacher, prohibitionist, and newspaper publisher. Senn was a progressive long before there was any progressive movement in South Dakota, and as a young man he had boarded at the Norbeck home while teaching school nearby. He often talked to this farm lad about politics, and in the Populist vein he pointed to railroad, grain elevator, and banking abuses. When these things are considered it is not so surprising that Norbeck joined the progressives.

Furthermore, he had never been a conservative in his business activities. People considered him radical when he abandoned well-drilling machinery which had been standard equipment for forty years or more and built a well-drill to suit his own desires and needs. He had never been a man to reject ideas because they were new or different and it was not difficult for him to alter or adjust his thinking to changing economic, social, and political conditions. The status quo was not sacred. Although he had never supported the Populists, that was a matter of indifference, not political conviction.

15 *South Dakota Legislative Manual,* 1907, pp. 378-79.

Before the Crawford-Elrod campaign of 1906, Norbeck showed very little active interest in political matters and the extent of his activity, outside of his brief term as township constable, was limited to membership on the Redfield council. His father, a member of both the territorial and the first state legislatures, warned his son against the wiles of politics and advised him to stick strictly to business. But it was unlike him to remain neutral on any important issue and when the crucial campaign approached, Norbeck threw his influence to Crawford and before final victory he and South Dakota's progressive leader were "dear friends." Crawford called on Norbeck for reports on the Spink county race, referring to him as a "sincere friend who I know can be fully trusted."[16] He told Crawford that he was too occupied to "keep a real close watch" on the political situation but that he believed "everything will be reasonably satisfactory to our side this fall;" a correct prediction.[17] A week later he expressed the hope that Crawford would be a candidate for the United States Senate in 1908 because "I think you would line up with a different crowd when you get to Washington." "You can call on me from time to time for anything which may be in my power to do for you," he concluded.[18]

Far more interested in well-drilling than politics, Norbeck's influence was strictly local in that vital campaign. It was important though in that he became definitely aligned with the progressive cause and intimately acquainted with the leaders. Also he began to grasp some of the issues at stake. Plaintively, he informed Crawford that at least one of the "machine men" from Spink county rode to the state Republican convention in Sioux Falls on a railroad pass![19]

Although Norbeck was not one of South Dakota's first progressives, within two years after the Crawford-Elrod campaign, he was one of the inner circle. Besides Crawford, this progressive nucleus consisted of S. X. Way of Watertown, O. S. Basford of Redfield, John Sutherland of Pierre, E. L. Senn, F. M. Byrne of Faulkton, W. C. Cook of Sioux Falls, Thomas Thorson of Canton, Olaf Eidem of Brookings, A. W. Ewert of Pierre, and R. O. Richards of Huron. With the exception of Ewert and Norbeck, who might be classed in the upper economic brackets, most of the progressive leaders represented the substantial middle class citizen of South Dakota. Way, Basford, Senn, and Cook were all newspaper publishers of average means.

Of this group S. X. Way, publisher of the Watertown *Public Opinion*, probably had the greatest influence on Norbeck. Way had moved to Dakota in 1907, after having been active among the progressive Republicans who brought A. B. Cummins to power in Iowa. Tom Way, his brother, had been one of Cummins' campaign managers in 1904. With this background it

16 Coe I. Crawford to Norbeck, undated, September, 1906. Crawford MS.
17 Norbeck to Crawford, July 30, 1906, Crawford MS.
18 *Ibid.*, August 6, 1906.
19 *Ibid.*

was natural for him to assume a position of leadership among South Da-kota's progressives. By 1908 he and Norbeck had formed a close personal and political friendship which was broken only when Norbeck died twenty-eight years later.

John Kelly, editor of the liberal Sioux City *Tribune* and Way's friend of Iowa days, was another man whose philosophy made a sharp and lasting impact on the well-driller. Way convinced Kelly of Norbeck's worth to the progressive cause and this started another friendship and mutuality of in-terest and purpose that stood the test of many years.[20]

Early in 1908 notice began to be taken of the possibility of Norbeck running for the state senate. His devotion to progressivism was unquestion-ed, and many believed that a prominent business man would substantially strengthen the progressive ticket. In some ways he was admirably fitted to enter politics. His principal assets consisted of a wide acquaintance over the state, a reputation as a successful and honest business man, and financial independence. The latter was very important since most of the progressives were of only modest means.

The perpetuation of progressive principles was uppermost in his mind when he announced his candidacy for the state senate on May 9, 1908. In a form letter sent to the voters of Spink county he stated his reasons for entering the political race:

> I am anxious to do all I can to promote the cause for which the Pro-gressive Republicans stand. I deem it highly important that a pro-gressive legislature be elected so that none of the reform laws enact-ed two years ago may be repealed. It is in my judgment, necessary to go yet further along the same lines. . . . If elected, I shall give my entire time and attention to the duties of the office. I have no politi-cal debts to pay; no political enemies to punish.

He also stated that he favored a "national law protecting depositors in National banks, and a state law protecting the depositors in state banks," a two-cent passenger rate, the regulation of public service corporations, and the election of Coe I. Crawford to the United States Senate.[21]

The techniques of the politician came readily to Norbeck, and soon he was waging a heated battle for the progressive cause in Spink and surround-ing counties. On June 4, four days before the primary, he wrote: "we are putting up the hottest campaign that Spink county ever had."[22] His op-ponent, N. P. Bromley, had the support of the stalwarts, illustrating how the party was becoming bitterly divided at the grass roots level. In assuring his own nomination and working for the entire progressive ticket, he received an ample initiaton in rough-and-tumble politics; and he liked it.

Norbeck's business success proved to be a genuine asset politically as

20 Sioux City (Iowa) *Tribune*, September 30, 1936.
21 Form Letter, Norbeck to the Voters of Spink County, May 9, 1908. Norbeck MS.
22 Norbeck to H. C. Shober, June 4, 1908. Norbeck MS.

the farmers looked upon him as a "practical" man and not a "politician." He appealed especially to rural voters because he was so much like them in appearance and action, and it was with this group that he exerted his greatest influence.[23] Despite the fact that he was worth between $100,000 and $200,000, farmers viewed "Old Pete," as he was affectionately known to many, as one of their own.

It soon appeared that the well-driller had little to learn from the more seasoned politicians. Just before the election, for example, he wrote to Lars Swanson, one of his crew foremen, urging him to have as many of the drilling crews as possible in Redfield on election day. Furthermore, he told Swanson to make sure that crew members had their citizenship papers properly filled out and certified so they could vote. "I am depending on you getting in every crew that possibly can get away," he added.[24] To another friend he stated: "It is absolutely necessary to station a good progressive Republican at the polls, both for the City and for the Township to see that our friends are given proper instructions in marking of the ballots."[25] His electioneering methods brought him the nomination, and in the November election he defeated his Democratic opponent by 700 votes out of a total of approximately 3000.[26]

When Norbeck arrived in Pierre for the legislative session early in January, 1909, South Dakota's new capitol building was almost completed. It was an imposing $600,000 structure, which, from its hilltop, looked majestically out across the mighty Missouri. Norbeck had little difficulty in adapting himself to his new environment. He knew many of the legislators, especially the Scandinavians who usually made up about one-third of the membership. This helped ease the transition from bossing well-drilling crews to the art of legislative procedure. For a newcomer he received good committee appointments, including the chairmanship of the Committee on Railroads.

A statute increasing the number of peremptory challenges allowed the prosecution in criminal cases was the only bill sponsored by Norbeck which became law during his first legislative term. In the fight over the bill's passage, he made a reputation as a formidable opponent on the senate floor. After his spirited fight the Sioux Falls *Daily Argus Leader* remarked:

> The legal representatives of the senate say they will move before the Supreme Court at its next session that Peter Norbeck, the Artesian Well man from Spink County, be admitted to the practice in the courts without any further examination, alone on his showing in the senate yesterday when the bill came to allow the state an equal number of challenges with the defense.[27]

Norbeck was not a good speaker but he made careful preparation before a senate debate. And although his language was often crude, he was level-

23 Norbeck to P. W. Schoonmaker, November 20, 1912. Norbeck MS.
24 Norbeck to Lars J. Swanson, June 4, 1908. Norbeck MS.
25 Norbeck to Mr. Freehoff, June 4, 1908. Norbeck MS.
26 Records of the Spink County Auditor, Redfield, South Dakota.
27 Sioux Falls *Daily Argus Leader*, February 8, 1908.

headed and deliberate and depended on logic to meet his opponent's arguments.

As chairman of the Committee on Railroads, he helped obtain a great deal of regulatory legislation. Among the laws passed were a maximum two cent a mile passenger rate and a measure requiring railroad locomotives to install electric headlights. The railroads were also forced to install certain other safety appliances and to make specified reports to the State Railroad Commission. This legislation put his progressive principles to the fiery test because it resulted in a personal financial loss when the two principal railroads in the state temporarily ceased giving well-drilling contracts to his firm.[28]

This first flurry in politics detracted little in either time or interest from his chief work, well-drilling. The legislative session was limited to sixty days, thus consuming relatively little time in a two year period. In 1908 he began to branch out into fields other than well-drilling. Perhaps after fifteen years the thrill and excitement were wearing off. One new outlet for expansion came from the formation of the Inter-State Surety Company which was soon doing a large bank-bond business. Norbeck was one of the chief stockholders in this $100,000 corporation.[29]

Norbeck also invested some money in the Carrizo Copper company. This was a purely speculative venture fostered by one of his friends, Kent E. Keller, later a United States Congressman from Ava, Illinois, and nourished by the money of those whom Keller could persuade to buy stock in the enterprise. As president of the company, Keller had raised considerable money among friends in South Dakota, Governor R. S. Vessey at one time serving as treasurer of the company. Since Norbeck was not in the habit of throwing his money into ventures of which he knew little or nothing, he accepted Keller's invitation to inspect the mine sites at first hand.

On February 1, 1910, he and Mrs. Norbeck accompanied a party which left for the mines at Ayutla and Jalisco, Mexico. He was much impressed with business possibilities across the Rio Grande and wrote Governor Vessey from Mexico City that he planned to buy another thousand dollars worth of Carrizo stock upon his return home.[30] But he was much less impressed with the Mexican people. Energetic and bustling with activity, he developed an intense dislike for the slow-moving, siesta-taking Mexicans. He took home a life-long contempt for the people south of the border.

Although Keller was an energetic promoter, he was unable to get the mines operating on a profitable basis and by 1912 Norbeck's stock became worthless. The $3,300 which he lost in this venture was philosophically charged off to "experience," but he remarked that it was not worth a single penny more.[31]

28 Norbeck to W. S. McLain, July 29, 1911.
29 Record of Incorporation filed in the office of the South Dakota Secretary of State, Pierre.
30 Norbeck to R. S. Vessey, February 21, 1910. Norbeck MS.
31 Norbeck to George Ellsworth, September 24, 1917. Norbeck MS.

When he returned from Mexico in 1910, the primary campaign was in full swing. The state Republican party was more sharply divided than two years earlier and the situation in South Dakota merely reflected in a small way the division between the same forces on the national level. Senator La-Follette and others were urgently demanding that their party adopt progressive principles and, according to many, President Taft had betrayed the cause of true progressivism. The division was augmented over the fight on the Payne-Aldrich tariff in 1909, when the bill was bitterly attacked by the midwest insurgents, including Crawford.[32]

Norbeck had been only partially right when he predicted that Crawford would "line up with a different crowd in Washington." During the tariff debate he wrote the senator that the tariff was "too high as a general thing and unnecessarily so on many things. . . . This feeling regarding the tariff does not seem to be limited to progressives," he explained. "Some of the stalwarts express themselves just as freely. . . . In my opinion you will not make any mistake by staying with the insurgent Senators. In the opinion of South Dakota people they are about right."[33] But his hopes that Crawford would stand against the tariff to the bitter end were dashed when the Dakota senator weakened and supported the bill when it came from conference committee. He explained his action by saying the South Dakota legislature urged him to stand by schedule K, the woolens schedule.[34] This was the first time that Norbeck showed any unusual interest in the tariff question.

Soon after the tariff fight in Washington, the South Dakota progressives formed the Progressive Republican League of South Dakota. Norbeck became a member of the seven-man resolutions committee, which brought in a statement putting the progressives on record as "unalterably opposed to Cannonism."[35] They were actually protesting Speaker Cannon's conservatism. The liberal faction now had an organization through which they hoped to continue control of the party. Any such objective, however, meant a continuous conflict with the conservatives.

Both factions had a full slate of candidates for the primary of 1910. The stalwarts were led by Congressmen Charles H. Burke and E. W. Martin, and former Governor Elrod. The progressive ticket was headed by Governor Vessey. In a hotly contested campaign, the progressives were successful generally in nominating their state ticket, but Martin and Burke were returned to Washington. Norbeck assumed an active role in the campaign and was re-elected to the state senate with ease.

Upon his arrival in Pierre for his second session, Norbeck turned down

32 Richard C. Baker, *The Tariff Under Roosevelt and Taft* (Hastings, Nebraska, 1941), pp. 76-107.
33 Norbeck to Crawford, May 26, 1909. Crawford MS.
34 Baker, *The Tariff Under Roosevelt and Taft*, p. 100
35 Copy of the Minutes of the Huron Meeting, September 15, 1909. Norbeck MS.

the position of president pro-tempore of the senate.[36] He wanted to be free to concentrate on his legislative objectives. Chances for enacting his program seemed bright because his brother Enoch was a leader in the House of Representatives. Together they made a good legislative team. He introduced bills providing for additional court reforms, a bank guarantee law, state rural credits, a "Blue Sky" statute, an improved primary election law, and a tax commission. Without exception, however, he was unable to push through even one of these bills. In the main they were blocked in the House where, in spite of Enoch's efforts, they were defeated.

In spite of this failure to carry through any substantial part of his legislative program, he worked his way to leadership; so much so, in fact, that his name was prominently mentioned as a gubernatorial candidate. "I learn from a number of newspapers that you are strongly mentioned for Governor," wrote Dr. H. F. Ratte, a prominent progressive. "It would please me if you would give me permission to boost for you. . . . We [progressives] want a candidate in whom the people will have full confidence. A man in whom progressiveness bubbles over in his every action and Pete, believe me, you are that man."[37] A Pennington county committeeman echoed similar expressions of confidence and good will. Norbeck, however, rejected all of these overtures, insisting that he could not leave his business and advising his supporters that he harbored no political ambitions beyond the state senate.[38] But to himself he did not deny that he had political aspirations!

His political influence and activity up to 1911 had been mostly in backstage conferences and through private contact. Repeatedly the progressive campaign strategists tried to persuade him to assist with the speaking engagements, but each time he begged off. He was deeply conscious of his inadequacy as a public speaker. A somewhat shrill voice with poor modulation, and a heavy Norwegian accent, which became more pronounced when he was excited, did not lend themselves to artful public presentations. With a commanding personality which inspired enthusiasm and created confidence, he realized that his best political results came from personal contact.

In the summer of 1911 his friend Kent Keller convinced him that they should spend a month in Chicago attending a traveling speech institute operated by Dr. S. S. Curry of Boston. Keller advised his Dakota friend that private voice instruction would help materially in overcoming his speech defects and that an improved speaking manner would be necessary before the next presidential campaign. "You are going to orate in that campaign *much* and do it *gracefully* too," Keller insisted.[39]

Norbeck left for Chicago on August 6 and enjoyed his four week stay

36 Norbeck to Mrs. Norbeck, January 4, 1911. Norbeck MS.
37 Dr. H. F. Ratte to Norbeck, April 6, 1911. Norbeck MS.
38 Norbeck to E. L. Senn, August 16, 1911. Norbeck MS.
39 Kent E. Keller to Norbeck, July 20, 1911. Norbeck MS.

there. His acquaintance with Dr. Curry started an intimate friendship that lasted for many years. He worked hard but progress was slow and his speech improvement was slight.

Norbeck had scarcely returned home from his second term in the legislature when an interesting and heated local election occurred. Again it was the old question of prohibition. Nicholson was running for alderman and his election meant a victory for the "drys" in Redfield. Norbeck and Nicholson wanted Redfield genuinely dry as a protection for their employees who sometimes spent money for whiskey that should have gone for groceries. Furthermore it was unsafe to have a workman around a well rig who was under the influence of liquor. A lively battle ensued with no holds barred and only a few days before election the result was still much in doubt. But the well-driller knew how to win elections. The day before the voting, he called in several well-drilling crews who voted for Nicholson the following day. This was enough to carry the issue by a very slight margin. Norbeck and Nicholson "came in for all kinds of cussing," because they herded their "damned Swedes" to the polls, but another victory, however minor, had been achieved.[40] Norbeck was learning his politics well and the taste sharpened his appetite for more.

CHAPTER IV

A ROOSEVELT REPUBLICAN

"Well, I like it alright, I think I will announce my candidacy for a third term when I get home. I guess we had better close out the well business and put our time to politics. There ain't so much money in it but there is surely less grief and more fun."[1] Thus Norbeck wrote to his associate Nicholson prior to adjournment of the 1911 legislature. The "political bug" had bitten him. He was not only enjoying local politics but he was taking a lively interest in the new and rapidly unfolding national developments.

The feeling of LaFollette and many of his supporters that Taft should not receive the Republican presidential nomination in 1912, and that a more dependable progressive should be selected, brought on January 21, 1911, the formation of the National Republican Progressive League. Its stated purposes were to promote "popular government and progressive legislation."[2] When the National League asked that corresponding state organizations be formed, the South Dakota progressives immediately responded. Although they had created a state league almost two years before, they were anxious to work in close harmony with the new national organization. Norbeck, Senn, Vessey, Basford, and other leading progressives signed a call for a meeting to be held in Pierre on February 25.[3] W. H. Roddle, a well-known progressive from Brookings, was elected president of the new league.

Within a short time Roddle was forced to resign and the question of electing a new league president faced the group. The progressives needed an experienced leader, a man with tact and good judgment who would not unnecessarily alienate conservatives, and one in whom the rank and file of the progressive voters had confidence; after looking over the possible candidates, they decided on Norbeck. He accepted reluctantly.[4]

Upon becoming president of the league, Norbeck put intense energy into the work, much of which was directed toward securing LaFollette's nomination for president. Since 1909, he had displayed a warm personal feeling for the Wisconsin Senator. During the tariff fight he had sent him a flattering congratulatory message, saying: "if there were a few more like you in the United States things would soon be different. We have been trying to fight along the same line in this state, as you have done, but we have not got very far yet."[5] Moreover, he had subscribed for LaFollette's

---

1 Norbeck to C. L. Nicholson, February 14, 1911. Norbeck MS.
2 Robert M. LaFollette, *Autobiography*, pp. 494-96.
3 Form Letter, Norbeck MS.
4 John Sutherland and O. S. Basford to Norbeck, May 13, 1911. Norbeck MS.
5 Norbeck to Robert M. LaFollette, July 27, 1910. Norbeck MS.

Weekly Magazine even before publication began in 1909, and he promised other subscribers in South Dakota.[6]

Norbeck's outspoken support of LaFollette contributed to an open fight between the South Dakota progressives and conservatives over the selection of delegates to the national convention in 1912. John Sutherland told him that some Republicans wanted to unite "for the good of the party." But Norbeck replied: "I am more anxious to see something done for the good of the people than for the good of the party. I think they [those who wanted to unite the party] can best serve the interests of the Republican party by having the party right on public questions."[7]

When LaFollette began an active campaign for the presidential nomination in July, 1911, the South Dakota progressives came eagerly to his support. Previously, Norbeck had expressed the opinion that South Dakota would go for LaFollette "if the lines were fairly drawn between him and President Taft."[8]

In September he called a meeting of the progressives at Mitchell to organize the state for the coming campaign. The day before the gathering he wrote: "the Republicans in South Dakota should nominate LaFollette even if it [is] very apparent that Taft will later get the nomination." Believing that the West and Northwest were the most progressive parts of the nation, he argued that it was the duty of those sections to express their sentiments vigorously.[9] The dominant expression at the Mitchell meeting agreed with Norbeck and definitely favored LaFollette as the Republican candidate.[10]

In reply to a letter from Walter L. Houser, LaFollette's campaign manager, Norbeck asserted: "There is in my judgment no reasonable doubt about LaFollette . . . carrying this state in the next primaries by a good majority. LaFollette's strength lies . . . in the confidence the people have in him, based on their knowledge of his work in Madison and Washington."[11]

Early in October Houser invited him to attend a progressive conference in Chicago about the middle of the month, adding that his "counsel and familiarity with the issues and conditions in the country would be of great assistance."[12] Norbeck accepted, probably feeling quite flattered. At the three day meeting starting on October 16, representatives from thirty states were present.[13] The South Dakota delegation, including Senator Crawford and Norbeck, supported a resolution endorsing LaFollette for the Republican presidential nomination.

6   *Ibid.*, November 13, 1908.
7   Norbeck to John Sutherland, October 14, 1911. Norbeck MS.
8   Norbeck to O. S. Basford, May 13, 1911. Norbeck MS.
9   Norbeck to Thomas Sterling, September 27, 1911. Norbeck MS.
10 Mitchell *Daily Republican,* September 29, 1911.
11 Norbeck to W. L. Houser, October 5, 1911. Norbeck MS.
12 W. L. Houser to Norbeck, October 2, 1911. Norbeck MS.
13 LaFollette, *Autobiography,* p. 532.

After spending several days in Chicago, Norbeck went to Aviston, Illinois, to look after his business interests. The failure of the Carrizo Copper company had not dampened his enthusiasm for new business ventures. Again it was his friend Kent Keller who urged him to broaden his activities; this time it was oil. One of the fields being developed around 1910 was located in southern Illinois, about forty miles east of St. Louis. After he and Keller had investigated the opportunities, Norbeck began drilling there with one of his large rigs in the fall of 1911. He had earlier incorporated the Siva Oil company through which he leased about 1000 acres of land near Aviston. This was a closed corporation with Norbeck as president.

During his absence, South Dakota's progressives, led by John Sutherland and O. S. Basford, staged an aggressive campaign for LaFollette. Norbeck returned to South Dakota on December 28 in order to be with his family for a few days and also to survey personally the political situation. Before leaving again for the oil fields he attended a state-wide progressive rally at Sioux Falls. The convention enthusiastically endorsed LaFollette for president and bitterly denounced Taft and his administration.[14] "The boys went home with a determination to win and with the feeling that they would succeed in carrying the state for LaFollette at the June Primaries," wrote Norbeck, and he added: "I will soon be back from St. Louis so I will be able to do my share of the fighting."[15]

In choosing a campaign slogan the progressives seemed to anticipate a possible desertion of LaFollette, although his supporters dominated the meeting. The motto "LaFollette Roosevelt Progressive Republican Principles," was selected in order to unite all progressives, especially to hold those in line who were demanding Roosevelt's candidacy. This left the way open to support Roosevelt in case he should become a candidate later. The Colonel's name was not prominently mentioned at the Sioux Falls meeting, but there was a strong undercurrent of Roosevelt sentiment only waiting for leadership! Governor Vessey, although he was working for LaFollette, let it be known that he was ready to support the Colonel.[16]

The first oil well had been completed by the time Norbeck returned to Aviston. That he had the spirit of a true wildcatter is seen in his remark, "while we did not make a paying well out of it, we had a splendid showing. It certainly looks better than it ever did before."[17] A short time later he expressed even more optimism: "we are well pleased with the outlook here and if we did not have such heavy investments in South Dakota we would be greatly tempted to transfer our operations."[18] But his enthusiasm was premature.

14 Sioux Falls *Daily Argus Leader*, January 12, 1912.
15 Norbeck to A. H. Wheaton, January 20, 1912. Norbeck MS.
16 George E. Mowry, *Theodore Roosevelt and the Progressive Movement*, (Madison, Wisconsin, 1946) p. 206.
17 Norbeck to W. A. Carlson, February 28, 1912. Norbeck MS.
18 Norbeck to O. S. Basford, March 6, 1912. Norbeck MS.

With a good but unprofitable showing from the first well, others were started and more land was leased. A number of friends wanted to "get in on the deal," but Norbeck was not encouraging. "We may lose every cent we put in," he told them.[19] He was never under any illusions as to wildcat oil ventures and explained to a friend that "we are not going in any heavier than we can afford to lose what we are putting in. That is the only safe plan in this kind of business."[20] It was well that he assumed that attitude because he lost several thousand dollars when none of his wells proved profitable. He accepted his losses in a sporting way and credited his failure to the "lack of ordinary luck."[21]

By the time he returned to South Dakota in March the political picture had undergone a profound change. Roosevelt announced that he would seek the Republican nomination on a progressive platform. Since 1910 he had been espousing policies upon which he previously had been silent, policies which seemed to leave no doubt about his progressiveness.

A great many progressives throughout the nation believed that the Colonel would make a much stronger candidate than LaFollette and a large number of them were in South Dakota, normally a LaFollette stronghold. The position of South Dakota's progressives was not an easy one. Should they abide by their endorsement of LaFollette given in Chicago, and later at Sioux Falls, or should they support Roosevelt, whose popularity definitely outshone that of the Wisconsin Senator? Various primary election results were giving added evidence of Roosevelt's mounting popularity. But South Dakota progressives, as well as those of the entire Midwest, divided, one group supporting Roosevelt, the other LaFollette.

Norbeck was slow in arriving at a decision. In April, 1912, long after many of his progressive friends had left the LaFollette camp, he wrote to Houser: "I am a LaFollette man and want to see him President, but among the progressive voters in the county, [sic] is quite a large percentage who are Roosevelt men and there is another very large element who will support LaFollette or Theodore Roosevelt, whichever they think has the best show of winning against Taft, whom they cannot support."[22] This was a common feeling among many progressives, not only locally but in the entire Midwest. It also indicated that Norbeck might swing to Roosevelt. But he was under rather a definite committment to LaFollette, since in an earlier letter to Houser he asserted that "I am at your service from now on, until the campaign closes."[23]

By May a majority of the state's progressives had concluded that Roosevelt had the best chance to win and they flocked to his standard. The Huron *Daily Huronite,* a conservative paper, chided the progressives

19 Norbeck to Dr. S. S. Curry, March 30, 1912. Norbeck MS.
20 Norbeck to Jacob Johnson, October 21, 1911. Norbeck MS.
21 Norbeck to Dr. S. S. Curry, June 11, 1913. Norbeck MS.
22 Norbeck to W. L. Houser, April 15, 1912. Norbeck MS.
23 *Ibid.,* April 5, 1912.

for their lack of consistency and stated that when they saw LaFollette could not win they "got on the Roosevelt bandwagon."[24] It was later charged by the Taft Republicans that Sutherland, LaFollette's state campaign manager, when stung by the "Roosevelt bee," unceremoniously dumped a large consignment of LaFollette literature into the Missouri river![25]

At first Norbeck showed signs of regret at this trend, but he had to admit the stampede to Roosevelt. In February, even before Roosevelt formally announced his candidacy, he attended a Governors' conference with Governor Byrne and there he found the LaFollette movement seriously declining. To his friend Dr. Ratte, he wrote: "I honestly believe the best we can do at this time is to elect Roosevelt and while I do not think him as good a progressive as LaFollette, I do believe we can elect him over Taft—and thereby hold the progressives together to do efficient battle in 1916."[26] "I feel that he is probably after all the only reformer we have in the United States who is consistent and aggressive enough to bring about results," he wrote of LaFollette a short while later. "It is sad to think of Crawford's administration in South Dakota as compared with the first LaFollette administration in Wisconsin and I am afraid even a comparison would be to Roosevelt's disadvantage. He would have accepted half that the bosses offered and started a Hurrah."[27]

But having made his decision, Norbeck became a most vociferous Roosevelt supporter. Even though he did not believe that Roosevelt was as good a progressive as LaFollette, it is perhaps not surprising that he threw his support to the former president. He held the previous Roosevelt administrations in high esteem and agreed with his "practical" middle-of-the-road policies. Furthermore, he admired the Rough Rider's energy, ambition, versatility, and aggressiveness. These were characteristic of the well-driller.

In June he attended the Republican national convention in Chicago and he described his five days there as "pretty lively."[28] Like thousands of others, he firmly believed that Roosevelt was, as he put it, "beaten by fraud." He did not openly favor a third party movement, however. "I did not commit myself to the independent Roosevelt candidacy," he said, "nor did our delegation do so, but they are friendly to the proposition and will no doubt support the independent progressive ticket this fall."[29]

When S. X. Way, South Dakota's national Republican committeeman and Norbeck's political adviser, was approached by the Roosevelt men, he replied: "No I won't bolt, but . . . I'll go back to South Dakota and arrange for a slate of Regular Republican Presidential electors pledged to vote for

24 Huron *Daily Huronite*, May 30, 1912.
25 Pierre *Daily Capital Journal*, October 9, 1912.
26 Norbeck to H. F. Ratte, February 18, 1912. Norbeck MS.
27 Norbeck to Thomas Thorson, March 2, 1912. Norbeck MS.
28 Norbeck to Enoch Norbeck, June 25, 1912. Norbeck MS.
29 *Ibid.*

Roosevelt instead of William Howard Taft. If you fellows are smart you'll do the same thing, start a third party and you'll just split the Republican vote and elect a Democratic president."[30] The South Dakota progressives returned home to follow his advice.

When the Republican state convention met on July 2 it was controlled by the progressives who refused to pledge the electoral votes to Taft, the regular Republican nominee. This meant there would be no Taft electors on the ballot, thus no way to vote for him in November. One must either vote for Roosevelt, who was formally nominated as the progressive candidate the following month, or Woodrow Wilson.

Under the Roosevelt spell, exhilarated by the thought of being soldiers at Armageddon, nothing seemed to matter but a Roosevelt victory. Fairness and political ethics were secondary if they interfered with the paramount object. Norbeck and the other South Dakota Bull Moosers worked with a zeal and enthusiasm unequalled in any previous campaign. Infected by the Rooseveltian spirit, Norbeck truly believed that he was battling for the Lord and political righteousness!

The progressives' tactics actually meant that thousands of Taft voters were disfranchised and if their procedure was not outright unethical, it was certainly unusual. In Nebraska, for instance, the Supreme Court ordered that the Taft electors must be listed on the ballot as "Republicans" and the Roosevelt men as "progressives."[31] William Allen White, one of the leading Bull Moosers in Kansas, explained to Roosevelt that it would be dishonest and indecent to disfranchise the Taft voters by forcing Roosevelt's name in the regular Republican column. Consequently the Rooseveltian electors in Kansas were placed on the ballot as "progressives."[32] But the South Dakota progressives worked with a vengeance.

John Sutherland explained: "We take the ground that Mr. Taft did not receive the legal nomination at the hands of the Republicans; that he is not in law or morals entitled to the vote of our electors, and we do not intend to give it to him. . . ."[33] It was somewhat unusual for a state organization to judge the legality of the national convention proceedings. "This is an outrage which our primary election law and the political free-booters have forced upon the people," complained the Pierre *Daily Capital Journal* bitterly. "The friends of Mr. Taft can do nothing but take revenge by voting for Johnson [Ed Johnson, Democrat] for Governor."[34] In any event S. X. Way had kept his promise and South Dakota went for Roosevelt by about 10,000 majority.

Norbeck was active during the entire campaign, contributing about

30 M. B. Ronald, "The Dakota Twins," *The Atlantic Monthly,* 158:316 (September, 1936).
31 Pierre *Daily Capital Journal,* October 22, 1912.
32 William Allen White, *Autobiography* (New York, 1946), p. 492.
33 John Sutherland to Coe I. Crawford, July 29, 1912. Crawford MS.
34 Pierre *Daily Capital Journal,* September 27, 1912.

$1000 in addition to making loans to progressive newspapers and signing notes so some of the progressive candidates could borrow money.[35] His own election as a third term senator proved to be the closest he had ever experienced. He had no opposition in the primaries, but the Democrats ran a strong man against him in the fall. His opponent, R. C. Styles, not only received Democratic support but the Taft men who sought revenge because of Norbeck's part in disfranchising Taft's supporters also backed him.[36] The conservatives carried two precincts against him in Redfield but the farmers again gave him a strong endorsement. To Norbeck this was especially flattering, since Styles was a farmer, an old settler in the community, and a man of good reputation.

In 1912 Norbeck spent very little time at home. Business trips to Illinois and campaign excursions scarcely allowed him to see his family. This was not unusual, however, and Mrs. Norbeck was resigned to meeting the home responsibilities. Because of frequent and lengthy absences from Redfield, he hired his brother, George, to take over the active management of his business. George had a small well-drilling business at Aberdeen before he started to supervise the Norbeck and Nicholson machines. This left Peter free for increased political responsibilities.

Having spent two terms in the senate, Norbeck returned to Pierre an experienced legislator in January, 1913. He again presented his program which had been defeated at the previous session. One of his bills provided for tax exemptions on farm buildings and certain classes of town dwellings; another would provide a state rural credit system; a third proposed a "Blue Sky" law; and the fourth called for a tax commission to replace the old Board of Equalization and Assessment.[37] Only in the latter instance did he succeed.

The campaign of 1912 and his work in the legislature in 1913 established Norbeck as one of the state's most powerful progressives. He also had become acquainted, not intimately, but on a working basis, with some of the national leaders. LaFollette, Beveridge, Henry Allen and others had campaigned in the state and Norbeck at one time or another had worked with them. He attained that position of leadership because of his devotion to the progressive cause and because of his astuteness. Furthermore, since he was consistently a heavy party supporter, there is no doubt but that his financial position added to his prestige in progressive ranks. Little was done among the progressives without first consulting him, and along with this increasing influence came demands that he seek a more important office.

Several friends strongly urged him to seek the governorship. P. W. Peterson, a Clay county leader, told him: "if you will come out in the field we will nominate and elect you."[38] "My business would have to be sacrificed

35 Norbeck to S. S. Curry, December 13, 1912. Norbeck MS.
36 *Ibid.*
37 *South Dakota Senate Journal*, 1913.
38 P. W. Peterson to Norbeck, June 3, 1911. Norbeck MS.

if I should put my time wholly to politics," Norbeck replied. "I have worked so hard to get the business built up that I do not feel like letting it go in that way. Not for the present at least."[39] While he temporarily turned aside the advice of his friends, he did not dismiss the possibility of seeking a higher office at some future time.

Upon his return home at the close of the legislative session, he was tired and disgusted with politics. His powerful physique was beginning to show the terrific strain of a hard and irregular life. He developed a bad case of inflammatory rheumatism during his stay in Pierre and after returning home he was confined to the house for over a month, much of the time in bed. With time to think over his political career he concluded that "progress" was slow and that his accomplishments were meager. Poor business prospects added to his discouragement. Drought and high hot winds during the spring, caused farmers to spend less for improvements, including wells. In addition, collections were almost impossible. He estimated that farm values in the James river valley had dropped twenty per cent, and even more farther west. His company had little more than held its own since 1910, and in 1913 its assets, excluding the partnership rigs, totaled only about $177,000.[40] Both 1910 and 1911 had been poor business years because of a severe drouth and farm depression. In the latter year he wrote: "everything is bum this year. There is [sic] not over one-third of the rigs running."[41] Moreover, losses sustained in the Illinois oil fields amounted to approximately $25,000.

One bright spot, however, was Oscar Nicholson's optimistic reports of oil possibilities in Wyoming. After the Illinois fiasco Norbeck and Nicholson moved one of their outfits West and did custom drilling at a profitable figure. As Nicholson's reports arrived, Norbeck decided to forget politics temporarily and go to Wyoming. He hired Professor J. E. Todd, South Dakota State Geologist, and together they spent a month investigating the state's oil sands. He did not hesitate to make another gamble in spite of his Illinois experience. By July, 1913, he announced that he would follow the oil game "for the next four or five years," adding, "it has immense possibilities and if handled conservatively on the right plan, looks like a fairly sure thing."[42]

An important political question awaited him when he returned from Wyoming in August. Should he accept the nomination for lieutenant governor which many newspapers and personal friends were urging him to do? Obviously he was attracted toward politics, but his first reaction was to follow his father's advice and stick to business. He wrote to Gjolme: "there is not only more profit but more pleasure in attending to business than

39 Norbeck to P. W. Peterson, June 7, 1911. Norbeck MS.
40 Norbeck and Nicholson, Annual Statement, 1913. Norbeck MS.
41 Norbeck to J. R. Hutter, May 19, 1911. Norbeck MS.
42 Norbeck to P. H. O'Neill, July 15, 1913. Norbeck MS.

mixing in politics. Of course, the campaigns are interesting . . . but the worry is too much and the results too few."[43] A short time later he said that he "had no intention of running for any office. . . . I want to stay home and attend to business now and will if they will only leave me alone."[44]

But his friends continued to insist that he enter the race. Both Governor Byrne and state treasurer Ewert declared that his candidacy would "strengthen the [progressive] ticket."[45] On December 12, obviously in the throes of indecision, he replied: "I think I will let this thing take its natural course." The following day, however, he sent word to Byrne saying he would accept the nomination if it came from popular demand, but he added: "I will not seek the office."[46]

This was a most important decision. He knew that if he accepted the nomination and was elected he would in all probability be the next candidate for governor and then for United States Senator. That was the course of the "apostolic succession," as it often worked out in South Dakota politics. While it did not mean the entire abandonment of business activities, it did imply that thereafter politics would be his chief interest. Perhaps the fact that he hired his brother to manage his company anticipated this course.

In both the primary and general elections of 1914 he ran approximately 3000 votes ahead of Governor Byrne. For a lieutenant governor to garner more votes than the gubernatorial candidate was unusual and was adequate testimony to his popularity with the rank and file of the voters.[47]

His new position suited neither his desire nor disposition. He liked the senate floor and secret conferences, not the position of a presiding officer. He did a great deal to restore party harmony, however, because, as one editor stated, "of his fairness and breadth of mind."[48] The feeling in the Senate is fine, he wrote, "Stalwarts and Democrats who have always fought me are really friendly this time."[49]

As lieutenant governor he played an important role in enacting one of his favorite measures, a law designed to protect deposits in all banks operating under state charters. He felt that this was one of his greatest achievements.

Although Norbeck's legislative accomplishments were modest, the period from 1908 to 1915 was one of the most important in his long political career. It was then that he learned the politicians' techniques and laid the foundation for his political organization which lasted for almost a quarter of a century. His vote-getting power rested on two common principles; organization and personal popularity. His business had taken him into

43 Norbeck to Hans K. Gjolme, July 14, 1913. Norbeck MS.
44 Norbeck to E. L. Senn, September 2, 1913. Norbeck MS.
45 F. M. Byrne to Norbeck, December 11, 1913. Norbeck MS.
46 Norbeck to Bryne, December 13, 1913. Norbeck MS.
47 *South Dakota Legislative Manual*, 1915, p. 398.
48 Mitchell *Daily Republican*, March 19, 1916.
49 Norbeck to R. J. Hutchings, February 5, 1915. Norbeck MS.

almost every community in the state with the result that he had formed hundreds of intimate friendships. In each precinct a "Norbeck man" guided the destinies of the "boss." This may have been a man for whom Norbeck had drilled a well, someone he had met in the state legislature or in his work with the progressive Republican group, or perhaps a person who believed strongly in his principles.

He kept in close contact with those in whose hands his political destiny lay. Frequent letters were sent to local leaders asking for their "size up" of the political situation. His friends in turn kept him informed of developments in each particular community. But he realized that correspondence, however effective, was not sufficient. So he maintained a close personal contact with all his supporters. He often left a main-traveled road and drove to the home of some farm friend to discuss the political situation. When in a town he would frequently go up one side of the street and down the other renewing old acquaintances and making new ones.

"The first rule in politics," he wrote to a political novice, "is to get out your vote; perfect such an organization in your district that your friends will cast their vote; there is nothing in politics one-half as important as this."[50] And Norbeck left nothing undone to achieve this. In his first campaign he paid the driver of a team and wagon five dollars to haul people to the polls. He feared nothing so much on election day as bad weather, a condition that normally reduced the farm vote. It is significant that his organization was based strictly on the farm vote. He made relatively little effort to carry the larger towns. By working through and with a large number of devoted personal followers, and throwing his success into the hands of the ordinary dirt farmer, he built and maintained an unbeatable machine. The distribution of loaves and fishes played no prominent part during the formative period of his organization.

Although he was an astute politician, he had numerous other advantages. In the first place, he was a Scandinavian and there were many of his nationality in South Dakota. The Scandinavian-American Republican State League, formed in 1889, was a constant Norbeck ally. He was a pioneer, born on a homestead, and had faced the rigors of frontier life. While he had been poor, through his own efforts he had become eminently successful in business; yet he was not considered wealthy or aligned with big business. His entire career coincided with the traditional concept of a successful man and a leader.

One of his greatest assets was the fact that he always remained so much like his rural constituents—just plain Pete. He was content to act the part of a well-driller even in public life. He possessed a warm affection for the common people and he liked to be with them and discuss their problems. What is more, he showed a desire to help solve them. These characteristics, along with his aggressiveness and natural qualities of leader-

50 Norbeck to W. R. Woods, February 27, 1922. Norbeck MS.

ship, made it easy for him to acquire followers. While his tendency to be aggressive and forceful created bitter enemies, they respected him as a worthy antagonist.

The well-driller's political, social, and economic philosophy was well developed by the time he occupied the lieutenant governor's chair. It strongly reflected the thinking of Theodore Roosevelt and some parts of his philosophy can be traced to the literature of the period. Not only did he read LaFollette's magazine, but his library included the works of some of the other stimulating thinkers of that period. He read and studied Herbert Croly's *The Promise of American Life;* William Allen White's *The Old Order Changeth;* Benjamin DeWitt's *The Progressive Movement,* and others. It is impossible to determine to what extent any of these or other books may have influenced him, but Norbeck's thinking often reflected the tenets of those various authors.

His reading was by no means confined to politics and his favorite book was Voltaire's *History of Charles XII of Sweden.* Time and again he read about the exploits of this dashing young king. To him Charles typified the greatness of his ancestors of whom he was intensely proud. He frequently bought extra copies and gave them to his Scandinavian friends as Christmas or birthday gifts.

By 1912 there were signs that Norbeck was moving to the left in his political thinking, as in his advocacy of a state financed rural credit system. He believed that the government should extend its power to alleviate economic distress and inequalities. Especially, when it came to helping his farm friends, he showed no hesitation in proposing government aid.

His desire to help the common man was the ultimate of his progressiveness. A bank guarantee law to protect the average person from deposit losses and a statute protecting people against the sale of bad securities illustrate this. In achieving progressive objectives he recognized the human element and he understood that he must work with people as he found them and not as he wished them to be. He recognized further that reform must come gradually. He once told Senn: "we can not have everything the way we want it, we can not reform the world or part of it as fast as we would like it but there is nothing left for us to do except to do the best we can under existing conditions."[51]

In almost every way by 1916 Norbeck was prepared for a more important political position. He knew practical politics, an absolute necessity for a successful administrator under the American democratic system; he was an experienced legislator; and he had at least some understanding of the major forces which were influencing American life. He did not have long to wait.

51 Norbeck to E. L. Senn, October 19, 1909. Norbeck MS.

CHAPTER V

TO THE GOVERNORSHIP

"Everything looks favorable for me in case I decide to become a candidate," said Norbeck about the approaching gubernatorial campaign of 1916.[1] Plaintively, he had written to Senn six years earlier that "the progressives of this state are surely handicapped for any leader who would hold the confidence of the people."[2] Little did he realize that eventually he would be that leader.

The Mitchell *Daily Republican* correctly expressed the situation when it said early in 1915: "there is a greater unanimity of belief that Peter Norbeck should be the next Republican candidate for Governor than has been behind any possible gubernatorial candidate in the history of the state."[3] And this sentiment was echoed by most of the leading Republican newspapers.

Norbeck was acceptable to all Republicans except a few members of the most conservative and bitter "Old Guard." By 1916 the party which had been torn asunder for ten years came nearer to unity than at any time since 1900. This was in keeping with the national trend which saw even Theodore Roosevelt return to the Republican fold. But in South Dakota the progressives dominated the party and it was a matter of the conservatives "going along." Nationally, the exact opposite was true.[4]

Norbeck formally announced his candidacy on February 24, 1916, promising the voters a "sound business administration." As might be expected, the leading plank in his platform called for a state rural credit system, a measure he had advocated since 1912. He proposed an extensive highway building program and legislation permitting the state to receive federal funds for road construction on a matching basis. The adoption of a budget system and a workmen's compensation law were also urged. In a bid for party unity, he stated that he would "enter the campaign free from all alliances and independent of all factions—a Republican in all that the name implies."[5]

Most Republican newspapers greeted his announcement enthusiastically. "There is not even a ripple on the Republican sea of harmony," said the Mitchell *Daily Republican*. And it added that the "vast majority of Republican voters" would back him to the limit.[6] The Sioux Falls *Press* called

1 Norbeck to Kent E. Keller, February 18, 1915. Norbeck MS.
2 Norbeck to E. L. Senn, October 19, 1909. Norbeck MS.
3 Mitchell *Daily Republican*, March 19, 1915.
4 Between 1912 and 1916 the conservatives controlled the national Republican party machinery, and the progressives who bolted in 1912 had to return to the Republican fold on the conservatives' terms; that is, of course, if they wanted to return at all. In South Dakota, however, the progressives who controlled the party in 1912 were still dominant in 1916.
5 Pierre *Daily Capital Journal*, February 24, 1916.
6 Mitchell *Daily Republican*, March 20, 1916.

him a "clean-living, clear-headed, red-blooded and ruggedly honest citizen, . . . the type that's needed to maintain South Dakota's progress."[7] Other leading dailies were equally flattering, and the weeklies, reflecting the "grass roots" sentiment, were not surpassed in their praise of the well-driller.

The sharpest note of disagreement came from the conservative Huron *Daily Huronite*. It expressed the opinion that there was no good reason why he should be nominated and that at least one good reason existed for denying him the honor. It charged that he represented the "machine, the slate makers and the spoilsmongers." While admitting that he possessed ordinary competence, it argued that he had "no commanding ability as a statesman." A short while later the same newspaper said of Norbeck: "He is the machine."[8] The Sioux City (Iowa) *Tribune* scoffed at this accusation. "The only machine operated by Lieutenant Governor Norbeck," it said, "is one capable of tapping the artesian water and oil strata. . . ."[9] The Huron *Daily Huronite's* "machine" charge was true only to the extent that Norbeck did dominate the faction of the Republican party which was in control. Of course, if elected, he intended to use the party as a vehicle for carrying out a progressive program. The fact, however, that he later made a sincere attempt to work with all factions refutes the machine accusation.

Norbeck's friends capitalized on his successful business career. This strategy was based on the common belief that success in business fitted a man for political office. The Kadoka *Press* best expressed this when it exclaimed: "Boys, let's quit the politicians for once and elect a business man Governor by voting for Pete Norbeck."[10]

The primary campaign aroused much interest, although the outcome was never in doubt. Two other candidates also sought the nomination. R. O. Richards of Huron, father of South Dakota's primary law, ran on a platform demanding the adoption of a new primary statute. In 1912 the people had voted favorably on Richards' measure but it was so complicated that the legislature of 1915, with Norbeck playing an important role, repealed it and re-enacted the simpler 1907 law. But Richards now asked for repassage of his complicated and unwieldy bill.[11] Taking his cue from the Huron *Daily Huronite*, he also charged that Norbeck was a "machine candidate."

A second opponent was that perennial office-seeker, George W. Egan of Sioux Falls. This was his third attempt to reach the governor's chair, but because he did not present an attractive program to the voters and because of a questionable personal reputation, he had failed. He now sought the nomination on an economy platform and tried to prove the extravagance

7   Sioux Falls *Press*, February 24, 1916.
8   Huron *Daily Huronite*, February 24, and April 24, 1916.
9   Sioux City *Tribune*, undated clipping, 1916. Norbeck MS.
10   Kadoka *Press*, May 11, 1916.
11   Doane Robinson, *Encyclopedia of South Dakota* (Sioux Falls, South Dakota, 1925), p. 624.

of the Byrne-Norbeck regime.[12] When this failed, he attacked Norbeck personally and pictured him as having "hands as big as bushel baskets . . . feet eighteen inches long . . . [and] clothes that [did] not fit very well."[13] This description of the well-driller may have amused Egan's audiences, but it did not influence their votes.

Norbeck campaigned in every county in the state. He hammered home his rural credits idea and told farmers that, if elected, he would establish a state system where they could borrow money for as little as four per cent interest.[14] This appealed to debt-burdened farmers who paid as much as ten and twelve per cent in western South Dakota. Richards, however, insisted that the state should stay out of the farm loan business and charged Norbeck's advocacy of it as "a cheap bid for votes."[15] Norbeck also urged the adoption of a constitutional amendment which would permit other state internal improvement projects if they were found necessary and desirable. Some farmers were beginning to demand state terminal elevators to eliminate certain marketing abuses, but Norbeck told his friend Way:

> I have not been advocating state terminal elevators for the reason that the men at the head of the cooperative organization in this state have not reached that point yet. I doubt very much if there were a state wide meeting of the farmers co-operative elevator people, if they would by state wide vote at this time declare for state terminal elevators. Still I think a similar plan will have to be worked out within the next five or ten years. I have in mind now submitting a plan of this kind to the voters at the next general election. The cost would be considerable—probably a million dollars. The legislature would not be justified in appropriating such a sum of money as an experiment without first submitting it to the voters.[16]

This analysis no doubt represented current thought on the terminal elevator issue in South Dakota. While shying from this question, he did urge the creation of a state marketing office.

The election results definitely showed that South Dakota Republicans had confidence in "Old Pete." He polled 31,987 votes, while Richards and Egan together secured only 21,891.[17] William H. McMaster, a Yankton banker and progressive, was Norbeck's running mate. He also won by a substantial majority.

Orville Rinehart, a prominent Democrat, opposed Norbeck in the November election. Even the most enthusiastic Democrats doubted Rinehart's chances for victory unless he could capitalize on Wilson's prestige in the national race. Realizing this possibility, Norbeck attempted to rally all the Republican forces behind himself and Charles E. Hughes.

12 Mitchell *Daily Republican*, May 16, 1916.
13 Aberdeen *American*, May 9, 1916.
14 Mitchell *Daily Republican*, May 2, 1916.
15 *Ibid.*, May 16, 1916.
16 Norbeck to S. X. Way, September 9, 1916. Way MS.
17 *South Dakota Legislative Manual*, 1921, p. 278.

Diligent campaigning delivered South Dakota to Hughes by the slim margin of approximately 5,000 votes. But even this was a marked achievement in light of the fact that Montana, North Dakota, and Minnesota all went for Wilson. Norbeck, however, ran far ahead of the national ticket and defeated Rinehart by over 20,000 votes, the largest majority ever polled by a gubernatorial candidate in South Dakota up to that time.[18] Norbeck achieved still another distinction: he was the first native-born South Dakotan to reach the governor's chair. Eastern reporters do not always analyze western political situations correctly, but the New York *Times* was not amiss when it said: "He [Norbeck] is a South Dakota institution. The Missouri River, the Black Hills, and spring wheat are not more familiar to South Dakotans."[19]

Most of the editorial comment was favorable. But the disgruntled *Huronite* complained: "The machine is running well oiled and will grind out the grists for them [people] as they are wanted." It further predicted with considerable accuracy that "the people will be expected to elect Norbeck to the Senate four years from now and McMaster to the governorship."[20]

He and Mrs. Norbeck arrived in Pierre December 31. South Dakota did not have a governor's mansion, so they moved to a suite in the St. Charles hotel. January 2, the date of the inauguration, was brisk and clear with a northwest breeze blowing over the ice-packed Missouri. Presiding Judge J. H. Gates of the state Supreme Court administered the oath of office in the governor's reception room before a few officials and members of the Norbeck family.

When the lawmakers assembled, they were greeted with a comprehensive message. Governor Norbeck urgently recommended a rural credits system permitting direct state loans to farmers on real estate. Secondly, he suggested a careful study to determine the advisability of state hail insurance on farm crops. This proposition, although not originating with Norbeck, had been before the legislature at four previous sessions, only to be defeated. The legislators were also asked to investigate the feasibility of establishing a state coal mine. Furthermore, he advocated the acquistion of water power sites by the state and urged their development and operation. In keeping with his suggestion to Way, he recommended that the legislature explore the possibility of establishing terminal grain elevators within the state.

To some these ideas may have seemed radical and socialistic, but they were the consummation of eight or ten years of study and observation of some of South Dakota's most pressing problems, and reflected the spirit of agricultural unrest and discontent so prevalent in the Northwest. His recommendations represented a definite dissatisfaction with existing economic conditions and indicated his desire to aid the farmers through govern-

18 *Ibid.*, p. 315.
19 New York *Times*, October 1, 1916, Pt. VII.
20 Huron *Daily Huronite*, November 9, 1916.

ment action. As Norbeck viewed the matter, legislation of this type would put the government on the side of the common man as opposed to the power and influence of big business. To him the duty of government was "to safeguard all the interests of the people."

Norbeck also recommended legislation covering prohibition, protection for South Dakota's wild life resources, a road-building program, free text books for the school children, and a workmen's compensation law. In conclusion, he said: "You will agree with me that it is the province of the state to protect and aid the individual whether he be engaged in agriculture or some other enterprise."[21]

His address received praise from many quarters. Even the unfriendly Huron *Daily Huronite* concluded that "with some few exceptions Mr. Norbeck's first message . . . will strike the public favorably and it will be generally supported."[22] The *Daily Capital Journal* referred to it as the most "business like document ever presented to a legislature of South Dakota." It added, however, that in "some respects it is advanced in thought and purpose, is in reality somewhat socialistic."[23] This latter observation was certainly correct if the state was to enter all the business enterprises that Norbeck had suggested.

The legislature quickly followed Norbeck's leadership. The governor's pet measure, rural credits, was passed and approved on February 26. A commission was authorized to investigate the advisability of the state entering the coal mining business, and a committee was also appointed to examine the proposals allowing the state to establish flour mills and terminal elevators.

To many the establishment of state flour mills and terminal elevators was the most radical part of Norbeck's program. The Pierre *Daily Dakotan*, a most conservative newspaper, however, praised this recommendation. "A market commissioner and the establishment of terminal elevators would mean more to South Dakota than any one thing that could be done," said the editor.[24] The *Daily Huronite*, however, took a different view and claimed the governor's suggestion was "the bulwark erected against the campaign of the . . . Nonpartisan League that has swept North Dakota and is flowing over into South Dakota."[25] The outstanding characteristic of the League's program was its demand for state enterprises!

The report of the legislative committee appointed to investigate the establishment of terminal elevators gives a fairly clear picture of the early demand for state enterprises in South Dakota. As might be expected, opinion was sharply divided on this issue, although practically all of those interviewed favored creating an office of marketing commissioner.

21   *Peter Norbeck to the South Dakota Legislature,* 1917. A pamphlet.
22   Huron *Daily Huronite,* January 4, 1917.
23   Pierre *Daily Capital Journal,* January 3, 1917.
24   Pierre *Daily Dakotan,* January 4, 1917.
25   Huron *Daily Huronite,* January 4, 1917.

After interviewing personally or by mail several score elevator operators, farm leaders, and individual dirt farmers, the legislative committee recommended that no action be taken except to submit the issue to the people in the form of a constitutional amendment at the next election. As yet, the report said, state-owned terminal elevators and warehouses were entirely in experimental stages. While the legislators gave it only passing consideration, it is significant that a good many farmers favored the old Populist idea of creating warehouses where farmers could store their grain and receive negotiable certificates.[26]

Norbeck did not press the issue but carefully felt out public opinion. One person wrote to him: "I hardly think we are ready for state-owned elevators . . . although I admire your address on the question . . . as it shows your readiness to aid any and all industries of the state."[27] He finally supported the committee's recommendations. The office of marketing commissioner was created under a law which stated: "The business of marketing farm products in this state is declared to be affected with the public interest and to be subject to control by the state."[28]

Other legislation included enactment of a workmen's compensation law and the establishment of a highway department with a provision permitting federal aid for road building, as was provided under the Federal Highways Act of 1916. The legislature also passed constitutional amendments to be submitted to the voters at the next general election. Three of these would permit state hail insurance, a state cement plant, and water power development. The most radical amendment was one whereby the state could "own and conduct proper business enterprises . . . loan or give its credit to . . . any association, or corporation, and . . . become the owner of the capital stock of corporations."[29] This sweeping proposal would allow the state to engage in a wide variety of enterprises if approved by the voters. But the final responsibility would rest with the legislature.

Norbeck's suggestion for creating a unicameral legislature met with less success. A number of the state's leading progressives, including Senator Dowdell and W. C. Cook, attempted to pass a unicameral law. The governor supported the bill but did not make it one of his major objectives primarily because he thought its chance of passage was remote.

Few, if any, sessions of the South Dakota legislature went along more smoothly than the fifteenth. Norbeck was in complete control. There were no major factional fights or political battles so characteristic of by-gone days and as Steve Travis, veteran capital reporter, stated: "the Governor

26 "Report of the Joint Commission of South Dakota Legislature to Investigate establishing a Marketing Commissioner and Terminal Elevators," *South Dakota Senate Journal,* 1917, pp. 818-30.
27 Unnamed correspondent to Norbeck, January 15, 1917. C. M. C. Woodland MS.
28 *South Dakota Session Laws,* 1916-17, Chap., 225.
29 *Ibid.,* Chap., 163.

and the members of the legislature . . . worked in perfect harmony." He added: "Seldom does [*sic*] so many recommendations contained in a Governor's message become enacted into law."[30] One of the outstanding characteristics of the session was the dominant attention given to farm problems. The *Daily Argus Leader* commented that if the farmers wanted anything at Pierre, "all they have to do is ask for it."[31] The legislature went as far as the constitution permitted in meeting agricultural demands besides proposing the amendments previously referred to. The name "farmers legislature" aptly applied.

A "bone-dry" prohibition law was one of the major statutes that was not connected with farm needs. Norbeck had consistently favored statutory prohibition ever since his unfortunate experience with the Charles Mix county "wets" in 1892. On February 21 he signed the law surrounded by W. C. T. U. workers and representatives of the Anti-Saloon League. After signing the measure he paused and said: "Well, South Dakota's dry." This was the cue for the temperance representatives to strike up several prohibition hymns; but Norbeck did not join in.

In March the Governor and Mrs. Norbeck returned to Redfield. Norbeck attended to neglected business matters and then took a much needed rest. The citizens of Redfield welcomed him home by holding an informal reception in the Masonic Temple. Norbeck was a Mason, as well as a member of several other lodges, but he seldom took time to attend the meetings. The feeling toward him among local residents had greatly improved and he enjoyed the informal fellowship with his old neighbors.

In September he moved his family to Pierre. The children had not gone to Pierre in January, but stayed in Redfield to complete the school term. Norbeck rented a large ten bedroom house about four blocks from the capitol building. The spacious old living room was a favorite place to entertain his many friends. He liked to bring them home to a delicious dinner after which a comfortable evening was spent discussing oil prospecting, political appointments, or state problems. But usually politics was the main topic of conservation. An abundance of good Havana cigars added to the enjoyment. The Norbecks paid $100 a month rent, half of which was furnished by the state. It was not uncommon for household expenses to run $1000 a month and the $3000 annual salary scarcely met incidental expenses.

When not entertaining, Norbeck usually spent the evenings at his office. Many nights the lights in the governor's office on the second floor of the capitol burned until after midnight. An ordinary work day was from twelve to fourteen hours. He worked at the job of being governor just as he had that of drilling wells.

He was absent from Pierre during much of 1917. This was occasioned

30 Webster *Reporter and Farmer*, March 8, 1917.
31 Sioux Falls *Daily Argus Leader*, January 20, 1917.

by the extra duties growing out of the World War and also by developments in his Wyoming oil business. Since 1913 he and Oscar Nicholson had been prospecting in the Pilot Butte field. They had purchased some prospective oil land and leased additional areas where chances of success looked especially promising. A number of test holes had been drilled and altogether, including the Illinois venture, they had spent about $100,000.

Norbeck's hope of striking oil in profitable quantities was realized in the summer of 1917 when his drilling outfit struck a good gusher about twenty-five miles north of Lander. The well drew considerable attention in wildcat oil circles. Norbeck, however, was soon forced to sell his property. "It was necessary to do it," he stated, "as the big oil companies were getting to the point they would have ruined the value of the property."[32]

In August he and Nicholson sold their 160 acres and the leases on other oil lands to R. C. Megargel and Company of New York for $640,000.[33] The profits amounted to $560,000 of which Norbeck's share was about $190,000. He and Nicholson had an equal interest and a few friends held smaller equities. Norbeck received his share in installments from 1917 to 1919. As a result of this successful business venture and his well-drilling profits, his average income for those years was about $90,000.

By 1917 he had purchased extensive farm land and, while his exact acreage is unknown, he was reputedly one of the state's largest land holders. He was also a large stockholder in a $200,000 surety company, with additional investments in banks and other businesses. A conservative estimate of his entire holdings at that time would be $500,000. Late in the year a close friend wrote to him that "it should now only be another season's cereal crop till I can congratulate you on your entrance in the millionaire class."[34] While he fell far short of this, he probably was correct in his comment to Judge William Williamson: "Judge, if I had tended to business and stayed out of politics I could have become a millionaire."[35] Here was a true story of the Horatio Alger type.

The United States' declaration of war on Germany in 1917 created additional problems for all state governors. This was especially true where a considerable element was lukewarm toward prosecuting the war. Norbeck wanted his state to render outstanding service and he gave unstintingly of his time and energy. He directed the state council of defense, visited South Dakota troop encampments, aided in liberty bond drives, and helped the war effort in many other ways. Demands for speeches before patriotic rallies were heavy and the Pierre *Daily Capital Journal* pleaded with the

32 Norbeck to Royal C. Johnson, August 27, 1917. Norbeck MS.
33 Sales Contract, Norbeck MS.
34 John Berg to Norbeck, December 10, 1917 Norbeck MS.
35 William Williamson to Author, July 17, 1944.

people to be more considerate and give the governor "a breathing spell occasionally so he can catch up in his office."[36]

In September, 1917, the People's Council of America for Democracy and Peace, a pacifist organization, attempted to invade the state. It already had been outlawed by the governors of Illinois, Minnesota, and Wisconsin, but conditions appeared bright in South Dakota for a strong organization. The hopes of its members were lifted when during the preceding month the anti-war faction in Hutchinson county, led by thirty farmers mostly of German descent, wrote to Norbeck bitterly complaining about the war. They expressed dissatisfaction with the draft system and asked for a popular referendum on the selective service law. They also opposed the sale of liberty bonds and favored the repudiation of all war debts. They added that failure to get a favorable response would bring a demand for his resignation and that they would seek to defeat his party at the next election. This represented the disloyal sentiment in the state and encouraged the People's Council to further action.

In the meantime, the People's Council held a mass meeting at Parkston at which 500 people were present. Loud and prolonged applause greeted the reading of an open letter condemning Norbeck because he refused to sanction their gathering. But when another meeting was scheduled for Sioux Falls, the governor directed the state sheriff to prevent it.

Norbeck had to deal with a number of incidents of this type, but most South Dakotans were loyal. He exaggerated only slightly when he declared: "the people of the state are solidly behind the government in the prosecution of the war, and organizations like the People's Council will find they are not any more welcome than in other patriotic states."[37]

Everything pointed to a highly successful administration. Most of his legislative suggestions had become law, his popularity in all parts of the state had never been greater, and his political fences were in excellent repair. His personal fortune was even increasing. There was only one disturbing factor: the Nonpartisan League.

36 Pierre *Daily Capital Journal,* republished in the Mitchell *Daily Republican,* September 25, 1917.
37 Centerville *Journal,* September 6, 1917, and Columbia *Columbian,* September 21, 1917.

CHAPTER VI

NORBECK AND THE NONPARTISAN LEAGUE

The organization of the Nonpartisan League early in 1915 was essentially a protest of the spring wheat farmers of North Dakota against grain marketing abuses. Rumblings of discontent had never completely subsided since the days of the Populists, James B. Weaver, Ignatius Donnelly, and Richard F. Pettigrew, and now Arthur C. Townley, bankrupt farmer and Socialist, took the scepter from the Populists and led the most important rural revolt of the early twentieth century.

As previously shown, farmers in the North-Central states were protesting against unfair grain grading practices soon after 1900. In order to escape the results of monopolistic grain markets, a movement developed in North Dakota to establish a state-owned terminal elevator and in both 1912 and 1914 the people voted favorably on a measure permitting this. Much to the dismay of most farmers, however, the State Board of Control, which was authorized to determine the practicality of such a move, reported adversely in January, 1915.[1]

The American Society of Equity, a cooperative organization, brought pressure on the 1915 legislature to establish a terminal elevator, but the Equity committee which appeared before the legislature reportedly was told to "go home and slop the hogs."[2] This recalcitrant attitude paved the way for Townley to organize the farmers into a powerful political organization which ultimately gained control of the entire state government and threatened existing regimes in surrounding states. Townley was an ideal leader for such a movement. He was a master organizer and his agents traveled over the North Dakota plains calling the farmers to follow a new Moses into the Promised Land.

While in his state in 1916 Norbeck was elected governor with ease, the regular North Dakota Republicans fought a losing battle with a belligerent League which campaigned on a platform advocating extensive state-owned enterprises. Included were a state bank, state-owned terminal elevators, flour mills, packing plants, a rural credits system and state hail insurance.

Townley's organization gained sweeping victories in the house of repre-

1 None of the histories of the Nonpartisan League is adequate. See Paul R. Fossum, *The Agrarian Movement in North Dakota* (Baltimore, 1925); Theodore Saloutos, "The Rise of the Nonpartisan League in North Dakota, 1915-17," *Agricultural History*, 20:43-61 (January, 1946); and also Saloutos, "The Expansion and Decline of the Nonpartisan League in the Western Middle West," *Agricultural History*, 20:235-52 (October, 1946); Gilbert C. Fite, "Peter Norbeck and the Defeat of the Nonpartisan League in South Dakota," *Mississippi Valley Historical Review*, 33:217-36 (September, 1946). Material from this article has been used with the permission of the Editor.
2 Herbert E. Gaston, *The Nonpartisan League* (New York, 1920), p. 43.

sentatives, named all except one of the elective administrative officers, elected three members to the Supreme Court, and also elected a majority of those running for state senate seats. Governor Lynn J. Frazier took office in January, 1917, at the head of a League-dominated government. Only the state senate stood in the way of adopting the radical program as there were enough "holdover" senators to keep the League from controlling that body.

Supporters of the new farm movement were highly disappointed in 1917 when the senate refused to sanction changes in the constitution permitting the state to embark upon such undertakings. About the only concrete accomplishment of the League was the passage of a grain grading law. In fact, the South Dakota lawmakers enacted much more "farmer legislation" than did the League, by creating the office of marketing commissioner, establishing a state rural credits system, and by providing committees to investigate the feasibility of other state-owned enterprises.

Although the League had been temporarily frustrated in North Dakota, its leaders looked forward to ousting the refractory senators and gaining complete control two years later. In the meantime, national headquarters were opened at St. Paul, and Townley dispatched his most trusted lieutenants to spread the new gospel in surrounding states, particularly in South Dakota and Minnesota.

Since agricultural dissatisfaction was not confined to state boundaries, it was to be expected that the League would soon flow over into South Dakota. Norbeck and the Republican leaders did not lack information on the League's activities. J. D. Bacon of Grand Forks, North Dakota, a relentless League enemy, wrote to S. X. Way in May, 1916: "It might be well for you to keep a little tab on our papers regarding the Non-partisan League, for you will surely be up against the same kind of a game some day."[3] Way immediately passed this letter along to Norbeck. Commenting on Bacon's analysis, Norbeck admitted that the League had an appealing farm program and that its leaders were "wonderful" organizers. But he added: "There is less danger of them getting anywhere in South Dakota. Part of the trouble in North Dakota is a reaction from McKenzie [Alexander McKenzie] rule. . . ."[4]

Shortly after writing to Norbeck, Way met Bacon in Chicago and again the North Dakotan attempted to impress Way with the seriousness of a potential League invasion of South Dakota. But Way argued that his state already had so many "agitators" that it would be hard for the League to gain a foothold there.[5] Neither Norbeck nor Way seemed concerned about a League threat and during the first part of 1916 their interest grew from curiosity more than anything else.

3 J. D. Bacon to S. X. Way, May 30, 1916. Way MS.
4 Norbeck to S. X. Way, June 24, 1916. Way MS.
5 S. X. Way to Norbeck, June 23, 1916. Way MS.

It was not until early autumn that the South Dakota newspapers began paying much attention to the new farm organization. Late in September the Pierre *Daily Capital Journal* reported that people were beginning to "sit up and take notice" of the League and that the movement was well started in the northern counties.[6]

By December organizers moved to the state in full force and found many farmers receptive to their program. The Huron *Daily Huronite* emphasized this tendency by declaring that the League was "invading South Dakota in a forcible way."[7] A few weeks later the editor added that conditions in the state were favorable for such a movement.[8]

While the Sioux Falls *Daily Argus Leader* was speculating on whether the League would succeed or go the way of the Grangers and the Populists, other newspapers showed signs of political fright. When Governor Norbeck picked up his Pierre *Daily Capital Journal* on the evening of January 15, his eyes fell on an editorial which read in part: "There are 15,000 South Dakota farmers allied in the $16 membership of the South Dakota Nonpartisan League. Just keep your mind working a little and imagine . . . the the 1918 campaign."[9] Fifteen days later an article entitled "NONPARTISAN LEAGUE GROWS," appeared as front page news. Needless to say, Norbeck's mind was working more than "a little," and if he had ever taken Republican domination for granted such reports should have removed his complacency.

A close friend from Redfield wrote to him that "the Non-partisan crowd is coming down from the north like a swarm of grasshoppers."[10] To a pioneer Dakotan the meaning of such phraseology was crystal clear. And this was scarcely an exaggeration in view of the fact that by March, only two months later, the League claimed 20,000 members in the state.[11]

The League moved so rapidly that it even had representatives present during the last days of the 1917 session. W. H. Talmadge, speaking for the organization, expressed himself as being "highly pleased" with the accomplishments of the South Dakota legislature. "South Dakota," he said, "is the first state in the union . . . that has drafted a constitutional amendment to be submitted for a vote permitting state-controlled and assisted industries in every line—the very principle for which the League works." Talmadge claimed that League influence was a determining factor in getting this amendment through the legislature.[12] Talmadge probably greatly overestimated League influence because Norbeck had advocated the constitu-

6   Pierre *Daily Capital Journal*, September 27, 1916.
7   Huron *Daily Huronite*, December 6, 1916.
8   *Ibid.*, January 25, 1917.
9   Pierre *Daily Capital Journal*, January 15, 1917.
10 B. B. Haugen to Norbeck, January 29, 1917. Norbeck MS.
11 Pierre *Daily Capital Journal*, March 7, 1917.
12 *Ibid.*, March 5, 1917.

tional change during the 1916 campaign, almost a year earlier and before the League had even gained control in North Dakota.

If the laws enacted during the first Norbeck administration were pleasing to the League representatives, it was only accidental because as yet the organization was of no political force in the legislature. In fact, Talmadge admitted that his agents appeared in Pierre too late "to do anything with any other resolutions."[13]

Norbeck was too wise politically to ignore the seriousness of the League threat and he did not dare to continue indifferent. The worst feature about the League from his viewpoint was that it made heavy inroads on his chief source of political strength, the farmers. From his first entry into politics he had leaned heavily on members of this group. But now hundreds and even thousands of farmers, who had previously supported him, were making a new political alignment. The League leaders soon discovered, however, that they were no match for "King Peter," as his friends sometimes called him, and even Townley's organizational genius was no match for Norbeck's political acumen.

Norbeck's strategy for defeating the League included three broad principles. In the first place, he decided to contrast his record of achievement with the failure of the North Dakota Nonpartisan League program, which had been defeated by an unfriendly senate the preceding year. Secondly, he and his organization would support amendments to the South Dakota constitution permitting additional state enterprises, and finally, he would attack the League leaders as being radical Socialists and disloyal in the war. W. Harry King, chairman of the state Republican committee and an especially astute politician, was chosen to direct the campaign.

To present his program to the electorate, Norbeck wrote a forty-eight page campaign pamphlet which was given wide distribution. In this booklet he reviewed his term in office, evaluated his progressive legislation, and discussed new proposals reflecting his views on government and economics. He emphasized the assertion that his state already had more progressive legislation than North Dakota and that it would be folly to overthrow an administration characterized by performance in order to accept the Nonpartisan League program of promises.

Norbeck commented at length on the eleven major amendments coming before the people at the November election. He urged support of one permitting the state to purchase and operate plants for developing water power. He again advocated favorable consideration of an amendment which would allow the state to sell hail insurance on farm crops. Norbeck denied that it was socialistic, contending that it was "simply cooperative." He lent vigorous support to the amendment permitting the state to engage in various types of internal improvements. This was the proposal favored by the League and would allow the state to enter any type of business deemed

13 *Ibid.*

practical by the legislature; the only restriction was a provision forbidding the state to spend more than approximately $7,200,000 on any of the suggested projects. He also favored establishing a state cement plant and a coal mine. Norbeck, however, treated with caution the proposed amendment permitting the state to construct and operate terminal elevators, warehouses, flour mills, and packing plants. While favoring such ideas tentatively, he spoke of the many difficulties involved and of the advisability of having a committee of "competent and impartial" men to investigate and to make recommendations. He warned that this was absolutely necessary before "action was taken and the taxpayers' money is appropriated."

His message to the people ended with a two-page discussion of socialism. Norbeck had read numerous books on this subject and believed he understood its basic tenets. He denied being a Socialist, and asserted that the entrance by the state into certain lines of business was not socialism. After severely criticizing monopolies, he said: "Where men attempt to extort an unreasonable profit, it is the business of the government to step in and regulate it and where the regulation can be best had by government ownership and operation, this plan should be adopted." Like Roosevelt, Norbeck distinguished between "good" and "bad" trusts.

The entire pamphlet was an obvious bid for votes against the encroachments of the League.[14] It was not argumentative or combative but was simply an attempt to emphasize South Dakota's progressiveness and the Republicans' concern for the farmer. In commenting on the message, George B. Elliot, employee of the Watertown *Public Opinion,* made a most interesting observation. "It is pretty well accepted," he wrote, "that the progressive element of the Republican party has no quarrel with the main principles for which the N. P. L. stands. . . . The fight when it comes will be based upon the proper application of these principles and upon the best men to apply them. On principle alone we could all be members of the League without misplacing a hair."[15] Elliot was close to Way and Norbeck and his thoughts may have represented their beliefs. In any event, Norbeck's statement contained no substantial departure from his previous philosophy. He did not promise that South Dakota would go as far as the League along the road of state ownership, but he was willing to provide that possibility through additional constitutional amendments if the voters should demand it. This attitude was in sharp contrast with that of the North Dakota anti-Leaguers.

Perhaps Norbeck's general strategy to keep the League from gaining a foothold in his state is best expressed in his own words: "First, we supported every good suggestion that the farmers made. Second, we did not even oppose their going into new experiments of uncertain value, providing the risk connected with the venture was only nominal, for the farmers themselves

14 Peter Norbeck, *Message to the People of South Dakota* (Redfield, 1918).
15 G. B. Elliot to Norbeck, February 8, 1918. Way MS.

were the main taxpayers, so why should they not be permitted to have some experiments if they honestly and sincerely asked for it [*sic*] in the belief that it would better their conditions."[16] This statement is evidence that some of the measures proposed and supported by Norbeck were advocated because of political expediency. His calling a special session of the legislature in March, 1918, to pass on constitutional amendments permitting additional state enterprises is further substantiation of a desire to prepare for the League attack.[17]

The Aberdeen *Daily News* concluded later that Norbeck's advocacy of these principles was pure hypocrisy. It charged that in adopting a socialistic platform the "state administration was suffering from a severe attack of cold feet. . . . Townley had it scared so bad that it was ready to go any length to curry favor with the St. Paul boss."[18] As will be shown later, this charge was without foundation in fact.

Harry King told party leaders to base their campaign on the idea that the farmers "have been securing and will continue to secure all the legislation which they ask for. Especially such legislation as they think is proper and that which will stand up under the searchlight of 'Will it Pay.' "[19] Norbeck, King, and all the political workers kept hammering this point home during the entire campaign.[20]

Having informed the voters where he stood on matters of public interest, Norbeck began a vigorous campaign. It was unnecessary to fight the League in the primaries, since on February 26 its leaders decided not to enter candidates but to marshal all their strength for the November election.[21] This disappointed the Norbeck forces who hoped to come to grips with the League before it had additional time to organize. But looking forward to the November elections, the governor and his cohorts set out to smash the organization by branding its leaders as Socialists, who were disloyal.

During the First World War, when super-patriotism was thought to be virtuous, it was easy to brand leaders of the Socialist party and Nonpartisan League with charges of disloyalty. This method of combating the League was not peculiar to South Dakota; it was an effective method wherever used. Such criticism was confined chiefly to the League leaders and little attempt was made to brand members of the organization as unpatriotic. On one occasion, however, Norbeck did say, "I wish some publicity would be given to the disloyalty of League members," but he added: "this should

16   Norbeck to R. A. Nestos, November 5, 1921. Norbeck MS.
17   Amendments passed either for the first time or in a different form included those permitting a state cement plant and coal mine, hydro-electric development, and internal improvements. Of course, these still had to be ratified by the people to become effective.
18   Aberdeen *Daily News*, January 6, 1919.
19   Harry King to J. J. Murphy, March 1, 1918. Norbeck MS.
20   Carl J. Hofland, "The Nonpartisan League in South Dakota," Unpublished Master's Thesis, University of South Dakota (Vermillion, 1940), p. 42.
21   *Ibid.*

not be overdone."[22] This suggestion was obviously for political effect because he wrote a short time later that "the rank and file of the League, both in South Dakota and Minnesota, are loyal."[23] It was possible, however, to emphasize Townley's former socialist connections, and almost every anti-League editor in the state printed photostatic copies of his registration as a Socialist elector.

The newspaper campaign sponsored by the anti-League group was concentrated and effective. The conservative Sioux Falls *Daily Argus Leader* was probably the most bitter antagonist. In fact, editor Day wrote such vicious editorials that Harry King found it necessary to ask him to soften his tone because the League thrived on that kind of opposition.[24] The Norbeck campaign committee sent political reprint materials to about 200 newspapers throughout the state. The League had only two strong publicity mouthpieces; the Mitchell *Daily Republican,* and the League's own paper, *The South Dakota Leader,* a weekly published at Mitchell. The League also published a weekly at St. Paul, however, which went to all members.

Norbeck's League opponent was Mark P. Bates, a well-known and highly respected farmer from Letcher. The governor and the Republican strategists believed that if they could administer a crushing defeat to Bates the main strength of the League would be forever broken in South Dakota. But since Bates' personal reputation could not be successfully attacked, Norbeck and his supporters turned their main assault on Townley, Gilbert, Duncan, and other national League leaders. James E. Bird, Democratic candidate, campaigned on the sidelines with no hope of election.

As is often the case in political campaigns, the issues were not fought out squarely before the people. In this instance, the most publicized issue proved to be freedom of speech and personal protection for Bates and other League leaders. After League organizers, such as Townley, made statements that could be interpreted as disloyal to the nation, some of the county councils of defense attempted to stop all League meetings.

One of the first instances of this type occurred at Madison in February, 1918, when the League was prohibited from holding an organization meeting. Immediately upon hearing of this undemocratic incident Norbeck notified the county sheriff that "no political organization should be interfered with. It has the right to hold public meetings. None should be prevented except such as are held for the purpose of embarrassing the government in the prosecution of the war."[25]

But in spite of the governor's proclamation and his desire for freedom of speech and assembly, many League organizers were roughly handled, while others were barred from speaking in certain localities. The most

22 Norbeck to Harry King, May 2, 1918. Norbeck MS.
23 Norbeck to M. Q. Sharpe, June 17, 1918. Norbeck MS.
24 Harry King to C. M. Day, February 5, 1918. Norbeck MS.
25 Norbeck to Sheriff E. H. Kellar, February 4, 1918. Norbeck MS.

outstanding incident of this nature took place at Britton. When it was learned that Townley and Bates planned to speak there, a committee of local citizens appealed to the state council of defense to prohibit it. The council replied, however, that it was customary to leave such matters to the county council and unless actual statements of disloyalty were made, no molestation should occur. But regardless of this policy, when Bates, Townley, and other members of the party arrived in Britton, they were escorted out of town and as far as the state line under threat of physical violence.[26]

Bates, bitter over this action, now began attacking Norbeck on the grounds that as chief executive he was failing to uphold the constitutional freedoms of speech and assembly. Norbeck responded vigorously to this charge, informing Bates in a public letter, dated October 7, that freedom of speech would not be interfered with and that as long as he was governor all candidates seeking public office would receive full protection of the law. He further told his opponent that if it became necessary, he would personally escort him on any speaking engagement where there might be danger of violence.[27] Norbeck promised there would be no interference if Bates wanted to hold a meeting at Britton. He did not, however, offer similar protection for Townley and other League leaders whom he described as "radical socialist followers of Lenine [sic] and Trotsky."[28] Only three days after his letter to Bates the governor issued an order through the state council of defense barring Townley from speaking in South Dakota. This order was rescinded the next day, providing he made no more disloyal statements.[29]

Norbeck soon had an opportunity to prove his sincerity. On October 10, Bates was scheduled to speak at Bonesteel, a town in which the League was very unpopular. In fact, in the preceding winter the Gregory county council of defense offered serious interference with an attempted League gathering. Determined that this should not happen again, at least at Bonesteel, the governor made a 250-mile trip from Pierre to see that order was maintained.[30] Although Norbeck apparently made a sincere effort to protect his opponent, Bates continued to suffer restrictions and indignities from local fire-eaters. He charged Norbeck with lack of good faith and frequently commented that he had been "hunted down by Norbeck's henchmen."[31]

During most of the campaign, issues were submerged under a flow of words. Unjustifiable charges and counter-charges were the order of the day. Bates assumed the attitude of a martyr, while Norbeck accused him of having no issues except that of being mobbed! He charged that Bates actually refused protection, thinking incidents of the Britton type would bring political sympathy and votes. As a final resort, Bates accused Norbeck of

26 Hofland, "The Nonpartisan League in South Dakota," p. 49.
27 Sioux Falls *Daily Argus Leader,* October 9, 1918.
28 Norbeck to Henry J. Allen, April 21, 1919. Norbeck MS.
29 Hofland, "The Nonpartisan League in South Dakota," p. 50.
30 Pierre *Daily Capital Journal,* October 14, 1918.
31 Wessington Springs *True Republican,* October 17, 1918.

stealing his program, to which the governor replied: "If Norbeck stole your thunder as you claim . . . it was done before the League was born."[32]

During October the Norbeck forces waged a most concentrated campaign. Anti-League newspapers carried supplements with entire pages of exhibits designed to prove that the League leaders were disloyal. One of the favorite photostats, in addition to Townley's registration as a Socialist, was the facsimile of the blue card returned against L. J. Duncan in connection with the Third Liberty Loan. This copy quoted the Secretary of the South Dakota League as saying that "it was criminal for the Government to try to get money from people who had to work for a living."[33]

Norbeck's friends gave very wide distribution to a letter written by Theodore Roosevelt to S. X. Way. "As long as the League submits to the leadership of Messrs. Townley and LeSeuer, " Roosevelt declared, "it cannot escape the condemnation of good and loyal Americans." He asserted that the real purpose of the League "is to bring bolshevism in the United States. . . . Under the lead of men like Governor Norbeck," Roosevelt continued, "South Dakota during the last three years has done more for genuine progressive legislation than any other state in the union."[34] He added that he most earnestly hoped for Norbeck's re-election.

It was not only Republicans who supported Norbeck. One Democratic farmer said: "The only thing that a self-respecting Democrat can do is vote for the next best man [next to Bird] and that is Peter Norbeck."[35] Early in the campaign the editor of the Centerville *Independent* wrote to Harry King that "I am doing all for the Governor that a consistent democrat can do."[36]

The final days before election found most of the political strength in the state solidly back of Norbeck and bitterly opposing the League. Although many conservative Republicans did not agree with administrative policies, they looked upon Norbeck's re-election as the lesser of two evils. The most influential paper in the state, the Sioux Falls *Daily Argus Leader,* strongly opposed the governor's "socialistic" program, and Editor C. M. Day warned that if the state adopted the socialistic amendments it "would suffer for many years to come." He called the situation a most serious one for the people of South Dakota. But while endeavoring to defeat much of Norbeck's program, Day worked unceasingly for his re-election.[37]

Although some may have questioned the outcome, Norbeck never seriously doubted but that he would win. In August he wrote: "I do not anticipate any danger about the final results, but it keeps me campaigning."[38]

32 Huron *Weekly State Spirit,* October 17, 1918.
33 Supplement to the Chancellor *News,* October 25, 1918.
34 Huron *Daily Huronite,* November 2, 1918.
35 *Ibid.*
36 I. W. Cameron to Harry King, March 15, 1918. Norbeck MS.
37 Sioux Falls *Daily Argus Leader,* January 3, October 30, and November 4, 1918.
38 Norbeck to S. S. Curry, August 2, 1918. Norbeck MS.

Thirty days before the election he was less confident, but when the final votes were tallied Norbeck had polled more than both Bates and Bird combined. Of the 96,160 votes cast, he received over 51,000.[39] Constitutional amendments permitting various state enterprises also carried by substantial majorities.[40]

Norbeck's thumping defeat of the League may be attributed to several factors. In the first place, he directed a very effective political organization and his lieutenants were both devoted and ambitious. He directed the campaign skillfully by pointing to his own accomplishments and emphasizing the alleged disloyalty of League leadership. Furthermore, while the League in North Dakota had promised much, it had as yet produced few concrete results, since no substantial part of its program was enacted there until 1919, by which time the entire government was League controlled.

Norbeck had the distinct advantage in that a rural credits department, viewed with great favor by agricultural interests, had been established and was operating. Throughout the campaign he had taken every opportunity to capitalize on the popularity of this law. His general popularity with the farmers cannot be over-emphasized. This was contrary to the situation in North Dakota where the regular Republican candidates had, to a large extent, lost the confidence of the farm groups. Norbeck's ability to convince the voters, especially the farmers, that his program was progressive, yet not radical, largely accounts for the League's inability to unhorse him.

It has been frequently charged that Norbeck was able to defeat the League only because he "stole" its program. There is no doubt but that his willingness to establish state-owned enterprises, which the South Dakota farmers honestly believed would alleviate some of their difficulties, was a most important factor in turning back the "swarm of grasshoppers" from the North. But it is not true that he and the progressive Republicans "stole" the League's program. Norbeck's thinking, however, was influenced by the same forces of agricultural discontent which operated in North Dakota. His ideas did not originate with the League. For instance, one cannot say that rural credits was supported by Norbeck to meet the League threat when he had been advocating it three years before the League was organized. And the League's other objectives and ideas were also familiar to South Dakotans before this organization became a political power. It is true, however, that he made political capital out of his willingness to support constitutional amendments, which, if adopted, would permit state-owned flour mills, packing plants, and terminal elevators. And he did this, even though he was unfriendly to these proposals.

Norbeck was never willing to go as far in this direction as the League advocated, but he believed in going far enough to satisfy the people of

39 *South Dakota Legislative Manual*, 1919, p. 353.
40 *Ibid.*, 103. All constitutional barriers to an extensive program of state enterprises were thus removed.

his state. He was able to do this without compromising his basic economic or political principles as he was a firm believer in a limited extension of governmental powers.

Later Norbeck wrote to Governor Henry J. Allen of Kansas in reply to a letter relative to the League: "I believe the best way to meet the League proposition is to give the farmers every reasonable thing they ask for and refuse to go with them on the impractical."[41] And writing on the same subject to Senator James E. Watson of Indiana, he said: "It is my opinion that the so-called Townley organization got a foothold in North Dakota purely on account of unnecessary mistakes by republicans in charge of that state at that time."[42] Norbeck had avoided those mistakes.

41 Norbeck to Henry J. Allen, April 16, 1919. Norbeck MS.
42 Norbeck to James E. Watson, August 29, 1921. Norbeck MS.

CHAPTER VII

ROUNDING OUT HIS STATE PROGRAM

Norbeck dealt the Nonpartisan League in his state a mortal blow. He appeared as a heroic warrior to many anti-leaguers, who in North Dakota and elsewhere eagerly sought his counsel. Governor Henry Allen of Kansas, who had been fighting a rather weak branch of the League there for two years, asked him for his "closer view."[1] But to defeat the new farm organization was not the only important question before Norbeck, and one of more significance awaited him and the legislature of 1919. Should the Republicans carry out their platform and campaign pledges and proceed along the path of state ownership or should they retrench, now that the danger from the League was past?

The sixteenth legislative session began without fanfare. "Never before in the history of the state," said the Pierre *Daily Capital Journal*, "was Pierre so quiet on Sunday preceding the meeting of the legislature. . . . Everybody seems to be coming in with a satisfied feeling that they are going to start on a work that is in a manner practically outlined the same as a course of study in the school room."[2] The Huron *Daily Huronite* too noticed an "entire absence of the old-time warrior spirit which was rife in the earlier years of statehood."[3] In this spirit of "peace and harmony" the governor and the South Dakota lawmakers began tackling state problems.

Republicans differed sharply as to what course the administration should follow. Some opposed the "socialistic" program and argued that it would be folly to embark upon such questionable ventures, since the League threat had been erased. "It is true," wrote C. M. Day, "that the voters of the state endorsed the socialistic program but it is also true that at that time they had no statement . . . as to how many millions of dollars would be required to put the plan into full force and effect." He maintained that taxpayers in general and especially the farm owners would not want the state to plunge into doubtful experiments which might prove costly, and that after the citizens knew the cost they would "know better how far they want to go in the program of state socialism or whether they want to back out entirely."[4] The latter was Day's hope!

The Aberdeen *Daily News* in an editorial entitled "What will the Legislature Do?" commented in a similar vein: "This session of the legislature promises to be the most momentous . . . in the recent history of the state." It charged that instead of fighting, "the administration raised its hands skyward and cried 'Kamerad' when it saw the Townley cohorts approaching." Then, continued the editor, "in its efforts to out-Townley Townley, it caused

1 Henry J. Allen to Norbeck, April 9, 1919. Norbeck MS.
2 Pierre *Daily Capital Journal*, January 6, 1919.
3 Huron *Daily Huronite*, January 14, 1919.
4 Sioux Falls *Daily Argus Leader*, January 28, 1919.

to be adopted a platform so radical that the Townley program was the extreme of conservation in comparison. . . . It would be a costly piece of extravagance to keep the promises made in that platform. . . ."[5]

In contrast to those who would frankly repudiate the platform pledges, there were many people who believed the legislature had no choice but to carry out the mandate of the electorate. The Mitchell *Sunday Republican* observed that "Governor Norbeck should find . . . an opportunity to give the state the benefit of his own distinct success in business. . . . Failure by the administration to obey the virtual mandate of the voters in the adoption of these constitutional amendments will be fraught with far reaching political consequences."[6]

While the proper course of action was being widely and heatedly disputed, Norbeck went boldly ahead. The election had strengthened his political control enormously and most people realized that his wishes would govern the situation. If he wanted additional state enterprises, he would get them. If not, none would be created. His political power made it that simple.

His recommendations to the legislature coincided with his campaign promises and in no sense did he retreat from his advanced position on the state ownership issue. He again urged the adoption of a law allowing the state to engage in water-power development and recommended an appropriation of $50,000 for surveying dam sites on the Missouri river. He advocated the establishment of a state-owned cement plant and the passage of a state hail insurance law. And he also recommended that the state immediately take steps to operate a coal mine.

Concerning the establishment of flour mills, packing plants, and terminal elevators, he displayed less enthusiasm and was unwilling to make a positive recommendation. Rather, he placed the responsibility squarely upon the legislature, saying that these propositions should "not be treated lightly," and that "serious consideration" should be given to working out practical plans. With a note of caution he warned that no action should be taken until "all . . . information possible was secured."[7]

Personally, Norbeck opposed the state's entering the milling business and even during the campaign caution had characterized his discussion of the matter. Although he urged the constitutional amendment permitting flour mills and terminal elevators,[8] it seems clear that he doubted their feasibility and advocated them largely for political purposes.

He did not, however, hesitate to urge the establishment of state-owned stockyards. He explained that "private ownership of stockyards works to the disadvantage of both the shipper and the buyer." He believed if the state owned and operated them it would protect South Dakota livestock

5 Aberdeen *Daily News,* January 6, 1919.
6 Mitchell *Sunday Republican,* January 5, 1918.
7 *Peter Norbeck to the South Dakota Legislature,* 1919. A pamphlet.
8 Norbeck to R. A. Nestos, November 5, 1921. Norbeck MS.

producers. He failed to specify the advantages that might come from such an arrangement and his indictment of privately owned stockyards was of the weakest sort.

This was Norbeck's answer to those who charged during and after the campaign of 1918 that he had advocated League principles only because it was politically expedient. In later years, after part of the state enterprises failed, some of his apologists insisted that actually he never believed in them, but was influenced by Harry King, his campaign manager, who, they charged, was concerned less with principle than political victory.[9] But the fact that he proceeded to carry out his program after the League's defeat refutes this accusation and testifies to his sincerity of purpose.

Norbeck's economic philosophy grew out of the same rural unrest that was responsible for the League, and both turned to a degree of public ownership for the solution of their problems. There can be no doubt but that his thinking was influenced by the League, and that its work spurred him on to sponsor projects he might not otherwise have considered urgent. He supported that part of the state-ownership program which he believed was "practical," and which would go furthest toward solving the most pressing farm problems. While several of his state-owned projects failed, he was sincere in advocating them. He never expressed any regret over his gubernatorial program.[10]

His message to the legislature was not exclusively devoted to farm problems. Partially because of his limited schooling, he was always conscious of the state's educational problems. He told the legislators that South Dakota's rural schools were far below standard and urged state aid for rural-teacher training and for rural consolidated schools. Since the legislature of 1917 had not provided free text books as he had recommended, Norbeck again advocated this. The lawmakers now followed his suggestion. In order to aid returning veterans, he suggested that the state establish a soldiers' land settlement bureau to purchase and improve land for sale to veterans on reasonable terms. He also asked the legislature to create a state bonding department.[11]

Again, as was true in 1917, many of the governor's recommendations were enacted into law. A state bonding department was established, a state cement commission was set up and empowered to acquire property and to construct a plant, and another commission was created to begin coal mining operations. State hail insurance was also provided. Norbeck's veterans legislation was passed along with a law providing free tuition at state schools for all honorably discharged service men.[12]

Norbeck and the Republicans, however, repudiated that part of the 1918 platform which called for state-owned terminal elevators and flour

9 W. R. Ronald, in interview with Author, July 10, 1944.
10 Norbeck to E. L. Senn, January 13, 1923. Norbeck MS.
11 *Peter Norbeck to the South Dakota Legislature,* 1919.
12 *South Dakota Session Laws,* 1919. See Chaps., 318, 324, and 136.

mills. Just a few days before the session's end, a legislative committee reported adversely on these proposals. It asserted that since transportation facilities and terminal elevators were closely connected, regulation of one without ability to control the other would not bring about the desired results. Since only the federal government could effectively regulate railroad rates, committee members thought it would not be wise to establish a terminal elevator. The committee said it had arrived at this conclusion after studying the movement in Canada where it had generally failed, and then added significantly: "In North Dakota the agitation in regard to terminal elevators has been largely political and a study of the developments in that state is of little economic value."[13]

The Farmers' Union, which claimed a membership of 10,000, also bitterly opposed establishing these state industries. The Union's farm relief plan was to stimulate and strengthen the cooperative movement in the state. The organization's legislative committee recommended creating a state cooperative credits commission, similar to the rural credits board, with power to grant loans to legally and soundly organized cooperatives up to fifty per cent of their actual property resources. Thus, instead of luring the state directly into business, only state loans would be granted to enable the farmers themselves to improve marketing conditions by establishing terminal elevators, creameries, mills, or whatever industries they thought necessary.[14] Many believed that this scheme would insure better management than could be obtained under a completely state-owned system, because the cooperatives would not be subject to political pressures. Also it was thought that the farmers would be more interested in the industries' success because of their direct financial stake.

This difference in policy did not indicate a cleavage on economic grounds, because both the League's and Union's membership represented a fair cross section of South Dakota farmers. Their programs and objectives, however, were conflicting. The Union called for financing its enterprises through cooperative effort with some state aid, while the League wanted the state to furnish all of the funds for a wide variety of projects. The Union also fought the League because it did not want a strong competing farm organization in the state, and the officials were fearful that their organization might lose its identity. This was well expressed by the president of the Kansas Farmers' Union who warned his members to avoid League membership![15] The South Dakota legislature refused to adopt the Union's program, and it gave no heed to Norbeck's earnest request for state-owned stockyards.

The question arises as to how these proposals became so unpopular after the election when the people voted by a majority of over 15,000 to accept them. Norbeck explained that many people voted for these projects

13 See the report in the *South Dakota House Journal*, 1919, pp. 672-91.
14 *The South Dakota Farmer*, 18:8 (February 14, 1919).
15 Hofland, "The Nonpartisan League in South Dakota," p. 23.

simply because they believed the constitutional restrictions should be removed. This is no doubt true. But also many citizens probably voted favorably because they believed it would help head off the Nonpartisan League.

With most of his program on the statute books by March, 1919, Norbeck turned to the administrative tasks. He inaugurated a huge road building program and directed the investigation for hydro-electric development. The real crusader in South Dakota for harnessing the Missouri river was state historian Doane Robinson. For years he had tried to interest South Dakota's governors in his pet project, but they viewed his idea skeptically. But Norbeck took Robinson's proposal seriously and made the first real progress in that state. Under a $50,000 legislative appropriation, his commission employed two engineers to survey possible dam sites on the Missouri. On April 20, 1920, the engineers recommended three possible locations for hydro-electric dams, the most favorable being about four miles north of Mobridge. On the basis of their survey the engineers concluded that development by private capital was then impracticable, but that the state could safely undertake such a project.[16] The cost was estimated at between $9,103,000 and $13,325,000, depending on the location chosen.

Nothing more was accomplished during Norbeck's administration, but he had laid the groundwork for later developments. In 1921 the legislature had a spirited fight over which site should be approved. Consequently, none of the proposals was sanctioned. The next year a constitutional amendment was initiated to build a hydro-electric dam at Mobridge, but it was defeated.[17] It was not until over two decades later that the federal government took hold of this matter and Congress provided for a Missouri river basin development.

It was during Norbeck's second term as governor that he carried out his first ambitious conservation program. Few people knew of his interest in park development and conservation of wild-life resources, but the temperament of this rough and energetic well-driller contained much of the aesthetic. He was attracted to and loved natural beauty. A deer grazing in a protected glade in his beloved Black Hills, a flock of honkers winging northward, or trees, lakes, and mountains blended into a picture of serene beauty—to him were the embodiment of art in nature.

Preserving natural beauty and wild-life was more than an interest, it was a passion. Norbeck never explained the source of this but one of his close friends credited it to his "primeval and ancestral instincts."[18] His only answer was: "perhaps you are right."[19]

16   Daniel W. Mead and Charles V. Seastone, *Report of the Feasibility of the Development of Hyrdo-Electric Power from the Missouri River in the State of South Dakota,* April 20, 1920.
17   Doane Robinson, *Encyclopedia of South Dakota,* p. 529.
18   William Williamson to Elmer George, January 16, 1924. Norbeck MS.
19   Norbeck to William Williamson, January 17, 1924. Norbeck MS.

As previously pointed out, his interest in conservation was not a selfish one. He was not a sportsman and spent summer after summer in the Black Hills, a game and fish paradise, without every trying to shoot a deer or catch a fish.

One of his greatest ambitions was to establish a great state park in the Black Hills. This became his chief hobby. Beginning in 1905, he worked for over thirty years creating a park of unusual beauty and proportions. Its beautification and accessibility became almost an obsession.

After his visit to Custer county in 1905 and his advocacy of a state park, little was done until 1911. In that year most of the land which ultimately became Custer State Park was donated to South Dakota by the federal government in place of school lands which could not be transferred for various reasons. After this land transfer, situated in Custer county, Norbeck insisted more persistently than ever that it should be used for a game preserve and park, and in 1912 he proposed that the state game fund be used for this development.[20] When the legislature met in 1913, he encouraged Senator John F. Parks to introduce a measure creating a state game preserve on the 61,440 acres which the federal government had turned over to the state. He asserted that while "the bill was not introduced by me, it was really one of my pet measures."[21]

After considerable legislative maneuvering, the bill, including an appropriation of $15,000, was passed.[22] Norbeck estimated that only fifteen to fifty deer were in the general area, but that at least 4000 deer, 1000 buffalo, 1000 elk, 500 antelope, and 150 mountain goats should be the ultimate goal. Fortunately, the eight-by-twelve-mile area was ideal for a park and game preserve. It contained heavy forest land, mountains towering as high as 7,240 feet, rugged canyons, rapid flowing streams, and beautiful glades and meadows. Thus it was suited for animals whose habitat was either grassland or mountain country.

Norbeck spent much time in the Black Hills and personally supervised the forty-mile fencing project which was completed in 1914. Very few Dakotans were interested in his work and it was said that he "could count his supporters upon the fingers of one hand."[23] The Black Hills ranchers were the most annoying adversaries. They strongly opposed fencing part of their former range and as late as 1921 they frequently cut the wire to let their cattle graze in the game preserve. Residents in the eastern part of the state objected because of the expense involved.

But in spite of these obstacles, he continued his work, and after becoming governor, he was in a position to complete his park program. He told the 1919 legislature that an unusual opportunity awaited the state in the

20 Norbeck to State Game Warden, August 28, 1912. Norbeck MS.
21 Norbeck to Fred Hepperly, March 11, 1913. Norbeck MS.
22 Robinson, *Encyclopedia of South Dakota*, p. 77.
23 Norbeck to H. S. Hedrick, July 16, 1914; and William Williamson to Elmer George, January 16, 1924. Norbeck MS.

creation of a permanent state park. Since the land within the game preserve belonged to the schools, it was subject to sale at any time and he urged that money be appropriated to purchase the school land. He further recommended establishing a state park board to supervise this development.[24] A law embodying these recommendations was enacted and $200,000 was appropriated to begin the land purchase program.[25]

Although he was making steady progress, he was dissatisfied because the most beautiful part of the Black Hills, the Sylvan Lake, Needles, and Harney Peak area, was not included in the park boundaries. It was part of the Harney National Forest. In 1920 he enlisted the support of Congressman Harry Gandy of Rapid City who secured national legislation permitting the area to be enclosed within the park. The addition, constituting approximately 30,000 acres, was designated as the Custer State Park Game Sanctuary and was placed under the custody of the park board. Norbeck became chairman of this board. The federal government retained title to the land, maintained supervision over the timber, and provided a fire patrol, but otherwise it was controlled by the state.

The South Dakota park was now one of the largest, if not the largest, state park in the entire nation and compared favorably with some of the larger national parks.

By 1920 his work was attracting widespread attention—so much so, that a legislative committee called on him and proposed that the name be changed to Norbeck park. But he told the legislators that he wanted no personal advertisement because "it stands in the way of getting further work done."[26]

To establish the park was only part of the job as Norbeck saw it. It must be made accessible to tourists. He spent days walking and riding over the area laying out unusual roads through the seemingly inaccessible places of rugged beauty. With C. C. Gideon and Scovel Johnson, state engineer, he tramped the trails on foot because horses could not walk over much of the terrain. Working their way through towering granite cliffs and heavy forest, they finally traversed the entire distance of a road which would take tourists through the Needles. The governor's trousers were badly torn and his legs were scratched and bleeding. It was not easy to push his 240 pounds over such a difficult route. As he sat on a log breathing heavily, he turned to Johnson and said: "Scovel, can you build a road through there," to which the engineer replied: "If you can furnish me enough dynamite."[27]

Luckily for the artistic beauty of the park, Johnson had some conception of the kind of road construction Norbeck wanted, but heated controversies

24 *Peter Norbeck to the South Dakota Legislature,* 1919.
25 *South Dakota Session Laws,* 1919, Chap., 165.
26 Norbeck to Robert D. Jones, February 18, 1929. Norbeck MS.
27 C. C. Gideon, in interview with Author, July 14, 1944.

between him and the other engineers were common. His desire was to preserve the natural beauty and to build roads where the public could obtain the best artistic view. This often contradicted commonly accepted engineering principles, but his policies usually prevailed. By 1922 the Needles highway was completed, and Norbeck saw his first real effort in picturesque highway building bear magnificent fruit.

It is difficult to explain Norbeck's almost total lack of interest in the momentous problems of peace during 1918 and 1919. Perhaps he was too engrossed with his own legislative program, but in any event, he seemed little concerned with such important problems as world peace, the League of Nations, and the Wilson-Senate conflict.

He did develop a temporary enthusiasm for the League of Nations, and recalled years later that when President Wilson first presented the idea "it made a very strong appeal to me."[28] When President Wilson toured the country in the fall of 1919 seeking support which might force the Senate to ratify the treaty incorporating the League, he held a meeting at Sioux Falls. Although the newspaper report that Norbeck presided was untrue, he seemed to be strongly in favor of the League. At least a few days later he asserted that he favored ratification of the treaty "substantially in its present form."[29]

However, he thought certain reservations would make the treaty much more desirable. He believed that the Senate "should at least wash its hands of the Shantung provision," which transferred German rights in Shantung to Japan, and he added: "they [sic] might make several other reservations or interpretations, all to the advantage of this country."[30] But he did not elaborate on this point.

At times he seemed eager to have the United States participate in world affairs, and perhaps even take a leading part. "Personally, I am not afraid of the entangling alliance," he wrote, "and I do not feel the duties of America are limited to its boundaries. I would use American troops, if need be, to protect not only Belgians, but Armenians, Serbs, and Poles,—until such time as the boundary lines become recognized and established."[31] On another occasion he said: "I don't believe we have much to fear from joining in the League with the other nations,—and while I am not at all sure it will prevent wars, I feel it is a duty of America to help establish order in the world, and help protect smaller nations."[32]

But his flicker of internationalism was soon to disappear. During his senatorial campaign of 1920, he followed the lead of his party. Political advertising appeared saying, "A vote for Norbeck is a vote for a Republican Administration in Washington and against the Wilson League of Nations."[33]

28 Norbeck to F. Jean Ehrenfried, February 20, 1925. Norbeck MS.
29 Norbeck to W. S. Cook, September 27, 1919. Norbeck MS.
30 Norbeck to C. D. Erskine, October 7, 1919. Norbeck MS.
31 *Ibid.*
32 Norbeck to Cash P. Jordon, October 7, 1919. Norbeck MS.
33 Huron *Evening Huronite,* October 21, 1920.

Whether this was actually Norbeck's view or was published out of political expediency, it is impossible to determine. Nonetheless, he apparently saw no reason for departing from his party's strategy.

One thing is certain. His attitude toward the League of Nations was not consistent and did not grow from firm conviction. Rather, it was vacillating and seemed to follow the path of expediency. The former was characteristic of many people throughout the entire nation and especially in the Midwest. Norbeck's thinking on the problem reflected a bewilderment, an uncertainty, and failure to understand the fundamental principle behind world organization designed to maintain world peace, and the part the United States should play.

Four years in the state's highest office made little difference in "Old Pete," the well-driller and agriculturalist. Physically, he got a little heavier and grey hairs were more numerous, but that was all. Contemporaries saw him in the governor's office as one who might have left the farm or the well-drill only a short while before. His grey trousers were usually unpressed and unless Mrs. Norbeck watched him closely, his coat and trousers were often unmatched. And he inevitably chose clashing color combinations! To keep him properly dressed was one of his wife's greatest trials. In full dress and on dignified occasions, however, Norbeck assumed a distinguished appearance. But so-called proper dress interested him little. Frequently, he worked in his shirt sleeves and commonly received visitors in this democratic manner. On one occasion he wore a pair of khaki unionalls to his office. He had no superficial dignity and no suppressed pride. By nature he was thoroughly democratic.

During his years as governor, Norbeck was unable to give his well-drilling business much personal attention. He supervised operations only in a general way and most of the active management was left to his brother, George, and to Charles Nicholson. By 1918 his firm had drilled approximately 8,000 artesian wells and business continued good during the period immediately after the war. Once he declared that his firm "had at least six months work arranged for in advance, and some contracts had to be refused."[34] Most of the time he made money easily, although frequently he had little cash, having it tied up in investments.

But if money came readily, he gave it liberally and spent it freely. He was not a spendthrift, but checks for $500 and $1,000 to the Mitchell Methodist hospital and to the American Syrian Relief illustrate his generosity. He usually insisted, however, that his donations be given no publicity. "I don't like this kind of advertisement," he said to the hospital officials.

Norbeck's two terms as governor amply demonstrated his capacity for actuating his objectives and ideals. Although he had a tendency to analyze problems from the political angle, at the same time he clung tenaciously to

34 Norbeck to Karle E. Winter, November 21, 1919. Norbeck MS.

his principles. He generally followed a policy of persuading men's reason and enlisting their cooperation on the assumption that his position was correct. But he almost instinctively relied on his personality and good fellowship to achieve success. And occasionally he resorted to political strong-arm methods, as had been true in the 1912 campaign. While these were often successful, they left sore spots and created enemies who were as bitter as his friends were loyal. Yet no other South Dakota governor has ever exercised such a strong influence upon the legislature and none so impressed his personality upon events during an administration.

CHAPTER VIII

NORBECK AND SOUTH DAKOTA'S STATE-OWNED INDUSTRIES

Of all the legislation sponsored by Norbeck, he viewed the rural credits law as his greatest achievement. What could be more reasonable, he argued, than to loan state funds to farmers on real estate mortgages at cheap interest rates? What greater service could the state perform for the bulk of its population?

Since 1896, when he began to engage actively in well-drilling, he had been in constant and intimate contact with the farm credit problem. He knew the difficulties involved in securing sufficient funds for operational and improvement purposes. In fact, he actually extended credit to scores of farmers when they did not have enough money to pay for artesian wells.[1]

As he came in closer contact with the credit needs of South Dakota farmers, he began dreaming of a more liberal farm loan plan; and by the time he had served two terms in the state senate, he had developed what he considered a practical rural credits system.[2] He reasoned that the state could borrow money at cheaper rates of interest than an individual farmer, and could in turn loan the funds directly to farmers at an interest rate only enough higher to cover handling charges. He suggested that the state take real estate mortgages to secure the loans, repayable over a long number of years, preferably thirty, and on an amortization plan.[3]

In 1915 the legislature passed a resolution submitting the question of state rural credits to the voters at the 1916 election. As lieutenant governor, Norbeck was influential in getting the resolution enacted. Between the time the legislature submitted the amendment and the election, however, the Federal Farm Loan Act was passed. Many farmers believed that a state plan was then unnecessary. But during the gubernatorial campaign, Norbeck spoke in every county on behalf of his measure. He also succeeded in pledging the party platform and the campaign speakers to the idea.[4] Then he received such an overwhelming vote, the rural credits amendment was approved by a vote of 57,569 to 41,959.[5]

Characterizing the Federal Farm Loan law as entirely inadequate, Norbeck proceeded to actuate his own plan. He referred to this subject in his inaugural address of 1917 as "one of the most important matters . . . at this session."[6] A statute embodying his recommendations was quickly passed and signed on February 26, 1917.

1 Norbeck and Nicholson, Annual Statement, 1908.
2 Gilbert C. Fite, "South Dakota's Rural Credit System: A Venture in State Socialism, 1917-1946," *Agricultural History*, 21:239-49 (October, 1947). Material from this article has been used with the permission of the Editor.
3 Norbeck to Charles Woodland, December 14, 1912. Norbeck MS.
4 Norbeck to V. E. Anderson, May 8, 1922. Norbeck MS.
5 *South Dakota Legislative Manual*, 1921, p. 440.
6 *Peter Norbeck to the South Dakota Legislature*, 1917. A pamphlet.

The law provided for a rural credits board consisting of the governor and four appointees. The board was authorized to borrow money on the state's credit and lend it directly to farmers on real estate mortgages. Loans were to be repaid on the amortization plan in not less than five nor more than thirty years. Funds could be borrowed to purchase land, equipment, and livestock, to make improvements or liquidate indebtedness on land. No loan could exceed seventy per cent of the land's value, plus forty per cent of the insured value of the improvements. A single farm loan could not exceed $10,000.[7] The board was authorized to sell rural credit bonds to provide the necessary capital. Norbeck wrote most of the important provisions and the law incorporated his ideas.

The bill passed with very little opposition. Extension of governmental functions was popular and in the progressive tradition. Years later the Sioux Falls *Daily Argus Leader* declared that only a few "lone souls" believed the scheme would not work successfully and at a great saving to the farmers.[8]

It has been persistently claimed and generally believed that the rural credits act was adopted to meet the attack of the Nonpartisan League. This is untrue. The legislature passed the proposed constitutional amendment before the League was born, even in North Dakota, and the law was in operation by the time the League had any substantial strength in the state. It was an old idea with Norbeck, one for which he had built up a great deal of popular support. It was not adopted to counteract so-called radicalism. It coincided with League philosophy but that is all.[9]

The act was a model of simplicity. When a loan application was received, an examiner investigated the property on which the mortgage would be taken, and reviewed the character and reputation of the borrower. The board then acted upon the examiner's recommendation.[10] After the loan was approved, the rural credit commissioner usually sent the money, with the necessary papers, to the farmer's banker, who closed the transaction and returned the mortgage to the board. Often a loan was completed in a week and the only cost to the farmer was furnishing an abstract of title. Such a loosely managed system, however, could easily result in high appraisals, excessive loans, and consequent loss of capital. An unfortunate practice soon developed where loans were not personally inspected by a department official. Letters were simply written to two or three local men who were familiar with the applicant.[11] Since a man would be asked to evaluate his neighbor's farm, he had a tendency to recommend the maximum!

7 *South Dakota Session Laws*, 1916-17, Chap., 333.
8 Sioux Falls *Daily Argus Leader*, August 16, 1944. The majority of the state's daily newspapers, as well as the farm journals gave the law enthusiastic support.
9 Norbeck to G. H. Henry, May 20, 1925; Norbeck to Mr. Mitchell, October 18, 1923. Norbeck MS.
10 Peter Norbeck, "For the Whole Family," *The Country Gentleman*, 85:4 (February 14, 1920).
11 Norbeck to W. C. Allen, December 18, 1924. Norbeck MS.

The first rural credits board consisted of Norbeck, C. M. Henry, J. E. Zeibach, Alfred Zoske, and A. W. Ewert. All of these men had wide business experience and were considered capable. Ewert, president of the Pierre National Bank of Commerce, was made treasurer. He was a progressive and a long time friend of Norbeck.

The first farm loan was made on October 20, 1917, and by July, 1919, six months before Norbeck left the governorship, the board had made loans aggregating $13,431,750. No official statements had been publicized before Norbeck's administrative responsibility ended in January, 1921, but the executive accountant reported that everything was in a satisfactory condition.[12]

Governor McMaster, chairman of the board from 1921 to 1925, called for an official report in 1922. Upon reading it, many South Dakotans began to doubt the wisdom of their farm loan plan. On June 30 of that year outstanding rural credit bonds totaled $41,500,000. This heavy obligation caused much uneasiness among many citizens; but the report carried an optimistic tone, concluding that "no losses of consequence are apparent."

At the same time, however, the board, perhaps unknowingly, disclosed a grave difficulty. It said that because of the unprecedented slump in farm prices during 1920 and 1921, it had felt obliged to "pursue a liberal policy towards borrowers." Where the farmers were found unable to pay their interest when due, the board asserted it was necessary to grant "forbearance."[13] It did not take a financial expert to realize the seriousness of a situation where the state had to meet interest obligations regularly on over $40,000,000, when it could not collect its payments on schedule. Taxpayers commenced to wonder if they might not be called on to keep the state financially solvent.

By June, 1924, the department had made 11,693 farm loans totaling over $45,000,000. The aggregate of rural credit bonds was $47,500,000. The average loan per acre amounted to fourteen dollars and seventy-one cents, while the appraised value of the secured land was thirty-five dollars and nineteen cents. Considering the character of much of the land, both the loans and the appraised value were clearly excessive.

Considerable criticism of the system developed before and during the 1923 legislative session; but after a special committee investigated the department it concluded that "no losses of consequence are likely to occur."[14] This conclusion was reached even though the state was obtaining many tracts of land through foreclosure!

By the latter part of 1924 rumors were widespread that all was not well in the department. When the legislature assembled in January of the

12 *Seventh Biennial Report of the South Dakota Executive Accountant,* 1923-24, p. 125.
13 *Report of the South Dakota Rural Credit Board,* 1922, p. 7ff. Cited hereafter as the Report of the Rural Credit Board.
14 See the report in the *South Dakota Senate Journal,* 1923.

following year, a resolution proposing an investigation was passed. Much to the surprise of everyone, Ewert refused to appear before the committee until he was summoned with a subpoena. When he did appear, he refused to bring the rural credit records demanded by the committee. On the same afternoon, following his appearance before the committee, he closed his bank which held about $400,000 in rural credit funds, thus making the records unavailable to the state officials until a national receiver had been appointed.[15]

Ewert's actions seemed to substantiate the rather general suspicion that something was wrong in the department. The committee soon proved this to be true. It was disclosed that the rural credits records were terribly confused and some of them were intermingled with Ewert's bank and personal files. It was also found that many deposits had been made in banks uncertified by the board, and that Ewert consistently kept more rural credit money in his own bank than was allowed by law. Furthermore, the committee revealed that Zoske had manipulated funds for personal advantage and for the benefit of his bank at Draper.

Another interesting disclosure showed that approximately seventy-five per cent of the loans had gone to liquidate indebtedness and that forty per cent had gone to pay notes and mortgages held by banks. With bankers administering the law locally, no doubt much of this had gone to redeem the bank's bad farm paper. While there were sufficient paper assets to pay the bonded indebtedness of $47,500,000, it was apparent that the taxpayers must aid in final liquidation. Loans totaling 12,116 had been made and about one-third, or 4,300, were in default as to interest or principal. Of this number 465 had been foreclosed or were in the process.

The committee concluded that there was no proof of defalcation or embezzlement, but that rural credit moneys had been handled in a "most questionable" manner. Finally, the legislators charged that perhaps Ewert had used the power which accompanied disbursement of rural credit monies to further his own political position and the political interest of those to whom he was responsible. This obviously referred to Senators Norbeck and McMaster, and the so-called progressive Republicans.[16]

Norbeck's correspondence throughout 1924 and early 1925 indicates that he was unaware of the serious condition in the department. On January 21, before the Ewert difficulty was publicly known, he wrote to State Senator Alan Bogue that he was certain the committee would find the rural credits department in excellent shape.[17] When the Ewert episode occurred, he criticized the treasurer for not cooperating with the committee and then added: "I care less about the political future of men than I do about the

15 "Report of the Select Legislative Committee," *South Dakota House Journal,* 1925, p. 783 ff.
16 *Ibid.,* p. 718ff.
17 Norbeck to Alan Bogue, January 21, 1925. Norbeck MS.

great advantage now secured by the enemies of the state rural credit system; they will try hard to discredit it."[18]

The 1925 legislature immediately passed a law prohibiting additional loans. No further rural credit bonds could be issued except for purposes of paying outstanding indebtedness. This directed the board to liquidate, thus putting South Dakota out of the money-lending business after about six and one-half years. An interim commission was appointed to carry on a more extensive investigation.

Some acquaintance with South Dakota's political situation in 1925 is necessary to understand the investigation, and what followed. The Republicans were sharply divided. Norbeck led one faction and Governor Carl Gunderson headed the other. This division had become accentuated in 1924 when Norbeck helped defeat Gunderson's friend, Thomas Sterling, in his race for United States senator. Likewise, Gunderson caused Norbeck and his friends as much political embarrassment as possible. Revelation of irregularities in the rural credits department offered Gunderson unusual opportunities.

The department became the center of an intra-party fight. Norbeck's political enemies tried to capitalize on the department's unsatisfactory conditions and he and his colleague, Senator McMaster, who was elected in 1924 with Norbeck's support, fought back with vigor. Even before the committee report of 1925 had been made public, ugly rumors circulated in Pierre to the effect that Governor Gunderson was "after" Norbeck and was attempting to "pin something on him."[19] Norbeck insisted that he should not be held responsible for the department's condition since he had left the governor's chair almost five years earlier, at which time everything was reported in good shape. "They cannot involve me in anything wrong," he wrote.[20]

To prove that he had been unfaithful to his trust, it was charged that Norbeck profited personally as president of the rural credits board from 1917 to 1921. He was accused of having given rural credit deposits to certain bankers and then getting a personal loan from the same institution. Norbeck and the bankers both denied this and it seems highly unlikely that these charges contained any truth in light of the fact that his annual income during those years was about $90,000.

He replied that his political enemies were endeavoring to destroy the rural credits system and were using its apparent failure as a means of removing him from the United States Senate. This assertion gained credence when his opponents used this as their chief issue in the campaign of 1926!

Norbeck sharply rebuked the legislature for abolishing the loaning provisions of the act. He declared that when the treasurer failed properly to

18 Norbeck to Francis Case, February 28, 1925. Norbeck MS.
19 Harry King to Norbeck, February 21, 1925. Norbeck MS.
20 Norbeck to S. X. Way, February 17, 1925. Norbeck MS.

fulfill his duties, the sensible thing to do was to appoint a new treasurer and not abandon the system. He added that discontinuance of loaning operations was "the hardest blow ever struck by the state legislature against its basic industry."[21] He argued that a friendly administration was needed to operate the department.

But it seemed impossible to keep the rural credits debacle out of politics. On the morning of October 8, 1925, the United States grand jury impaneled at Pierre passed a resolution accusing Norbeck and McMaster of "dereliction and malfeasance" of duty in connection with their administration of the department. The resolution stated that both former governors knowingly permitted Ewert to disobey the law. Although it was outside of its jurisdiction, the grand jury asked the governor or attorney-general to make an investigation to determine whether or not this asserted dereliction of duty constituted "criminal offences."[22] However, Buell Jones, attorney-general, refused to institute a suit because of lack of incriminating evidence.

Meanwhile, Ewert was indicted on charges of misapplication and embezzlement of rural credit funds amounting to $211,437.59. He was convicted and sentenced to eleven years in the state penitentiary. It was found that he had manipulated rural credit monies through a dummy company for his own personal gain.

The interim commission reported to the legislature in 1927. It revealed that the total bonded indebtedness was $45,000,000. But before all the bonds were retired an additional $27,570,586.25 would be due in interest. This meant that $73,070,586.25 would be necessary for complete liquidation. With shrinking farm values it was becoming increasingly apparent that the taxpayers must come to the rescue. They did not have long to wait. In 1928 South Dakota's citizens were called on to help meet the department's deficiency and a special tax levy of $1,000,000 was initiated.[23] The remaining history is mostly one of liquidation and it is estimated that the taxpayers will have contributed $57,000,000 to the project by 1960 when liquidation will be completed.[24]

Why was this venture such a disastrous failure and to what extent was Norbeck, father of the system, responsible? By far the greatest contributing factor was the agricultural deflation following World War I. Most of the rural credit loans were made when the price of land was high and consequently they were seriously inflated. To make matters worse, the board did not lower its loans proportionately as land prices decreased. For instance, between 1919 and 1921, when South Dakota land values

21 Quoted in the Minneapolis *Sunday Tribune*, September 20, 1925.
22 Pierre *Daily Capital Journal*, October 8, 1925.
23 *Report of the Rural Credit Board*, 1928, p. 11.
24 "Special Report of the Rural Credit Department," 1945, p. 7. A mimeographed pamphlet.

dropped almost one-half, the board's loans only declined on an average of two dollars an acre. Loans were simply too generous.

Second only to the agricultural depression, the most serious difficulty was the apparent impossibility of separating the system from factional politics. In the first place, the easy credit system had been a popular political move for Norbeck and his faction of the Republican party. In 1918 and 1920, when the system was yet popular, Norbeck took every opportunity to use it to strengthen his political campaigns. When the system failed it was only natural that the anti-Norbeck crowd attempted to discredit him. Some officials actually gloried in losses and used this in two major campaigns in an attempt to defeat Norbeck. He, being the father of the plan, felt obliged to defend it. He boasted that anyone who opposed the rural credits system would have to meet him on the political battlefield.[25] This placed the department in the midst of an intra-party whirlwind and the taxpayers reaped the results.

A third difficulty was failure to work diligently in collecting the department's assets. When the deflation struck in 1921, Governor McMaster publicly declared that so long as he was in office no rural credits mortgage would be foreclosed if the farmer made a determined effort to pay.[26] For all practical purposes, this meant a moratorium on rural credit payments, while at the same time the state had to meet its obligation to bondholders. Leniency in individual cases was a necessity and often good business, but to establish it as a general policy meant that many farmers who were able to pay did not do so. Millard Scott, who in later years probably did more than anyone to liquidate the department, asserted in 1945 that one of the most important factors contributing to failure was "a lax and unbusiness-like collection policy."[27]

Another reason the plan failed was because the board made many poor or doubtful loans. When the deflation set in and bankers found themselves burdened with mortgages of uncertain value, they often encouraged their mortgagees to get a rural credit loan. When this was done, the banker secured his money and left the state with a mortgage of questionable worth. Consequently, the rural credit department received more than its share of poor loans.[28] And some loans were obtained with no thought of repayment. It was a virtual sale to the state. The system's laxness in this regard helped create losses and could have been easily corrected by appropriate legislation.

There were also other weaknesses. The small margin between the interest paid by the state and that received on farm mortgages was never enough to build a reserve fund to care for delinquent payments, losses,

25 Norbeck to Chet Leedom, February 21, 1927. Norbeck MS.
26 Fred Christopherson, "A State Goes Into Business and Out Again," *Nation's Business,* 17:48-50 (May, 1929).
27 "Special Report of the Rural Credit Department," 1945, p. 7.
28 Christopherson, "A State Goes Into Business and Out Again," pp. 48-50.

and department operating expenses. The department never operated on an entirely self-sufficient basis. The use of rural credit money to bolster tottering state banks also occasioned some loss. Approximately $850,000 was lost through bank failures. Not to be overlooked was the fact that during the 1920's the entire system was repudiated by South Dakota's citizens. State ownership became unpopular and the loss of public support was a serious blow.

Norbeck cannot escape partial blame for the rural credit debacle. He certainly was not guilty of any intentional wrongdoing or of any personal dishonesty. But his judgment proved weak on several occasions. The fact that he inaugurated the plan during an inflationary period was his worst mistake. He made no attempt to modify a loosely drawn and liberally administered law during the 1919 legislative session. His great faith in the future of South Dakota and his belief that farming would continue profitable there clouded his usual good business judgment. The fact that a majority of South Dakota's citizens agreed with him does not excuse him. Furthermore, while the board which he appointed appeared to consist of honest, conservative business men, two members proved to be bad selections. And Norbeck must also bear some responsibility for dragging the rural credits system into politics. By his own admission, he took full advantage of its popularity when it was popular with the voters.

On the other hand, he cannot be held responsible for the policies of his successors. There is no substantiating evidence that he used the department for personal gain, and his honesty was above reproach. A majority of South Dakota's voters continued to believe that he had honestly and conscientiously administered the trust placed in him.

The rural credits system had been operating over two years before the state began to mine coal and sell hail insurance, and it was not until late in 1924 that cement production started. Norbeck was firmly convinced that private companies charged exorbitant prices for these products and that the state could save its citizens untold millions by supplying them. Both in the case of coal and cement he frequently referred to "unfair competition" and "monopolistic prices." In 1919 he told the legislators that "it is good business judgment" to engage in the coal mining business. A state-owned mine, he asserted, would furnish coal at cheaper rates and the resulting competition would force lower prices for all coal sold in the state.[29] Besides bringing about lower coal prices, he hoped to stimulate the use of lignite which was abundant in northwestern South Dakota.

His idea regarding establishing a cement plant was the same. He declared that the risk of "unfair competition from without the state is too great. The state can well afford to operate such a plant at cost in order to re-establish competition and reduce the price to the consumer."[30]

29 *Peter Norbeck to the People of South Dakota*, 1919. A pamphlet.
30 Peter Norbeck, *Message to the People of South Dakota* (Redfield, 1918), p. 10.

That substantial popular demand existed for these projects, there is no doubt. The coal mine, cement plant, and state hail insurance amendments passed by substantial majorities.[31] Referring to coal mining and cement production, the Pierre *Daily Capital Journal* asserted: "This appeals to us as being not only wise but selecting the two industries that most vitally affect the masses of the state."[32] The Sioux Falls *Daily Argus Leader,* a bitter opponent of the state in business, said of the cement plant: "This is another case of the state going into business where it has material advantage over private enterprise."[33] Many South Dakota farmers strongly endorsed the idea of state hail insurance. This was not because they suffered greater hail losses than farmers in surrounding states, but because they had become imbued with the state-ownership philosophy which was so popular in that area.

Norbeck personally supervised locating the coal mine, a task that took over six months and an expenditure of almost $17,000.[34] While there were large quantities of lignite in northwestern South Dakota, the best fields were located too far from the main railway lines to make their purchase practicable. After drilling over 100 test holes around Firesteel, Isabel, and in Perkins county, the commission decided that the best prospects were not in South Dakota, but near Haynes, just across the line into North Dakota. A mine there could be purchased reasonably and it was near the main tracks of the Chicago, Milwaukee, and St. Paul railroad. Norbeck fully realized that the commission would invite sharp criticism by purchasing a mine outside the state boundary, but in light of the transportation difficulties, the mine near Haynes was purchased.

Norbeck closed the deal on August 31, 1920, and later remarked that he "drove as hard a bargain as I would if I had been buying it for myself." The mine contained an estimated 1,500,000 tons of coal, and other property was included in the transaction. The approximate cost was $45,000. If too much was paid, he said, "the responsibility is on me."[35]

The 1919 legislature appropriated $150,000 to initiate the mining venture, but because of poor management another $35,000 had to be given the mining commission in 1921. This made the state's total investment $185,000.

In keeping with Norbeck's policy, the state began selling its highest grade lignite at $3.50 a ton, or about one dollar cheaper than the commercial firms in the area. Most of the coal went to the state institutions, and by

31 *South Dakota Legislative Manual,* 1919, p. 103. The coal mine, cement plant, and hail insurance amendments passed by majorities of 15,626, 12,330, and 15,223 respectively.
32 Pierre *Daily Capital Journal,* January 7, 1919.
33 Sioux Falls *Daily Argus Leader,* October 13, 1920.
34 Norbeck to Dennis O'Leary, November 1, 1921. Norbeck MS.
35 *Ibid.*

1922 they were buying it for cost, or about two dollars a ton.[36] The sales policy provided for giving these institutions preference and any surplus was sold to private concerns at only a small profit. An attempt was made to fulfill the original objective of supplying coal as cheap as possible.

A little over 200,000 tons had been mined by 1926 and a surplus and reserve of $67,673.22 had accumulated.[37] Nothing had been refunded to the state treasury, however, as the surplus was used for expansion and development. But this represented the height of the mine's prosperity. Inefficient management and gradual depletion of the coal supply proved to be the beginning of the end. Matters drifted along until 1931 when a legislative committee was instructed to make a thorough investigation of the mine. It was found that only about 150,000 tons of coal remained and it appeared as though the state's original investment could never be returned. Also much poor management was revealed. Among the committee's recommendations was one calling for the state to abandon the coal mining business immediately, provided the mine and equipment could be sold at a reasonable figure.[38]

But the mine was not sold until 1934 in the midst of the depression. In March of that year, after having produced 499,363 tons, it was sold for $5,500. The state's loss was reported to be $174,077.40.[39]

Many citizens, however, including Norbeck, believed that this experiment in state capitalism had saved the taxpayers much more than the stated loss. It was argued that cheaper fuel prices to the state institutions had actually saved many thousands of dollars. As previously emphasized, Norbeck's original idea had been to furnish cheap fuel to the state institutions and to force coal prices down by creating competition. The institutions got cheap fuel because they purchased many tons at cost, plus freight. E. O. Roush, who directed mining operations, estimated in 1922 that Northern State Normal saved nineteen per cent on its fuel bill.[40] The state engineer concluded in 1928 that the state mine had reduced the price of out-of-state coal by about fifty cents a ton throughout much of South Dakota, because of its competition.[41] Seventeen state institutions used state coal in 1924, totaling forty-two per cent of their entire consumption. Other plants also saved money. The Pierre *Daily Capital Journal* claimed that the Pierre public utilities plant spent $50,000 a year for coal until it changed to state lignite, when the expense was reduced to $21,000.[42] Mayor J. E. Hipple of that

36 "Report of the Special Committee Appointed by the Legislature to Investigate the South Dakota Coal Mine," February 25, 1925, p. 3. Cited hereafter as, "Report of the Special Committee."
37 *Report of the Coal Mining Commission*, 1926. p. 2. A pamphlet.
38 "Report of the Joint Committee Appointed to Investigate the Coal Mine," *South Dakota House Journal*, 1932, pp. 198-9. Cited hereafter as "Report of the Joint Committee."
39 Sioux Falls *Daily Argus Leader*, August 23, 1935.
40 *Report of the South Dakota Coal Mining Commission*, 1922, p. 5.
41 "Report of the Joint Committee," pp. 8-9.
42 Pierre *Daily Capital Journal*, November 2, 1933.

city said: "The state coal mine in my estimation has saved the people of South Dakota millions of dollars, by forcing the coal trust to revise prices, and by direct saving by those who have patronized the state mine."[43] The strongest substantiating evidence for this viewpoint came from the New York Municipal Research Bureau, which indicated in 1922 that very definite savings were being accomplished.[44]

But this conclusion was not unanimous. The Sioux Falls *Daily Argus Leader*, while admitting some benefits, thought it very unlikely that they approximated $174,000.[45]

A fair conclusion seems to be that in spite of some mismanagement, the mining venture cost the state little, if anything. It is impossible to determine, however, whether the savings fell short of or exceeded the investment. In any event, it should not be judged in terms of profits or loss to the state treasury, because profits were not the objective. Rather, it was low coal prices and here it was successful.

While coal production began in 1920, there was considerable delay in getting the cement plant operating. Norbeck's commission, after inspecting various sites, adopted a resolution just before he left office locating the plant at Rapid City. Construction was delayed, however, and the plant was not completed until 1924. The first carload of cement was shipped in January of the following year. By that time the $2,000,000 which had been raised by selling cement bonds was expended, and the legislature loaned the cement commission another $275,000 for operational purposes.[46]

The commission established the policy of selling cement through the recognized trade channels and at prevailing market prices. In fact, the sales manager presented a sales policy identical with that of the Portland Cement Association! Governor Gunderson bitterly bemoaned this fact. He asserted that "it was clearly the intent of the people of the state, when they authorized construction of the plant, to secure . . . cement at cost of production and delivery." "South Dakota," he concluded, "is supposed to be fighting the cement and other trusts, yet, in this case, we are apparently submitting to their terms and regulations."[47] Norbeck also opposed this policy. But the commission's view prevailed and there was no attempt to lower substantially the price of cement.

Operating on a strictly business basis, the plant prospered. During two decades over 8,000,000 barrels of cement were manufactured and sold for over $21,000,000.[48] In July, 1943, the cement bonds were completely

43   J. E. Hipple to Norbeck, March 10, 1930. Norbeck MS.
44   Quoted in the *Twelfth Biennial Report of the South Dakota State Engineer,* 1927-28, pp. 43-4.
45   Sioux Falls *Daily Argus Leader,* May 5, 1936.
46   Cement bonds were sold in 1921 and 1923.
47   "Carl Gunderson to the South Dakota Legislature," *South Dakota Senate Journal,* 1925, p. 31.
48   *Twenty Years of Progress and Successful Operation,* p. 29. A pamphlet published by the cement commission in 1944.

retired, and a year later $1,250,000 was returned to the state's general fund. The revenue from a general tax levy in the twenties to retire cement bonds and pay interest amounted to $1,240,912.47.[49] Thus the cement plant is entirely free of debt, the taxpayers are out nothing, and on July 1, 1944, the state's general fund had a surplus of over $9,000 from the plant's operations. To achieve success, however, the price of cement was not materially lowered to South Dakota citizens, which was the original purpose.

Several factors contributed to this result. During the period from 1939 to 1945, war requirements created an unusual demand. The plant, too, has been singularly free from politics and most of the time has been blessed with good management. The consistent policy has been to make profits and not lower the price to the consumer. Finally, exemption from taxation and relatively cheap capital have also contributed to its success.

The state hail insurance law of 1919 provided that existing administrative machinery be used to administer the project, under the direction and supervision of the state insurance commissioner. Norbeck believed that compulsory insurance was necessary if the plan was to succeed, and his idea was carried out. The total crop land was subject to a premium tax, unless specifically exempt upon application by the farmer before June 1 of each year. When the assessor gathered information on other taxable property, he was to determine the number of crop acres cultivated by each farmer. He then reported this to the county auditor, who assessed a premium tax against the crop land. The amount was first determined by the legislature, but later by a commission. The farmer received ten dollars an acre protection against hail loss. Premiums were paid to the county auditor like other taxes, and the collections were then deposited with the state hail insurance department which paid the losses.[50] It was actually a mutual plan operated and controlled by the state.

After operating two years, the state hail insurance fund totaled $900,000. This amount had accrued after paying all hail losses, and in spite of the fact that state insurance was only about fifty cents an acre for ten dollars protection. This was only a little more than half that charged by commercial firms.[51] It is no wonder that Norbeck's enthusiasm for this system increased.

In 1929, after operating ten seasons, the hail insurance department had carried a total risk of $236,006,790. South Dakota farmers had been paid almost $10,000,000 on hail losses and the department showed a balance of $46,900.86. But this figure was deceiving, because in order to keep the system solvent it had been necessary to borrow $600,000. This was necessitated because most of the assets were unpaid tax premiums.[52]

49 *Ibid.*, p. 27.
50 *South Dakota Session Laws,* 1919, Chap., 243. The office of Deputy Commissioner of Hail Insurance was created to supervise this business.
51 Sioux Falls *Daily Argus Leader,* December 5, 1919.
52 *Report of the South Dakota Hail Insurance Department,* 1929, p. 14.

By 1930 the business of the department had declined almost one-half from that of ten years earlier. This was due, first of all, to the decreased amount of hail insurance being purchased during the economic depression. As was true with the other state enterprises, the hail insurance department suffered from the marked reaction against the state in business and it lost public support. Furthermore, politics played an unhealthful role after 1927, and there were frequent changes in personnel which did not permit the creation of an effective adjustment force. Also there was increased opposition from private companies.[53] An additional factor, and one that can scarcely be over-emphasized, was that many farmers resented the law's automatic insurable feature. There were many instances in which farmers did not fully understand the law or perhaps they failed to file an exemption before the deadline. Therefore, if they did not want the state insurance, they resented paying the premium tax. This was especially true if they had suffered no loss that year. While failure to file an exemption was the farmer's fault, the so-called "forced insurance" created a lot of enemies.[54]

Considering these factors, it is not surprising that the department was abolished in 1933. The liquidators endeavored to collect enough unpaid premiums to pay the department's $263,000 indebtedness, but they were unsuccessful. The legislature of 1941 appropriated this amount to liquidate the business. The department had $269,570.48 on its books three years later with practically no chance of making any substantial collections.[55]

The uncollectable assets, which total more than the amount contributed by the legislature, indicated that premiums were sufficiently high to cover the losses and operating expenses. The difficulty arose when the insured did not pay his premiums. The state assumed that chance when it passed a law operating on such a basis. It should have been clear to Norbeck and to all the lawmakers that some taxes always are in arrears and that some are uncollectable, and therefore, that some premiums would never be paid. If another method of premium payment had been devised, success might have been possible. No commercial insurance company could or would operate if the premiums were not fully paid, and the state should have followed a similar policy.

In spite of this criticism, however, the scheme can hardly be deemed a failure. Because of decreased insurance rates, it saved the farmers of South Dakota, assuming that hail insurance is an economic asset, a total of $7,465,000 between 1919 and 1929, or an average annual saving of about $600,000.[56] Norbeck believed that state competition not only gave the

53 D. E. Walker to Norbeck, November 13, 1930. Norbeck MS.
54 L. M. Larson to Author, January 16, 1945. Larson was county auditor in Clark county.
55 W. A. Mueller, South Dakota Insurance Commissioner, to Author, November 29, 1944.
56 D. E. Walker, Deputy Insurance Commissioner, to Norbeck, November 13, 1930.

farmers cheaper insurance, but was instrumental in forcing private companies to adjust their dues and to give more liberal and more prompt adjustments. This business, more than any of the other enterprises, probably represented the state's best opportunity to be of service to its farmers.

Norbeck, a son of the progressive movement, who was nurtured on agricultural discontent and unrest, led the South Dakota farmers a considerable distance along the road of state socialism. He never believed that some type of utopia lay at the end of this course. But he was firmly convinced that certain economic ills could best be eliminated through a limited degree of public ownership. The fact that failure ran rampant through most of the businesses, did not cause him to abandon his basic principle. It was the weakness of those who operated them, and not the principle that was wrong, he argued.

CHAPTER IX

A WELL-DRILLER GOES TO WASHINGTON

The possibility that any of Norbeck's popular state enterprises would eventually fail, costing the taxpayers millions and himself political embarrassment, was far from his mind on the evening of March 19, 1920. He and General Leonard Wood, Republican presidential aspirant, relaxed in the quiet comfort of the spacious Norbeck living room. And as the smoke rose lazily from their cigars, they discussed the turbulent political situation.

South Dakota's primary election was only a few days away and Wood's chances of obtaining the support of the state's national convention delegates were being seriously threatened by the rapidly growing strength of Illinois' Frank Lowden. As the evening wore on, Norbeck's nomination to the United States Senate received only scant consideration. His nomination and election were assured. Most South Dakota Republicans accepted his candidacy as a matter of course. It was the proper reward for a popular governor. But whether South Dakota would support his friend Wood was much more in doubt. Even though the Norbeck political machine was bending every effort in his behalf, the general's strength was fading.

Norbeck's friendship for Wood was not of long standing. It had been only the preceding summer that they had become well acquainted at the dedication of a Roosevelt monument near Deadwood. He later admitted that he had been captivated by Wood's personality and character, and concluded that he was a man of genuine presidential stature.[1]

Norbeck had not been so exuberant over a candidate since 1912. Wood is the "natural successor of old Theodore Roosevelt," said the well-driller. And he added that Wood had the "progressive support and was right on the farm question."[2] His personal feeling of friendship for Wood obviously clouded his political judgment. Some of his statements reveal an unusual naivete. "Wood is a poor man," he wrote, "but he has thousands of friends who will contribute [to his campaign] small amounts."[3]

From the viewpoint of a progressive, it would have been much more logical for him to support Johnson, Roosevelt's running mate in 1912. But of Johnson, he said: "His location and position on the League of Nations . . . prevents him being a national favorite at this time."[4]

Norbeck's statement that Wood had the progressive support was only partly true. He had the Norbeck progressives behind him, but such a leading South Dakota liberal as W. R. Ronald of the Mitchell *Evening Republican* supported Lowden, who generally had the farm support. While

---

1 Herman Hagedorn, *Leonard Wood a Biography*, 2 vols., (New York, 1931), II, pp. 346-9.
   2 Norbeck, "Memorandum," 1935. Norbeck MS.
   3 Norbeck to O. S. Basford, December 29, 1919. Norbeck MS.
   4 *Ibid.*

the Sioux Falls *Daily Argus Leader* also backed Lowden, editor Day worked for Norbeck's re-election, calling him a "big two-fisted, broadshouldered man, who is never neutral and is always to be found where the shells fly thickest—exactly the type of man South Dakota wants in Washington."[5] Norbeck's position was not consistent. He expressed an ardent desire to send a progressive Republican to the White House, but he did not support the most progressive candidate, and he even admitted that Wood would probably not be a popular president.[6]

While most of his efforts went to secure Wood presidential delegates, he did not altogether ignore his own campaign. He boasted of his record as governor, pointing to the state rural credits act, the state coal mine, hail insurance, and other laws for which he had been responsible. The conservative Republicans showed limited activity and supported Judge Richard Haney of Mitchell, but Norbeck's 13,000 majority amply demonstrated his popularity and the political bankruptcy of South Dakota's conservatives. The Wood delegates to the national convention achieved victory with greater difficulty, winning by approximately 5,000 votes.[7] In the last stages of the campaign Lowden's popularity rapidly increased and it is probable that without Norbeck's support Wood's defeat would have been assured.

Norbeck attended the national Republican convention in Chicago as head of South Dakota's delegation. He opposed Harding's nomination to the end. All the South Dakota delegates voted for Wood through the ninth ballot, and even on the tenth and last, over half of them, including Norbeck, refused to climb on the Harding bandwagon.[8]

The November campaign developed into a rather dull three-way race between Norbeck, U. S. G. Cherry, Sioux Falls attorney and Democrat, and Tom Ayres, representing what remained of the Nonpartisan League. The Mitchell [Sunday] *Morning Republican,* which had opposed Norbeck in the primary, aptly summarized the political chances of his opponents when it said they had about as much possibility of defeating him as a "cat with tallow candle legs striving to get through Hades."[9]

The League of Nations issue played an inconspicious role in South Dakota's 1920 election. The state platforms merely reflected the position of the national parties and the candidates all but ignored the question. As previously pointed out, Norbeck simply followed the party line, but did it without much interest or enthusiasm. He emphasized what he termed the unfitness and bungling of the Democrats, and his campaign was almost exclusively devoted to state problems.

The futility of the opposition's efforts became obvious when Norbeck

5 Sioux Falls *Daily Argus Leader,* March 15, 1920.
6 Norbeck to Harry King, September 30, 1919. Norbeck MS.
7 *South Dakota Legislative Manual,* 1927, p. 179.
8 *Proceedings of the National Republican Convention,* 1920, pp. 183-225.
9 Mitchell *Morning Republican,* October 28, 1920.

rolled up 92,267 votes, while Ayres and Cherry together received only 81,192.[10] The prediction of the Mitchell *Morning Republican* had not been far amiss, and that of the irritated Huron *Daily Huronite* editor, who four years earlier had forecast this result, proved to be exactly correct.

Norbeck went alone to Washington late in March, 1921. His family remained in Redfield where the children were attending school. The senator and his old friend, William Williamson, South Dakota's freshman congressman, obtained quarters at the Congress Hall Hotel. Williamson's companionship meant a great deal to Norbeck during the twelve years they spent together in Washington, and he relied heavily on Williamson's counsel and advice.[11]

His first impression of Washington was anything but flattering. To him capital life was highly artificial, pretentious, and unattractive. The lonesomeness that comes only in a bustling, crowded city made him long for the open prairies. At times during those first lonely days in Washington, his desire to return home became so strong that he seriously considered resigning, giving up his political career, and again assuming active management of his business.[12]

On April 11 Senator Sterling, dignified, well groomed, and looking every bit a senator, announced that his colleague was present and ready to take the oath of office. Eight years earlier this heavy, somewhat rough looking man beside him, whom he was about to escort down the aisle, had been largely responsible for sending him to Washington. Sterling could have hardly imagined then that the well-driller would eventually join him. Certainly he did not perceive that within four years more the Norbeck machine would help defeat him by throwing its support to McMaster, who was more progressive.

Norbeck found the senators from his section an interesting group. He already knew a number of them and his friendliness and good fellowship made further acquaintance easy. North Dakota boasted Porter J. Mc-Cumber and Edwin F. Ladd. The latter had gained national fame as a crusader for pure food and drug legislation and as president of North Dakota Agricultural College. McCumber, a conservative and high tariff man, had been an administration wheelhorse since 1899, and was soon to gain recognition as co-author of the McCumber-Fordney tariff bill. Nebraska still supported progressive, independent, and capable George W. Norris, although Democrat Gilbert M. Hitchcock, Wilson's line general during the peace treaty struggle, was about to be repudiated. From Kansas came Arthur Capper, former governor and publisher of numerous farm journals. Small, mild-mannered, and highly sensitive, Capper's personality hardly seemed in harmony with his vigorous newspaper policy. Along with Capper

10 *South Dakota Legislative Manual*, 1923, p. 314.
11 William Williamson to Author, February 26, 1945.
12 Norbeck to G. W. Wright, December 26, 1921. Norbeck MS.

came Charles Curtis, distinguished by his Indian blood, clever politics, and unswerving loyalty to conservative Republicanism. Iowa voters were still supporting Senator A. B. Cummins, leader of the state's progressive movement, but whose progressiveness was growing noticeably fainter with the passing years. William S. Kenyon, organizer of the senatorial Farm Bloc, also represented the Tall Corn state.

And there was "Old Bob" LaFollette, fighter for progressive causes, independent of party bosses, and leader of many political liberals. There were also Frank B. Kellogg and Knute Nelson from the North Star state. Kellogg's service in the Senate and to his party was soon to be rewarded with the office of Secretary of State.

Influential Republicans from outside of Norbeck's section included William E. Borah, isolationist, reputedly liberal, fearless, and an outstanding orator. California boasted Hiram Johnson, bitter League of Nations foe and losing vice presidential candidate in 1912. There was Henry Cabot Lodge, old and embittered, and George Moses of "Sons of the Wild Jackass" fame and Senate satirist, who held leading positions in party councils. And so did James E. Watson of Indiana, who in Norbeck's judgment epitomized conservatism of the worst kind. These were only a few of the men with whom Norbeck found himself and with whom he became intimately acquainted. With some of them he agreed on political matters, with others he violently disagreed. But he soon learned to work with them all and to enjoy a wide friendship in the Senate, with both conservative and progressive senators. Of this group Norris and Hiram Johnson became his closest personal friends.

Congress was slow in starting to work. Norbeck, with characteristic energy and enthusiasm, was impatient at the inaction and delay. He had yet to learn that he was a member of the world's greatest deliberative body! He established himself in the office of his Democratic predecessor, Edwin S. Johnson, and also retained Johnson's secretary, Julian Blount. Thus many details which might ordinarily have taken considerable time for a new senator to learn were easily and quickly disposed of by Blount, who had been in Washington for twelve years.

Norbeck was given what he considered very desirable committee assignments. They were Agriculture and Forestry, Banking and Currency, Public Lands and Surveys, and Mines and Mining.[13] While these might have been something less than satisfactory to one coming from a state of greater political importance and to one of greater political ambitions, Norbeck was content with the appointments. His first choice was Agriculture and Forestry. He hoped to play a leading role in framing badly needed farm legislation. His strong interest in conservation made him appreciate the Public Lands assignment, a committee which handled most

13 *Congressional Directory*, 1921, p. 191.

of that legislation. He showed less interest in Mines and Mining and practically none in Banking and Currency.

During the first few weeks of the session, the committees held only infrequent meetings. Norbeck attended an occasional gathering of the Banking and Currency committee, but usually found too few members present to do business. Therefore, he spent his time fulfilling requests from his South Dakota constituents and caring for his correspondence. He began the practice of giving every letter his personal attention, one which he had to abandon in later years. He also found an opportunity to read a great deal and almost every day he would send a secretary to the Library of Congress for books, or to one of the administrative departments for statistical data. And he did not overlook patronage possibilities during those early days of the session. Much to his regret, he found that he was unable to place his most worthy supporters in desirable positions.[14] He admitted to friends that a senator's patronage was not as extensive as he had imagined. Furthermore, his colleague, Senator Sterling, who was a close friend of the administration, received most of the choicest appointments. This foreshadowed the split between Norbeck and Sterling.

Washington offered some attractions that Norbeck thoroughly enjoyed. His interest in art made him familiar with most of the great medieval and modern painters and sculptors. While this may seem like an unusual interest for a man of Norbeck's background, few things gave him more genuine pleasure than to spend hours in an art gallery. He also found pleasure in visiting the zoo, and seldom spent any length of time in a city without enjoying this hobby. It was not uncommon for him to visit one or more of these favorite haunts, which included museums, two or three times a week. His daily routine included a walk, sometimes as long as ten or twelve miles. In this way he remained close to nature for which he always had such a deep appreciation. He may also have hoped that this exercise would help reduce his 224 pounds![15]

In September his family arrived in Washington. Within a month they were living in a modest eight-room house quite a distance from the Capitol, but close to high school. The two youngest children, Selma and Harold, lived with their parents; the oldest daughter, Nellie, registered at Goucher College in Baltimore; and Ruth remained in South Dakota to attend college. Norbeck found living in Washington unexpectedly expensive, and he wrote that almost everyone he knew was having difficulty living on his salary. He admitted that his salary was insufficient to maintain his home and keep the children in school.[16] However, the Norbecks lived well.

Norbeck's political policy in Washington was one of moderate progressivism. As a candidate for the Senate, there had been no doubt in his

14 Norbeck to H. S. Hedrick, April 28, 1921. Norbeck MS.
15 Norbeck to Nellie Norbeck, August 1, 1922, Norbeck MS.
16 Norbeck to Harry King, November 6, 1921. Norbeck MS.

mind what course he would pursue if elected. He stated that his purpose since entering public life always had been "that of trying to do something to better the conditions of the average man and woman."[17] While believing he was a progressive, he remarked: "I want to have my feet on the ground and stand for the things that are sound and will work out in practice. Otherwise, we get so much reaction that it results in little or no progress."[18] His statement may sound hollow to those who have seen the failure of his state enterprises, but at the time they seemed "practical."

Theodore Roosevelt's middle-of-the-road progressivism was still his ideal. He hoped that the Republican party would again accept the progressiveness of Roosevelt's day. He took pride in listing himself as a "Theodore Roosevelt Republican" in the *Congressional Directory*. Both contemporary Republican conservatism and Townley radicalism were distasteful to him.

When he first arrived in Washington, Norbeck hoped it would be possible to give his party whole-hearted support. But he never thought of giving up his privilege of vigorously and uncompromisingly opposing it, when he thought it was wrong on fundamental issues. "I am anxious that the Republican Party be kept in power," he wrote, "but more anxious that it justify itself in being kept in power."[19]

To him, the Republican party had a monopoly on intelligent and constructive legislative policies. The Democrats, in his judgment, were politically bankrupt, unworthy of public confidence, and lacking in leadership. Norbeck thought his personal republicanism was something about which he could boast; and he often did.

While progressive, he did not view himself as radical, in spite of a state record which to many seemed to border on state socialism. He believed that most of the so-called radicals were impractical. A firm believer in progress, he thought radicals were greater impediments to progress than conservatives or "standpatters." "One refused to step forward," he asserted, "except when he is compelled to; the other is stepping forward too often and often steps in a hole, for he is an advocate of radical and impossible things and he generally does not know what he is talking about—he just means well and is all mixed up."[20] Progress, he said, must be orderly and in tune with the times.

Norbeck met "all kinds" of progressives and observed all shades of progressivism in Washington. "Some mean well," he said, "but just don't understand. Some mean well and understand how to destroy but have nothing constructive about them. Some are progressive for votes only.

17 Norbeck to H. E. Hvistendahl, April 8, 1922. Norbeck MS.
18 Norbeck to Tom Ayres, April 5, 1922. Norbeck MS.
19 Norbeck to Carl Riddick, April 9, 1921. Norbeck MS.
20 Norbeck to H. E. Hvistendahl, April 8, 1922. Norbeck MS.

Some are so radically progressive that they cannot see the interest of the farmer at all, but want to serve every whim and demand of organized labor."[21] He recognized, however, that his position was becoming less popular and that radicalism and conservatism were both gaining ground. He asserted that the "middle ground is gradually becoming smaller and neither of the extremes are right."[22] Thus he launched upon his sixteen year senatorial career with a belief that moderate and practical progressivism was the sensible course, and he seldom deviated from that path. Why should he? Had not he successfully led the South Dakota Republicans against the onslaught of the Wilsonian Democrats and Townley's Nonpartisan Leaguers?

21 Norbeck to Charles N. Herreid, September 15, 1922. Norbeck MS.
22 *Ibid.*

CHAPTER X

FIGHTING FOR THE FARMERS

One of the most perplexing problems confronting the Sixty-seventh Congress was the agricultural depression. Probably no senator in the nation's capital had a more intimate knowledge of the effects of farm deflation than did Norbeck. There were few, too, who were more desirous of remedying conditions in this sick industry.

Having experienced growing prosperity for twenty years, he now found himself for the first time since 1900 in embarrassingly stringent circumstances. "My business at Redfield," he said, "that has made good earnings all but one year in the last twenty years, will hardly pay expenses. The oil business that ought to have brought me $10,000 a month is costing me $100 a month for a watchman. The farms that ought to make me money are running at a loss. Nothing is sure except interest and taxes."[1] Such was his financial plight.

His experience was typical of hundreds of thousands of people who depended on agriculture for a livelihood. A sharp decline in agricultural prices and values beginning in the summer of 1920 resulted in an acute farm depression by 1921. The collapse of agricultural prices, while those of non-farm commodities and wages remained relatively high, created an alarming disparity between farm income and that of other economic groups. As a result of these conditions, many farmers found themselves in a most distressing position.

While the World War was by no means solely responsible for the catastrophe which overtook the farmers in 1920, it was a great disruptive force in the normal development of American agriculture. The war abnormally stimulated prices, encouraged vast acreage increases, expanded both foreign and domestic markets for food products, and generally brought an unnatural prosperity to the nation's farms. Little did the farmer realize, however, the economic consequences of great interrelated international forces such as war and peace. Less did he understand that much of his prosperity was built on the shifting sands of these events.

There were many factors contributing to the sharp decline of agricultural prices in 1920 and 1921. During the war the government guaranteed minimum prices for certain farm commodities. Shortly after the armistice, however, the United States abandoned artificial price supports. This came at a time when our foreign markets began to decline, resulting, to a considerable extent, from the curtailment of United States loans to European nations. Suddenly, foreign countries found themselves suffering from an acute dollar shortage and they were unable to buy American farm produce, at least in customary quantities. These nations could not accept huge

1 Norbeck to S. X. Way, September 29, 1921. Norbeck MS.

amounts of American surplus agricultural commodities so long as our tariff policy restricted the sale of European goods in the American market. Consequently, most European nations encouraged greater agricultural production at home, thereby denying American producers part of their previous outlet.

Foreign markets were not only shrinking, but Canada, South America, and Australia were growing and exporting many crops which competed directly with United States farm products in the world markets. The virgin land of these countries was producing heavily and cheaply.

Furthermore, changes, unconnected with the war, were taking place which vitally affected American agriculture. Lighter and more varied diets lessened the demand for staple food products, such as wheat. Tractors were rapidly replacing horse power, releasing millions of acres, formerly needed for animal feed, for the production of food crops. Too, the population increased less rapidly after 1918 than it did before the war, partially because of immigration restriction and a decrease in the birth rate.

It would be misleading to intimate that the agricultural depression was confined to the United States. It was a world-wide phenomena with Eastern European grain growers and New Zealand and Danish farmers suffering along with the producers of staple crops in the United States. The drop in farm prices was closely related to the general economic chaos existent throughout much of the world. And neither was the depression restricted to agriculture. It was present in most industries. The agricultural situation is to be differentiated, however, because farm prices fell first, dropped most rapidly, and ultimately went lower than the prices of non-agricultural commodities. It was this disparity about which the farmers complained and which commanded the attention of farm leaders during the twenties and early thirties. It should not be overlooked, too, that the farmers' plight continued to some extent because they were unable to adjust their production to changed conditions as readily and with the same effect as industry.[2]

Although Norbeck arrived in Washington feeling that he knew relatively little about many national problems, he did not plead ignorance regarding agriculture. In fact, he had some very definite ideas on farm problems, their cause, and their solution. He believed the greatest obstacle confronting farm prosperity was the lack of a profitable market; that is, a price for agricultural commodities which would bring the farmers' purchasing power up to 100 per cent of its pre-war level. The government, he said, must be empowered to maintain "a price level that would insure the farmers a fair reward for their labor."[3] He was not adverse to using the

2 See the *Joint Committee of Agricultural Inquiry Report*, 67 Cong., 1 Sess., House Report, 408, Pt., I, p. 36; See also E. R. A. Seligman, *The Economics of Farm Relief* (New York, 1929), p. 14ff; Carl T. Schmidt, *American Farmers in the World Crisis* (New York, 1941), Chap II; Clarence A. Wiley, *Agriculture and the Business Cycle Since 1920,* University of Wisconsin Studies in the Social Sciences and History, No. 15 (Madison, 1930), p. 14 ff.

3 Norbeck to C. M. Day, September 8, 1921. Norbeck MS.

public treasury, if that should be necessary, to achieve what he termed "agricultural equality." An obvious need existed to lift the purchasing power of the farmers' dollar. Using 1909-1914 as the base period, the farm dollar was worth eighty-five cents in 1920 in relation to non-agricultural products, and by 1921 it had dropped to sixty-nine cents. When the purchasing power of farm products in terms of all commodities is considered, the farm dollar was worth slightly more; ninety-three cents in 1920 and seventy-nine cents in 1921.[4]

Many senators believed that most of the farmers' troubles could be solved by providing, in one way or another, additional credit facilities. Norbeck, however, along with a few others in Washington, began probing at something more fundamental; namely making the tariff effective on exportable agricultural products whose price was largely determined by the world market. In 1922 he wrote: "Slowly but surely, the idea is getting home that it is the surplus, and that the way to stimulate the market is to find some way to dispose of the surplus. Sell it at a good price, if we can; sell it at a poor price if we must; give it away if we cannot do better. . . . In other words, let agricultural products have the same benefit of a similar control that big business gives its products."[5] Here was the idea later embodied in the McNary-Haugen bill and which, at the time Norbeck wrote, was being urged as a solution to the farm problem by George N. Peek and Hugh S. Johnson of the Moline Plow Company. Norbeck was one of the plan's earliest congressional supporters.

A second hardship suffered by the farmers, he believed, was that of high freight rates. His criticism of the railroads and campaigns against unreasonable transportation charges were as old as his public career. Freight charges, he argued, added tremendously to the cost of production. His viewpoint was substantiated by the Joint Commission of Agricultural Inquiry created by Congress in 1921 to study the farm problem. The Commission reported that railroad rates were unduly high on farm commodities and recommended "immediate reduction."[6]

In the third place, he believed that the "arbitrary" policy followed by the Federal Reserve Board in 1920, when it sharply curbed post-war inflation, was responsible for many of the farmers' difficulties. "I believe they [Federal Reserve Banks] could have prevented the wild speculation that took place two years ago," he wrote in 1921, "and I also feel that when they did put on the brakes they put them on altogether too suddenly and

4 Bureau of Agricultural Economics, *The Agricultural Situation,* vol. XI, No. 3 (Washington, 1927), pp. 20-22. Professors Warren and Pearson state in their book, *The Agricultural Situation,* that in 1921 the farm dollar in relation to all non-agricultural products had a purchasing power of 72 instead of 69. It should be noted that not all farm commodities were in the same situation. Quite a number of commodities, including cotton and dairy products, had greater purchasing power than before the war.

5 Norbeck to C. M. Henry, December 7, 1922. Norbeck MS.

6 *Joint Committee of Agricultural Inquiry Report,* Pt., III, p. 3.

too hard."[7] It was commonly held in the Northwest, and other agricultural sections of the country, that the Federal Reserve Board had caused unnecessary hardship in the farm areas by calling in its loans in 1920. Whether or not this was true, a good argument could be advanced and the idea persisted.[8]

Norbeck was one of that group in Washington which felt that the national government should devote its attention first of all to restoring agricultural prosperity. He believed this could be accomplished, or partially so, by law. So strong did this feeling become among certain members of the Senate that early in 1921 they banded together to formulate a definite legislative program for agriculture. Because of their unity and aggressiveness, they became known as the Farm Bloc. The first meeting was called by Senator William S. Kenyon of Iowa and was held in the Washington offices of the American Farm Bureau Federation on May 9. Norbeck did not attend but he, Senator Charles L. McNary, and other well known farm leaders soon became affiliated.[9] Most of the legislation enacted as a result of Farm Bloc pressure in the early twenties was of limited value, but attempts were made to cope with the fundamental problem of restoring equality between farm and non-farm prices.

In 1921 Senator Norris introduced a bill authorizing the creation of a government financed Farmers' Export Corporation to assist in financing the exportation of farm products.[10] Norbeck immediately threw his support behind this proposal because it seemed to get at the basic problem as he saw it. The Norris bill, however, met a hostile Republican majority which claimed it would put the federal government in business. The administration leaders immediately proceeded to destroy the principle involved, and Senator Frank B. Kellogg of Minnesota offered an amendment which simply authorized the War Finance Corporation to give additional credit to agriculture. Getting Kellogg to offer the amendment was a smart maneuver, because he was a member of the Farm Bloc. Thus some of the Bloc members had been placated and the obnoxious Norris proposal was sidetracked. Norbeck opposed this amendment, charging that it would bring no real farm relief, but he was not in Washington to vote against it.

The failure of the Norris bill was the first in a long series of defeats, beginning in 1921, for those in Congress who believed the only way to solve the fundamental farm problem was to abolish or segregate the surplus.

7 Norbeck to C. M. Day, September 8, 1921. Norbeck MS.
8 Arthur S. Link, "The Federal Reserve Policy and the Agricultural Depression of 1920-21," *Agricultural History*, 20:166-75 (July, 1946). Link concludes that the Federal Reserve Board did not purposely deflate agriculture.
9 Gilbert C. Fite, "Activities of the Farm Bloc in the Early Twenties," Unpublished Master's Thesis, University of South Dakota, Vermillion, 1941.
10 Alice M. Christensen, "Agricultural Pressure and Governmental Response in the United States, 1919-29," Unpublished Ph.D. Thesis, University of California, Berkeley, 1937, p. 79.

This, according to most authorities, would make the tariff on exportable farm products effective and give American producers the world price plus the import duty.

Norbeck quickly observed why the northwestern farmers were unable to get any helpful legislation from Congress. In addition to the vigorous and ever-present administration opposition to any price-fixing or subsidy schemes, he noted that senators and representatives from the agricultural regions could not unite on any single program. For instance, his own colleague, Sterling, while nominally a member of the Farm Bloc, was a solid supporter of the Harding administration. Senator Porter McCumber of North Dakota believed that a high tariff was the solution to most of the farmers' ills, and he would not cooperate with those attempting to devise a method to dispose of the farm surplus. Inability of the north-western senators to cooperate on any significant legislative program for agriculture was one of the principal reasons why no legislation of conse-quence was passed in behalf of the farmers before 1927.[11] Norbeck also ob-served that the Farm Bloc, in spite of agitated eastern journalists, would not remedy this situation. The Bloc's chief debility, he asserted, was its "padded" membership; that when it became popular with rural constituents, some senators "came in for cover."[12] For example: "When Kellogg found the Farm Bloc was strong, and he was losing standing at home because he was not a member, he attended the meeting for five minutes, and a great deal of publicity was given in Minnesota to the fact that he attended Farm Bloc meetings. On the other hand, Senator Norris . . . who is probably the best farmers' champion in the Senate has refused at all times to affiliate with the Bloc as such because he understands the leadership as well as the membership."[13] Another difficulty was that conservative Republican leaders realized, as well they might, that much of the Bloc's apparent militancy was for home consumption. They were not convinced, nor should they have been, that Bloc threats would be translated into opposition votes. This was especially true as it related to the progressive Republicans who were affiliated with the Bloc. Norbeck analyzed this situation with unusual penetration. "The Progressive Republicans here are as a rule quite disappointed," he said, "but when I talk with the most rabid of them, they say as between Democratic or Penrose control, they would have Penrose. . . ."[14]

Senator George Moses delighted to heap ridicule on the Bloc. As a satirist, he was at his best when he pictured the Farm Bloc to his amused

11 The first McNary-Haugen bill was passed in 1927. Another reason that more substantial farm legislation was not passed before was that the South and Northwest did not unite before 1926.
12 Norbeck to C. M. Henry, June 25, 1922. Norbeck MS.
13 *Ibid.* Senator Norris wrote to the Author in 1941 saying that he had never been a member of the Farm Bloc, chiefly because of the reasons Norbeck gave in 1922.
14 Norbeck to S. X. Way, May 11, 1922. Way MS.

colleagues as consisting of twenty lawyers, one editor [Capper], and one well digger.[15] Norbeck was proud of his profession and received Moses' comment in the spirit in which it was intended, although he probably resented the reference to a "digger" rather than a "driller."

The principal Farm Bloc legislation was the Intermediate Credits Act of 1923. It was over this bill that Norbeck began opposing what he considered throwing sops to the farmers. He insisted that credit was not the real need and he felt confident on this point. Who in the Senate knew more about rural credits than he? Was he not the father of one of the most liberal state rural credit systems in the nation, and were not the South Dakota farmers in a distressed condition in spite of generous credit facilities? He believed that the Bloc was wasting its time and was ignoring the basic problem. Therefore, in December, 1922, while most of the Bloc members were working on the Intermediate Credits Act, he introduced a measure providing for extending $250,000,000 government credit to European purchasers of American farm products.[16] This plan was in some ways similar to the Norris proposal and it met with the same objections. Some of his constituents were the first to lampoon it. The Sioux Falls *Press* declared that "practically all of the so-called farm aid proposals in Congress are loose-jointed affairs and the Norbeck proposal to finance foreign buyers is easily the worst of the lot."[17] The bill was reported favorably by the Senate Agriculture Committee in January, 1923, but it was sidetracked for the Intermediate Credits measure.[18] Norbeck was fighting mad and a spirited battle ensued within the Farm Bloc organization. Several Farm Bloc meetings were especially "stormy" and, according to Norbeck, he did not "spare the [Bloc] committee for its failure to bring in a substantial bill that would mean something to the farmer."[19] When Kenyon resigned from the Senate late in 1922 and Capper came to head the Bloc, Norbeck referred to it as an "enigma." Of Capper he wrote: "it remains to be seen how long a man can be a lion in Kansas and a lamb in Washington."[20]

Norbeck's opposition to the Intermediate Credits Act did nothing to increase his popularity with his colleagues. He remarked: "They think I am a bad egg." He insisted, however, that he would oppose the measure if he had to do so alone and "even if it takes me off the reservation."[21] But his opposition proved futile. He was the only senator who registered a protest when the measure became law on March 3, 1923. Time and experience proved that his position was approximately correct. Frieda Baird and Claude L. Benner, authorities on this legislation, state that it is highly

15 Washington *Evening Star*, January 19, 1922.
16 New York *Times*, December 10, 1922, pt., I, p. 2.
17 Sioux Falls *Press*, January 26, 1923.
18 Sioux Falls *Daily Argus Leader*, January 24, 1923.
19 Norbeck to P. W. Dougherty, December 13, 1922. Norbeck MS.
20 Norbeck to B. B. Haugen, July 11, 1922. Norbeck MS.
21 Norbeck to C. M. Henry, December 22, 1922. Norbeck MS.

doubtful whether it lowered the general interest rates and that only modest claims can be advanced for the system.[22]

Norbeck opposed farm legislation which he was certain would not give substantial aid because he believed the enactment of makeshift laws made it more difficult to obtain additional government help of a more fundamental nature. When the farm leaders accepted a measure passed by Congress, opponents of government aid expected the farmers to be satisfied. But when the law proved inadequate and the farm representatives asked Congress for additional legislation, their enemies could, and did, plausibly charge that the farmers' demands were insatiable. Therefore, he believed that when the farm forces found themselves strong in Congress they should pass a fundamental law, one designed to restore the farmers' purchasing power. Because he actually thought the Intermediate Credits Act would make it more difficult to obtain further legislation, he opposed it. While this was the first time he stood alone against a bill he deemed worthless, it was not the last.

The following year, 1924, found Norbeck again working for farm legislation. In collaboration with Congressman O. B. Burtness of North Dakota, he introduced the so-called Coulter plan, providing that $50,000,000 be made available by the federal government to loan to northwestern farmers who found themselves handicapped by the one-crop system, for which, according to Norbeck, the government was partially responsible because of its plea for greater wheat production during World War I. The money was to be used to purchase pigs, chickens, and particularly milk cows. A Northwest Agricultural Conference meeting in Washington in February, 1924, endorsed the plan,[23] which, however, was defeated in the Senate forty-one to thirty-two.[24] Norbeck's departure from his basic contention that profitable markets were the farmers' chief need, and that the tariff must be made effective on staple agricultural commodities, was occasioned by the belief that nothing more substantial could be obtained for the Northwest at that session. He repeatedly emphasized in discussing the bill that it was not designed to solve any fundamental farm problems, but that it would be helpful in a limited area.

At the same time the South Dakotan was supporting legislation which he believed would solve the farmers' basic problems. At its Washington meeting, the Northwest Agricultural Conference submitted a minority report which favored legislation to control the farm surplus and recommended the passage of the McNary-Haugen bill, which had reached Congress for the first time.[25] Norbeck had been pushing this idea since 1922. Two years

22 Frieda Baird and Claude L. Benner, *Ten Years of Federal Intermediate Credits* (Washington, 1933).
23 Chester C. Davis, "The Development of Agricultural Policy Since the End of the World War," *Yearbook of Agriculture*, 1940, p. 308.
24 *Cong. Rec.,* 68 Cong., 1 Sess., March 13, 1924, p. 4084.
25 Davis, "The Development of Agricultural Policy Since the End of the World War," p. 308.

later the scheme had many adherents both in and out of Congress. The plan embodied in the bill had been presented to the National Agricultural Conference of 1922 by Peek and Johnson, and its legislative sponsors became Senator McNary and Congressman Gilbert Haugen.[26]

The bill proposed to segregate the exportable agricultural surplus of the basic crops, thereby preventing it from depressing the domestic market. With the surplus removed from the market, it was believed that the price would rise above the world price, approximately the amount of the tariff, or to a "fair exchange value." This was defined as the relation which had existed between the price of farm commodities and that of non-agricultural goods during the period from 1904 to 1914. In other words, the purchasing power of farm commodities was to be raised to pre-war levels. In order to dispose of the surplus, the first McNary-Haugen bill provided for an agricultural export corporation, capitalized at $200,000,000, which was to purchase specified farm commodities when a surplus caused depressed markets. The corporation might sell the surplus abroad at whatever it would bring, or hold it at home for a higher figure. Any loss on the segregated exports was to be paid by the farmers themselves through an equalization fee.[27]

From the first time he read the plan, Norbeck could not restrain his enthusiasm for its adoption. Likewise, his constituents manifested a lively interest. To S. X. Way he wrote: "Every letter from the bankers relating to the McNary bill is practically a whole-hearted endorsement. Many farmers write about it as though it is the straw that is going to save them from drowning. A few farmers are skeptical and a few are ferninst."[28]

The bill was first introduced in the Senate in January, 1924. Norbeck labored diligently for its passage, as he was very anxious to obtain some helpful farm legislation during that session. Four months passed, however, and still no action had been taken on the proposal. He became greatly concerned after Congress agreed to adjourn around June 1, less than a month away. On May 8 he announced his intention of introducing the McNary-Haugen bill as a rider to the Mellon tax reduction measure. Senator Walter Edge immediately protested but Norbeck insisted that the time was ripe to consider the bill. For several days he had been preparing a speech favoring the McNary-Haugen measure and he now proceeded to express his views, while the advocates of the administration's tax bill looked on with undisguised annoyance.

This was really his maiden speech on the Senate floor. For three years he had worked quietly and talked very little in the Senate chamber. He spent his time "learning the ropes," establishing friendships, and gaining the confidence of other senators. Besides, he realized that he was more

26 Darwin N. Kelley, "McNary-Haugen Bills, 1924-28," *Agricultural History*, 14:170-80 (October, 1940).
27 *Ibid.*
28 Norbeck to S. X. Way, February 12, 1924. Norbeck MS.

influential in personal contact than as a speaker. He often insisted that those who spoke the most accomplished the least, and during his first eight years in Washington he spent only about eight hours addressing his colleagues.[29] It was when he felt something should be said and no one else would say it, that he was constrained to speak. This seemed to be the case when he decided to review the entire farm relief question for his unwilling colleagues.

He first exploded a blistering attack on the "trust-made prices" of the things the farmer had to buy. Armed with statistics and data from various government departments, he showed conclusively that farm commodities were cheap in terms of purchasing power, and he attacked the administration's plan of cooperative marketing as being of no importance in solving this fundamental problem. Furthermore, he pointed out that adjustment of American agricultural production to meet the domestic market was important, but that relief from this source would come too slowly to prevent "disaster that is near at hand." He answered the argument that the McNary-Haugen bill would develop an increasing surplus by saying that if this did occur, it could easily be corrected by giving a governing board the power to penalize "those individuals, those communities, or those states that increased the production by increased acreage." Finally, he accused Congress of lacking sincerity and courage in dealing with the farm problem, and took those to task who opposed the bill because some of the principles were new.[30] His address showed a firm grasp of the farm situation and a considerable understanding of agricultural economics. But it made little impression on his colleagues, primarily because most of them were bitterly hostile to the general principle embodied in the bill.

Norbeck wanted to tack the measure to the tax bill so a vote could be secured at that session. Normally it would first have to be considered in the House because of its revenue feature. But he realized that he could not carry out his threat of fastening the farm bill to such an important part of the administration's program. Privately he stated: "I saw from the beginning I could not get by with it, but I did not dare to tell anyone I was just running a bluff and trying to force some promises out of the bosses."[31] In that he was successful.

On May 10 both the House and Senate leaders gave assurances that the McNary-Haugen bill would receive attention before June, and Norbeck received a specific promise from the Senate that the bill would be the order of business immediately after the House had disposed of it.[32] While it seems that the House would have considered it at that session in any event, evidence points to the fact that the House and Senate leaders were in con-

29   Norbeck to P. W. Dougherty, December 9, 1929. Norbeck MS.
30   *Cong. Rec.*, 68 Cong., 1 Sess., May 9, 1924, pp. 8185-93.
31   Norbeck to W. H. King, May 19, 1924. Norbeck MS.
32   *Cong. Rec.*, 68 Cong., 1 Sess., May 10, 1924, p. 8263.

ference and the House agreed to take up the measure in seven or eight days. With this assurance, Norbeck withdrew his plan of trying to obtain a vote in the Senate before the House had acted. On June 3 much to his displeasure but not to his surprise, the House defeated the proposal by a vote of 223 to 155.[33] This ended the first attempt to secure this plan of farm relief. Seemingly, those who championed the McNary-Haugen principle had labored in vain; actually much progress had been made as additional supporters had been gained.

Norbeck delighted to tell his conservative eastern colleagues a story which he considered illustrative of the situation if the Republicans did not stop feeding political promises to the Northwest, while producing no tangible farm relief. As the story went, an Irishman stepped into the offices of the superintendent of the Chicago, Milwaukee, and St. Paul railroad and said: "Me name is Casey. I work in the yards. I want a pass to Minneapolis." The superintendent turned and said: "Casey, that is not the way to ask for it. Come back in an hour and see if you cannot be more polite." In an hour Casey returned, walked into the office, doffed his hat and said: "Me name is Casey. I work in the yards. I got a pass over the Northwestern. You can now go to hell with your jobs and passes." That, said Norbeck, was exactly what the farmers were going to tell the Republican party.

33 *Ibid.,* June 3, pp. 10340-41.

Peter Norbeck at age nineteen, 1889
Karl Wegner Collection

Charles Nicholson (left) and
Peter Norbeck, 1906
Karl Wegner Collection

Peter Norbeck (center) and brothers George (left) and
Enoch (right), date unknown *Karl Wegner Collection*

Lydia Anderson and Peter Norbeck on their wedding trip
to Niagara Falls, June 1900 *Karl Wegner Collection*

Water well drilled by
Norbeck and Nicholson,
Redfield, South Dakota, 1902
South Dakota State Historical Society

Peter Norbeck at his desk
in the South Dakota Senate,
date unknown
*University of South Dakota
Special Collections and Archives,
I. D. Weeks Library*

Norbeck family at Redfield, 1911.
The children are (from left) Harold, Selma ("Sally"), Nellie,
and Ruth. *Karl Wegner Collection*

Governor Norbeck signing the "bone dry" law, 1917
South Dakota State Historical Society

Norbeck as head of the
South Dakota delegation
to the Republican National
Convention, 1920
Karl Wegner Collection

Peter Norbeck and
Colonel Edmund W. Starling
of the Secret Service (left) at
the White House, 1928
Karl Wegner Collection

Peter Norbeck (third from left) with members of the Mount Rushmore Commission, date unknown. At far right are Doane Robinson and John Boland. William Williamson stands fourth from right.
South Dakota State Historical Society

Peter Norbeck (left) and Calvin Coolidge at Mount Rushmore dedication, 10 August 1927
University of South Dakota Special Collections and Archives, I. D. Weeks Library

Peter Norbeck, Calvin Coolidge, T. Gilbert Pearson of the National Association of Audubon Societies, and Minnesota congressman August H. Andresen (left to right) at the White House, 13 February 1929
South Dakota State Historical Society

Gutzon Borglum at Mount Rushmore, date unknown
South Dakota State Historical Society

CHAPTER XI

REBELLION IN THE NORTHWEST

Norbeck had scarcely arrived in Washington when he began expressing disgust and disappointment with the Republican administration of which he was a part. This was not entirely due to the Republican attitude on the farm problem. To him the lack of general "progressiveness" was deplorable. "My view," he said, "is that there is as much need for progress within the party as there was in the days of Roosevelt and that the party must keep in accord with the spirit of the times. That it must move forward on sane lines but can not exist on the glories of the past."[1]

He deeply resented what he called the abandonment of Roosevelt's policies and longed for the return of a progressive to the White House. "I wish we had Teddy Roosevelt here bossing the machine for about a year," he lamented to an old friend. "The crooks would be kicked out; progress would be made; selfish interest would be curbed; public confidence would be restored. . . ."[2] To another South Dakota progressive he asserted that the government needed a "moral awakening."[3] This was good Roosevelt doctrine!

He was convinced that unless the Republicans followed a more progressive course they would eventually face grave difficulty at the polls. Few men in Washington could interpret the political sentiment of the Northwest more accurately than he, and national leaders often consulted him on the political situation. And he never hesitated to speak frankly. Replying to a letter from Henry W. Rose, manager of the Republican National News Service Bureau, in 1922, he wrote: "I believe the national situation requires a better display of sincerity and earnestness on the part of our national leaders. The time is nearly ripe for a leader who can make an appeal on moral issues rather than on economic principles."[4]

Norbeck knew the forces of discontent in the Northwest. He was a product of them. Always close to the electorate in his own and surrounding states, he well realized that the unrest in his section, typified to some degree by the Farm Bloc, was not dangerous radicalism, as often portrayed by ill-informed eastern journalists. He understood it as simply a determined protest against economic and political conditions in that area.

Political revolt in the Northwest became increasingly pronounced in 1922 and 1923. Lynn Frazier, North Dakota's first Nonpartisan League governor, was elected to the United States Senate, defeating McCumber, administration standpatter, who had served four terms. Almost simultaneously, Smith Wildman Brookhart of Iowa, campaigning against "re-

1 Norbeck to Lewis Larson, September 16, 1921. Norbeck MS.
2 Norbeck to John Berg, May 10, 1922. Norbeck MS.
3 Norbeck to C. G. Sherwood, May 16, 1922. Norbeck MS.
4 Norbeck to Henry W. Rose, December 5, 1922. Norbeck MS.

actionary" Republicanism, was nominated and elected. Norbeck's brother-in-law, living in Iowa, wrote saying that the farmers were really not for Brookhart, but "voted for him as they have no other way to protest."[5]

In 1923 the Farmer-Labor candidate, Magnus Johnson, a real "dirt farmer" with a broad Swedish accent, defeated J. A. Preus, Republican, in Minnesota for the senatorship. Charles Adams, Preus' campaign manager, stated that "the best efforts of Republican workers were unable to overcome the evident feeling of unrest and dissatisfaction with economic conditions which found its vent in a vote of protest against the party in power."[6] Concerning this campaign, Senator Norris wrote to Norbeck saying: "I could not help but sympathize with him [Johnson] in his campaign. It seems to me that his election is a natural result of the conduct of the Republican party in Washington. We cannot back up Newberryism and fill offices with lame ducks and continually fool the farmer with half-baked propositions and expect to get away with it."[7] To the Harding administration, Johnson's election typified the ultimate in political radicalism.[8] Even Norbeck believed that Johnson was too radical, and he made several campaign speeches against him. But he was subsequently forced to admit that Johnson spoke a language "that has impressed Eastern leaders more favorably than any of us have been able to do."[9]

On July 12, 1922, Norbeck asserted that he had been studying the election returns from Iowa, North Dakota, and other states, and "was spilling no tears over what happened."[10] He was not surprised at McCumber's defeat and referred to his North Dakota colleague as one who would make a "splendid senator from the state of Pennsylvania."[11] In confering with Coolidge soon after he became President, Norbeck warned that unrest in the Northwest was leading toward serious political consequences. The President seemed unconcerned!

In October of the following year, Norbeck went to the White House for another conference with Coolidge. His main interest was farm relief, but they also discussed the general political outlook. Norbeck, seemingly naive, expressed the hope that conservative policies would not dominate the new president's program. Perhaps he was equally naive when he asked Coolidge to support surplus-control farm legislation. In any event, the interview proved highly unsatisfactory. "I got nowhere; I went home disappointed," he said.[12] Norbeck's correspondence throughout 1922 and 1923 clearly indicates a disgust with the Harding-Coolidge philosophy and

5 Norbeck to Frank M. Byrne, June 7, 1926. Norbeck MS.
6 New York *Times,* November 9, 1922, p. 3.
7 George W. Norris to Norbeck October 16, 1923. Norbeck MS.
8 Willis F. Johnson, *The Life of Warren G. Harding* (Chicago, 1923), p. 189.
9 Norbeck to Paul E. Bellamy, January 16, 1924. Norbeck MS.
10 Norbeck to H. A. Sturgis, July 12, 1922. Norbeck MS.
11 Norbeck to E. C. Miller, January 2, 1922. This remark was prompted by McCumber's high tariff policies.
12 Norbeck to A. T. Johnson, January 24, 1924. Norbeck MS.

policies. It would, of course, have been good politics to write depression-ridden farmers that no worth-while farm relief could be obtained because of administration opposition. Some senators might have done this to cover up their own lack of effort. This, however, was not Norbeck's case, because he was working diligently to secure the McNary-Haugen legislation.

It is not surprising that the two men could not agree on the farm problem. President Coolidge was against any government action that would directly or indirectly raise the price of farm products. He insisted that agriculture must rest "on an independent business basis."[13] He approved federal assistance for cooperative marketing, but that was all. Norbeck, on the other hand, had believed since 1921 that the federal government should assist in raising farm prices, even if the public treasury must supply the necessary funds. Their differences on agricultural policy only reflected the sharp contrast between entirely different economic and political philosophies, as different as South Dakota and Vermont.

While the president wished to keep him friendly, Norbeck always displayed a healthy independence and frequently refused to follow the Republican leaders. As a member of the Public Lands Committee, he voted to investigate the leasing of United States oil reserves at Elk Hills in California and Teapot Dome in Wyoming. The leases had been negotiated by Harding's Secretary of Interior, Albert B. Fall. As the investigations proceeded, it became apparent that Fall had promised away great quantities of the nation's oil reserve and that he had profited personally.[14] Secretary of the Navy, Edwin N. Denby, apparently stupid rather than dishonest, was believed by many senators to be connected with the affair and a clamor arose for his resignation. On February 11, 1924, the Senate passed a resolution urging that he resign from the cabinet. Norbeck was one of the ten Republicans who voted for this resolution, and he stated that if Denby had "any defense it is that he is incompetent."[15]

A few days earlier he had praised the work of Democratic Senator Thomas Walsh, chairman of the subcommittee investigating the Teapot Dome scandal. On the Senate floor he stated that "without the great ability, energy, and earnestness" of Walsh, the investigation would have resulted in nothing.[16] Privately he wrote: "Most of the Republican members and some of the Democratic members on the Public Lands Committee were not very anxious to stir up that Teapot Dome business. Senator Walsh had to fight his way through all along."[17]

This, however, was not his first trip off the Republican reservation. Two years earlier, as a green member of the Senate, he had voted to unseat

---

13 Claude M. Fuess, *Calvin Coolidge, The Man From Vermont* (New York, 1940), pp. 383-4.
14 Mark Sullivan, *Our Times* (New York, 1925), VI, pp. 265-71.
15 New York *Times,* February 13, 1924, p. 14.
16 *Cong. Rec.,* 68 Cong., 1 Sess., January 30, 1924, pp. 1683-4.
17 Norbeck to Harry King, February 2, 1924. Norbeck MS.

114

Senator Truman Newberry of Michigan, who was charged with spending nearly $200,000 in his campaign for the nomination in 1919. In this instance, he was one of only nine Republican senators opposing the Michigan man.[18] The Mitchell *Evening Republican* praised Norbeck highly and said his vote against Newberry was the "acid test" of progressiveness.[19]

In the light of Norbeck's differences with the administration, especially on the farm problem, it is not hard to understand why he announced late in 1923 that he would oppose the president's nomination in 1924. He declared that he would go to South Dakota, the first state to hold presidential primaries, and support Hiram Johnson. In a letter to W. R. Ronald, he revealed the purpose of this move:

> It is a protest against the powers that be at Washington. I want them to know there is a Northwest and that it is an important part of the Republican party. I do not want them to take it for granted that we are going to fall in line, no matter what they do. ... But if Johnson gets a big vote in South Dakota I believe it will be helpful in calling the attention of the party leaders to the fact that agricultural distress is a problem that cannot be ignored by the government in Washington.[20]

Furthermore, he lacked confidence in Coolidge and charged that he "can no more run this big machine at Washington than could a paralytic. What we need is a regular Teddy Roosevelt house cleaning. Hiram can do it: the proof of that lies in his California record."[21] Norbeck characterized Coolidge as lacking "initiative and punch. He is judicial, almost as judicial as Bill Taft," he said. He added that if Coolidge had any place in Washington it was on the Supreme Court.[22]

Having announced his support of Johnson, Norbeck had to carry the March primary for his candidate or lose much of his personal political prestige in the state. He received a jolt when the anti-Norbeck faction of the party gained control of the December proposal meeting and endorsed Coolidge. The president and his supporters jubilantly declared that this action truly represented an "outstanding expression of what the rank and file of Republicans throughout the country feel."[23] Even some of Norbeck's friends agreed. Paul Bellamy wrote to him that he could find only meager Johnson sentiment in South Dakota and that it was "nearly all induced or manufactured."[24] And Mrs. Norbeck, whose fondness for the Coolidges was undisguised, strongly opposed her husband's action. Norbeck explained to Harry King that Coolidge "has been and continues to be personally very

18 New York *Times*, January 13, 1922, p. 1. The resolution failed by a vote of 46 to 41, but Newberry resigned the following November.
19 Mitchell *Evening Republican*, January 4, 1922.
20 Norbeck to W. R. Ronald, November 27, 1923. Norbeck MS.
21 Norbeck to Charles A. Alseth, February 21, 1924. Norbeck MS.
22 Norbeck to Jacob Tschetter, February 19, 1924. Norbeck MS.
23 New York *Times*, December 6, 1923, p. 1.
24 Paul Bellamy to Norbeck, January 5, 1924. Norbeck MS.

friendly. In fact, both he and his good wife go out of their way in this line, greatly to my embarrassment." And then he added: "My good wife lectures me nearly every day for not staying with the President, in whom she believes so firmly and who she insists wants to be friendly."[25]

But to Norbeck this was a matter of principle. He directed a heated campaign during which he made over fifty speeches and traveled 2500 miles. His efforts were not in vain and Johnson defeated Coolidge by about 1110 votes out of a total of approximately 80,000.[26] It was clearly a Norbeck victory, even though a small one. The people had not voted for Johnson because they necessarily thought he would be a better candidate, but because "Pete" told them to.

It was in this election that he also helped to defeat his colleague, Sterling, a Coolidge supporter. He claimed to have no personal dislike for Sterling; in fact, he had been partially responsible for his nomination and election twelve years earlier. At that time, however, Sterling was considered progressive and had supported LaFollette. But with time he grew increasingly conservative, and when Norbeck arrived in Washington he found his old friend a staunch administration man. Norbeck now threw the power of his organization behind McMaster, who was progressive beyond a doubt and who was really a "Norbeck man," having served as lieutenant governor under him and then succeeding to the governorship in 1921.

Perhaps it is not without significance that Norbeck and Sterling experienced differences over patronage matters. In most cases Sterling's appointees were anti-Norbeck men. This meant that Norbeck would have damaged his own political strength by supporting Sterling again. His failure to aid Sterling caused S. W. Clark, Sterling's law partner and Norbeck's attorney for many years, to join the anti-Norbeck faction of the party and fight Norbeck vigorously.

Political differences were not alone to plague him in 1924. Disagreement between Norbeck and Nicholson led to dissolution of their company which had operated for twenty-three years. Norbeck bought most of the equipment and incorporated the Norbeck Company which was operated by his brother George, as the old Norbeck and Nicholson firm had been since 1912.

Following the South Dakota primary, he returned to Washington to work unsuccessfully for enactment of the McNary-Haugen bill. June 3, the day it was defeated in the House, he declared that he felt like going to the Republican national convention and making a "real fight" for agriculture.[27] A few days later he arrived in Cleveland in the same belligerent mood. He caused the platform subcommittee, which drafted the agricultural plank, a few uncomfortable moments by insisting that the farmers must have more than the customary flimsy promises. Without some genuine concessions to

25 Norbeck to W. H. King, January 31, 1924. Norbeck MS.
26 *South Dakota Legislative Manual*, 1927, p. 184.
27 Norbeck to W. H. King, June 3, 1924. Norbeck MS.

agriculture, he said, the party might look forward to a LaFollette surge in his section comparable to a "Kansas cyclone."[28]

The platform committee finally presented a plank pledging the Republicans to take steps to "place the agricultural interests of America on a basis of economic equality with other industries."[29] Norbeck asserted that the party leaders were not anxious to adopt such a plank because it tended to embarrass them in the fall campaign. The attitude of the convention, he declared, was to "praise Coolidge and say the Lord be thanked for the wonderful little man in the White House."[30] He noted soon after the convention that the Republican strategists were "trying to duck this specific promise" to agriculture.[31] Therefore, while he made some speeches for the national ticket in the fall campaign, they were without enthusiasm. He was active, however, in helping McMaster secure the senatorial seat.

Dissatisfaction with the regular Republican administration should logically have thrown Norbeck with the LaFollette progressives. Organized in Washington late in 1922 under LaFollette's leadership, the Republican malcontents soon became identified as the progressive bloc. They refused to support the administration's legislative program and embarrassed the Harding regime at every opportunity. Although several members of the Farm Bloc joined the progressive bloc, Norbeck remained aloof. He had always held LaFollette in highest esteem, but upon arriving in Washington he found the Wisconsin progressive somewhat hard to work with.

He did not believe the greatest accomplishments for progressivism could be made by working independently of his party and was always reluctant to be outside the party breastworks in a presidential year. It will be remembered that in 1912 he helped to manipulate the party machinery in his state so there was no third party and Roosevelt was the only Republican presidential candidate on the ticket. While he was unwilling to support LaFollette in 1924, as did Frazier, Ladd, and Brookhart, he hoped to liberalize the party from within. He might enjoy the defeat of Sterling and McCumber, who represented contemporary Republican conservatism in the Senate, but actively to oppose the president was another matter. LaFollette's 75,000 votes in South Dakota to the president's 100,000 indicated that Norbeck's warning of a political revolt was not altogether illusory.

In spite of his anti-administration activity, Coolidge courted his friendship. "The Republican Caucus and the Republicans as a whole, are treating me better than at any time since I arrived in Washington," he wrote after the primary election.[32] After Coolidge's re-election he was placed on the

28 This account is given by correspondent George F. Authier in the New York *World*, June 12, 1924.
29 *Proceedings of the National Republican Convention,* 1924, p. 101.
30 Norbeck to C. M. Henry, June 9, 1924. Norbeck MS.
31 Norbeck to J. C. Cheever, September 16, 1924. Norbeck MS.
32 Norbeck to Mrs. Paul Rewman, May 16, 1924. Norbeck MS.

Republican Senate steering committee. While he recognized this as an unusual appointment for one from his state, he was not blind to its purpose. The New York *Times* reported that the appointment was part of an attempt to mollify those progressives who had remained "anchored" during the LaFollette "storm."[33] At any rate, he noted the absence of that "go to h——attitude" of two years before.

It was not until early in 1925 that Norbeck and Coolidge became personally friendly. A little political horse-trading brought them together. C. L. Leedom, McMaster's campaign manager, wanted to be appointed United States Marshall for South Dakota. McMaster, anxious to reward a faithful servant, asked Norbeck to call at the White House and arrange for Leedom's appointment. Many South Dakotans opposed Leedom because of his bibulous habits; thus it was more than a routine matter. Since Norbeck had fought Coolidge in the primaries and had displayed an obvious coolness toward him in the November election, he hesitated to ask for any favors. After some hesitation, however, he went to the White House. Having discussed the Leedom appointment, the president said to Norbeck: "you know my veto of the postal pay increase bill is in danger of being over-ridden in the Senate and I would like for you to uphold my veto when it comes to a vote." Norbeck replied that he intended to sustain the veto because he opposed the principle of raising the wages of one group of workers when the purchasing power of the farmer was still so low. Nothing more was said about Norbeck's mission and he left without obtaining any promise from Coolidge.

A few days later, on January 6, 1925, he voted to sustain the presidential veto of the postal pay increase bill. Had he changed his vote, the bill would have been passed over Coolidge's veto, as the final count was twenty-nine to fifty-five.[34] Shortly afterward, Leedom was appointed.

But friendship with Coolidge did not mean that Norbeck was giving up his independence. In spite of strong pressure from the White House, he voted against the confirmation of Charles B. Warren, Coolidge's choice for attorney-general. The fact that he was the only Republican senator coming up for re-election in 1926 who voted against Warren, indicates the well-driller's independence, as well as the effectiveness of administration pressure.

On the question of foreign affairs Norbeck generally hewed to the party line, but even here he was sometimes rebellious. Soon after arriving in Washington he found himself at odds with the party chieftains on Latin American policy. President Harding recommended a settlement with Colombia to appease that country's feelings over United States action in acquiring canal rights in Panama during Roosevelt's administration. Senator Lodge guided a treaty through the Senate which provided for paying the Colombian

33 New York *Times,* December 5, 1924, p. 44.
34 *Ibid.,* January 7, 1925, p. 1.

government $25,000,000. Although an overwhelming number of senators favored this, Norbeck was one of the nineteen voting against it.[35]

He looked upon Latin Americans with positive disdain and was often outspoken in his willingness to uphold United States influence and power, at least as far south as the Panama Canal. About the only people who counted for much, in his judgment, were the Nordics. His intense ancestral pride caused him to scorn all Latins, whether they were in Europe or America.

But this was only one factor in shaping his views. His devout loyalty to Theodore Roosevelt stimulated his advocacy of a strong United States policy south of the border. "What would Roosevelt think of paying the Colombians $25,000,000," he snorted. "Roosevelt handled those outlaws just right, and in fact dealt very liberally with them." Furthermore, he noted that the treaty was not to right "the wrongs of Teddy Roosevelt, but to help big American business, and especially the oil men."[36]

Norbeck's action on the Colombia treaty was not typical of his relation to foreign issues. He lacked any vital interest in foreign affairs, therefore it is not surprising that he should be willing to go along with the administration in most instances. In many cases he hesitated to take any definite position and often was contradictory. He voted for the various treaties growing out of the Washington Conference, but without comment or interest.

During the 1920's he drifted with his party toward a more pronounced isolationism. This may have been hastened by his close association with Senator Hiram Johnson, one of Norbeck's closest friends. The Californian affectionately called him "my dear Uncle Peter." Norbeck may have been guided to a limited degree by Johnson's position, although in 1923 in considering Johnson as a presidential candidate, he declared that he did not entirely "share Hiram's views on foreign affairs."[37] In any event, public opinion during this period, especially in Norbeck's section, made it easy for a senator who had little fundamental interest in foreign affairs to drift along.

His growing isolationism became apparent when President Coolidge endeavored to obtain United States adherence to the World Court. As a member of the Republican resolutions committee in 1924, he voted to incorporate the World Court plan, but he later admitted doing this simply to gain support for the agricultural plank.[38] He was really much confused on this issue and the intense interest of his constituents added to his embarrassment. To one friend he complained that he had never received so many communications on any question since arriving in Washington.

35 *Cong. Rec.*, 67 Cong., 1 Sess., April 20, 1921, p. 487.
36 Norbeck to S. X. Way, May 16, 1921, and to P. W. Peterson, February 26, 1924. Norbeck MS.
37 Norbeck to W. R. Ronald, November 27, 1927. Norbeck MS.
38 Norbeck to Enoch Norbeck, January 27, 1927. Norbeck MS.

"The Women's Clubs and the educators and part of the Bar are for it," he said. The opposition consists of the general public, part of the bar, and the Klan leaders generally, who are sending a large number of petitions protesting against the plan."[39] A few days earlier he had written that "many people who are members of the Klan, have written me that they are opposed to the World Court. I am no enthusiast for this thing myself, but I believe with the reservations that it carries that it is entirely harmless (if not helpless)."[40] The Klan had a small and noisy membership in the state, but it had relatively little political influence. Norbeck would not cater to the Klan, and neither did Senator McMaster nor the state's congressmen.

When the matter came to a vote, with the five reservations, he supported the administration. But he told McMaster: "I am frank to say I am not stuck on this World Court, but the platform endorses it, and I see no other way than to keep quiet and vote for it."[41] In this instance he apparently allowed himself to be voted by his party.

Just before the end of Norbeck's first term the McNary-Haugen bill was again considered. Both the House and Senate defeated it by substantial margins.[42] The original bill had provided for the re-establishment of a "ratio price" for farm commodities, but by 1926 the emphasis had been changed to making the tariff effective on exportable farm products. This did not change the idea behind the measure, because to make the tariff effective the surplus must be removed.

Norbeck did not allow the opportunity to pass without taking a parting shot at those responsible for the bill's defeat. In a lengthy prepared speech he reviewed the entire farm relief situation since he had been in the Senate. He charged that business had received government aid in the form of increased tariffs and decreased taxes, but that the farmer was still crying in the wilderness. He also accused those who opposed the McNary-Haugen bill of having offered no other practical farm program. He reiterated all the arguments for his favorite measure, and attempted to refute the objections. Frank Lowden enthusiastically called it "a great speech." "It covered the ground in a practical, sensible way," he said, "and no definite answer has been made to your arguments."[43] But more than argument was necessary to influence an administration dead set against surplus-control legislation.

The administration's panacea for the farm problem, that of mildly encouraging cooperative marketing, received Congressional attention in 1926, when a Division of Cooperative Marketing was created in the Department of Agriculture. Norbeck viewed the act as of "comparatively little

39 Norbeck to Leslie Jensen, February 8, 1926. Norbeck MS.
40 Norbeck to Paul E. Bellamy, January 27, 1926. Norbeck MS.
41 Norbeck to William McMaster, December 10, 1925. Norbeck MS.
42 The House vote was 157 to 212. In the Senate the bill was considered as an amendment to the Cooperative Marketing Act.
43 Frank Lowden to Norbeck, September 7, 1926. Norbeck MS.

importance." He also warned the Republicans that the "radicalism" expressed in the 1924 elections was mild compared to what would follow if the inequality between farmers and other economic groups continued.[44]

He was dissatisfied with the course of his first term in Washington. He admitted that his accomplishments had been meager, and he gained no satisfaction from the fact that most of his colleagues were in a similar position. Most of all, he regretted that no substantial farm relief law had been enacted. He charged this to lack of unity among the farm forces. "We could have got farm relief," he wrote, "when the eastern section got their tariff bill. We could have got relief on two different occasions when the Mellon Tax reduction bills were pending. They needed our votes and we needed theirs. A compromise could have been reached."[45] But any opportunity that may have occurred had been dissipated and the only tangible accomplishment was that the farm relief adherents were steadily gaining recruits, both in and out of Congress. The idea of surplus-control legislation was finding more and more friends as the propaganda campaign gained momentum. Norbeck was more determined than ever to make a strong fight in the coming session for the McNary-Haugen bill. First, however, he must return home and test his political strength.

44 *Cong. Rec.,* 69 Cong., 1 Sess., June 15, 1926, p. 11289.
45 Norbeck to Buell F. Jones, October 2, 1926. Norbeck MS.

CHAPTER XII

THE FARM QUESTION AGAIN

The senatorial campaign of 1926 actually began the year before after it had been revealed that Ewert, Norbeck's appointee, had administered rural credit funds illegally. South Dakota politics had never been tranquil, and Ewert's defalcation injected a new and explosive issue into the election.

George Danforth, a Sioux Falls attorney and a conservative "stand-by-the-president" Republican, announced that he would contest Norbeck's Senate seat. But the well-driller, with his usual optimism, declared that he knew he could win against any opponent if he went "after it hard enough."[1] Nevertheless, the primary was watched with keen interest because of Norbeck's obvious coolness towards the administration. What did the voters in the Northwest really think of Coolidge after all? Perhaps the results of this first state primary election would give some indication.

Beginning his campaign in February, Danforth blamed Norbeck for the rural credits debacle and reiterated all the charges that had been made against his administration of that department. He further charged him with leading the state into "mad socialism" and with failure to supervise the state enterprises properly. Finally, he endeavored to connect him with the Ewert embezzlement and compared his faithlessness as governor to that of Albert Fall of Teapot Dome infamy.[2]

Thousands of copies of *Norbeck's Record,* as interpreted by Danforth, were printed and circulated widely throughout the state. Danforth and other conservative Republicans sharply criticized the senator for not supporting the president and accused him of doing nothing for agriculture while in Washington.[3] One voter, after receiving a copy of *Norbeck's Record,* put it in an envelop and sent it to him after scribbling across the top: "Have you got guts enough left to run on this record for a second term as United States Senator? If so, I may support you, as guts counts for a whole lot in politics."[4]

By all counts the most serious charges concerned the rural credits venture. South Dakotans were not particularly concerned whether their senator had supported the president, but it did matter whether he had the nerve to fight for the Northwest in the face of stiff administration opposition.

Just before the primary he made an extensive speaking tour; armed with legislative reports, rural credit statements, and other data he showed conclusively that when he left the governor's chair everything in the rural credits department was in good condition. And the voters believed him.

1 Norbeck to J. A. Stanley, February 2, 1925. Norbeck MS.
2 *Norbeck's Record,* published by the Danforth campaign committee, 1926.
3 Pierre *Daily Dakotan,* March 18, 1926.
4 R. W. Levitt to Norbeck, undated, 1926, Norbeck MS.

The Sioux Falls *Daily Argus Leader,* published in Danforth's home town, said that Norbeck had "made the mud dry up and blow away like the flimsy stuff it was. The charges have all been answered and Senator Norbeck stands stronger with the people of South Dakota than he ever has in his long and honorable career."[5] The electorate agreed emphatically with Editor Day, and Danforth received only 24,271 votes to 52,737 for Norbeck.[6]

The Mitchell *Evening Republican* credited the triumph to Norbeck's refusal "to be bound by the dictates of the standpat Republican leaders in Washington. He has refused to obey the whip of the East. He realized his duty to his constituents. He placed that duty above party loyalty."[7] Norbeck recognized the all important fact that his anti-administration stand in Washington was popular. The average South Dakotan took it for granted that his disagreements with Coolidge were part of his efforts to protect the state's interests.

The nomination practically assured his election in the fall campaign, but Governor Gunderson, Norbeck's friend of thirty years, failed to win a second term. There is no definite proof that he personally opposed Gunderson, but many of his friends did. Members of the Norbeck faction of the Republican party gave William Bulow, Democrat, active support and he was elected as South Dakota's first Democratic governor. Norbeck and Gunderson had disagreed over rural credit matters, and it cannot be overlooked that Gunderson had not cooperated well in developing Norbeck's favorite project, Custer State Park. While Gunderson was being defeated, Norbeck swamped his Democratic opponent by almost a two to one vote.[8] He was so proud of this overwhelming endorsement that, when the next *Congressional Directory* appeared, his majority was added to the nine lines of biographical data.

Considerable truth was contained in a story that circulated around South Dakota, illustrating Norbeck's political popularity. It was said that when a Scandinavian voter was asked at the primary election whether he wanted a Democratic or Republican ballot, he replied: "I don't know about that but I want to vote the Peter Norbeck ticket."

Norbeck returned to Washington a seasoned legislator and with increased prestige. During his first term such veteran northwestern senators as Sterling, McCumber, and Cummins had been rebuked by the voters, but "Old Pete," in tune with his constituency, had received a strong endorsement. The strange, lonesome feeling so strong in 1921 was much milder after he had served one term in the nation's capital. Through a powerful sense of duty and fearless honesty, he had won the respect and admiration of most of his colleagues. Many of them affectionately called the fifty-six

5 Sioux Falls *Daily Argus Leader,* March 22, 1926. Norbeck MS.
6 *South Dakota Legislative Manual,* 1927, p. 216.
7 Mitchell *Evening Republican,* March 25, 1926.
8 *South Dakota Legislative Manual,* 1927, p. 214. The vote was 105,756 to 59,128.

year old senator "Uncle Pete." Even those who disagreed with him on political and economic issues held him in high regard. Senator Walter E. Edge of New Jersey characterized him as "a good old solid representative of his constituency [with] a lot of old fashioned horse sense."[9]

The deep affection in which he was held in Washington was picturesquely stated in 1928 by Senator James Watson, who seldom agreed with Norbeck on national policies. Watson, discussing various members of the Senate with Charles Gates Dawes and William Hirth, editor of the *Missouri Farmer,* said: "One of the longest headed men in the Senate is old Pete Norbeck of South Dakota. He doesn't make much noise, and he is careful in taking a position, but when he does finally make up his mind on a proposition he goes in with both fists, and ninety-nine times out of a hundred he is right—and when he gets ready to go down the line he reminds me of an old bull going through a patch of Jimson weeds with his tail up in the air." "You are right," General Dawes laughingly replied. "Old Pete is one of the strongest men in the Senate, and a hell of a fine man besides."[10]

At the opening of the second session of the Sixty-ninth Congress, agrarian temperatures ran high. Spurred on by the belief that the agricultural depression could be lifted by an effective tariff on farm products, the farmers and their representatives were very vociferous. Leaders from the Northwest threatened to unite with those of the South in a war against the entire protective tariff system. Norbeck asserted that if the farmers did not get their share of protection, "they would tear down the tariff wall as Sampson [*sic*] had torn down the pillars of the temple."[11] The campaign for farm relief was assuming almost revivalistic proportions.

A formidable array of agricultural lobbyists was on hand to help convert any wavering souls to the surplus-control principle. George Peek, chairman of the American Council of Agriculture which was formed in 1924 to carry on the campaign for agricultural equality in Washington, was the outstanding leader. He was ably assisted by Chester C. Davis, former Commissioner of Agriculture in Montana, and Frank W. Murphy of Wheaton, Minnesota. Peek, Davis, and Murphy were the three most effective workers, but representatives of special farm organizations, and men like William Hirth of the *Missouri Farmer,* lent considerable aid.

While Norbeck was less vocal than some of his more oratorical colleagues, he was not idle. Late in April, soon after his return to Washington from the primary campaign, he organized a series of one o'clock luncheons which he called an "educational school" on farm problems. He invited various senators to hear Peek, Davis, and Murphy discuss the benefits of the McNary-Haugen plan. His main objective, of course, was to convince those senators who might still be open to conviction on the

9 Walter E. Edge to Author, February 21, 1945.
10 William Hirth to Norbeck, September 18, 1931. Norbeck MS.
11 "A Big Tariff Twister on the Horizon," *Literary Digest,* 90:5-7 (July 3, 1926).

measure. Writing on May 4, he stated that more than half of the entire Senate membership had at one time or another been present.[12]

The groundwork seemed well laid when Congress met in December, 1926. Senator McNary re-introduced his surplus-control bill and the Senate Agriculture Committee reported it favorably on January 22, 1927.[13] The bill differed only in details from the previous McNary-Haugen measures. It provided for a Federal Farm Board whose main objective was to promote orderly marketing and dispose of surplus basic agricultural commodities, including wheat, corn, rice, and swine.[14]

The Senate debate was not unusually bitter, partially because of the effective spade work done by the various farm organizations, special farm lobbyists, and interested senators and representatives. The bill passed the Senate on February 11, by a vote of forty-seven to thirty-nine, and six days later the House voted 214 to 178 to accept it.[15]

Unfortunately, Norbeck was not present to participate personally in this victory which he had done so much to bring about, but he was paired in its favor. Three days before the Senate vote was taken he was involved in an auto accident which hospitalized him for ten days.

President Coolidge sent a stinging veto message to Congress. He flayed the McNary-Haugen measure as economically unsound, asserting that such a law would bring about increased production, thereby aggravating the surplus problem. In his estimation the bill was unconstitutional and would lead to government regimentation and bureaucracy. Furthermore, he claimed that price fixing of farm products was abhorrent.[16]

Coolidge's action was no surprise to Norbeck. On the day the House passed the bill he had written a friend: "I presume the bill will be vetoed by President Coolidge."[17] Although he was disappointed, he had not been entirely satisfied with the bill when it left the Agriculture Committee. He had thought it would be safer to have a government board start handling a single commodity, presumably wheat, to see how the principle would actually work. Furthermore, he would have endowed the board with power to impose penalties to prevent increased acreage. But he admitted that here he was getting on "new ground."[18]

Although he had suggested acreage restriction in 1924 in answer to the argument that the McNary-Haugen bill would increase production through acreage expansion, he did not dwell on this point when speaking on the measure two years later. He seemed unable to decide on this problem which obviously bothered him. Publicly he would not admit this weakness

12   Norbeck to C. J. Moen, May 4, 1926. Norbeck MS.
13   *Senate Report*, No. 1304, Serial No. 8629, 69 Cong., 2 Sess.
14   *Ibid*. This bill omitted butter and cattle from the basic commodities and added rice. .
15   *Cong. Rec.*, 69 Cong., 2 Sess., February 11, 1927, p. 3518.
16   *Ibid.*, February 25, 1927, p. 4771 ff.
17   Norbeck to A. L. Berg, February 17, 1927. Norbeck MS.
18   Norbeck to Charles A. Howard, January 29, 1927. Norbeck MS.

in the bill, but privately he did. Thereby he tacitly agreed with the opposition's argument that the bill would tend to increase production through greater acreage.

This was one of the most difficult issues which faced the McNary-Haugenites and few of them met it intelligently on historical or economic grounds. Norbeck either was afraid to come out boldly for acreage restriction or actually believed that the threatened increase in the equalization fee would tend to curb excessive production. It is possible, too, that he may have thought it would work successfully for a few years and that any benefits would justify the plan.

After Coolidge's veto of the McNary-Haugen bill, threats against the administration came with increasing bitterness. Norbeck, however, attacked the problem from a different angle. During the spring of 1927 he took every opportunity to convince Coolidge that the Black Hills would be an ideal spot for his summer vacation. Norbeck had three purposes in mind. In the first place, such a trip would take the president into the very heart of the distressed agricultural area, and he thought perhaps if Coolidge could see and study some of the problems first hand he might be more sympathetic. Secondly, he realized that the president's presence in the Black Hills would bring national publicity for the Hills and his particular interest, Custer State Park. Furthermore, he hoped to enlist Coolidge's support for the carving of giant figures of Washington, Lincoln, Jefferson, and Roosevelt on Mount Rushmore. This project was languishing after two years of effort by Norbeck and a few other interested parties.

The first person to conceive the idea of carving figures of historical significance on some of the granite upthrusts in the Black Hills was the state historian of South Dakota, Doane Robinson. In December, 1923, he wrote to the artist and sculptor, Lorado Taft, asking if such work was feasible. Robinson said that he had some notable Indian chief in mind, perhaps Red Cloud.[19] Taft was ill, however, and unable to go to South Dakota to survey the possibilities. Norbeck, who in the meantime had received a copy of Robinson's letter to Taft, wrote to the state historian agreeing that something of this kind might be done, although admitting that he had never thought of it before.[20] From that time on Robinson and Norbeck were the two principal forces behind the idea, although Gutzon Borglum soon became interested.

South Dakota's general public was hostile to carving in the Needles. When Robinson suggested it during an address before the Black Hills Trail Association in Huron on January 22, 1924, most people considered it a destructive dream.[21] But Robinson was persistent. When he failed to secure

19 Doane Robinson to Lorado Taft, December 28, 1923. Norbeck MS.
20 Norbeck to Doane Robinson, January 4, 1924. Norbeck MS.
21 Doane Robinson, "Inception and Development of the Rushmore Idea," *The Black Hills Engineer,* 18:334 (November, 1930).

Taft to survey the possibilities, he wrote to Gutzon Borglum, who at that time was carving a Confederate Memorial on Stone Mountain near Atlanta.

It happened that Borglum was having serious difficulties with the Commission which was supervising the Stone Mountain work and it appeared that he would soon resign or be discharged. Borglum's interest in unique sculptural projects, along with his unlimited ambition, immediately attracted him to the Black Hills scheme. He promised to visit the area in the autumn.

Meanwhile Norbeck and Robinson agreed to meet Borglum and Governor Bulow in September. Together they could examine the granite mountain peaks. Both Norbeck and Bulow were unavoidably detained, but Borglum and Robinson surveyed the granite upthrusts upon which carving seemed possible. After viewing the Needles and surrounding structures, Borglum displayed great enthusiasm. He promised to return the following year and make a complete examination of the rocks. Before leaving Rapid City he praised the work Norbeck had done in the State Park, adding: "The present admirable park plans [sic] and roads are curiously in harmony with any sculptural plan."[22]

The following year Borglum returned. By that time his trouble with the Commission at Stone Mountain had reached such serious proportions that he was free to devote a great deal of time and energy to the South Dakota enterprise.[23] Late in 1925 he and Norbeck made a complete examination of the granite in various parts of the Black Hills. Borglum's first idea seems to have been to carve two giant figures in the Needles. But Norbeck dissuaded him. He told a friend: "I am trying to talk Borglum out of his Washington-Lincoln Siamese Twins idea." In this he was successful and at the same time he was insisting that Theodore Roosevelt be included in any busts that might be carved.[24] Borglum was receptive to this idea. "Recently Senator Norbeck injected into my mind the idea of using Roosevelt," he wrote to Robinson.[25]

Out of the many ideas that were suggested, it was finally decided to carve the figures of Washington, Lincoln, Jefferson, and Roosevelt on Mount Rushmore.[26] The idea of carving in the Needles was abandoned because of public opposition.

Plans to create a great national shrine dedicated to democracy advanced rapidly, and in 1925 both state and national legislation was obtained.

22 *Ibid.*
23 Borglum was charged with gross neglect of duty, attempts to use the Confederate Memorial for personal profit, use of undelegated authority, lust for money, and other deficiencies. *Statement by the Executive Committee of the Stone Mountain Confederate Monumental Association,* March 14, 1925. A pamphlet.
24 Norbeck to C. M. Henry, January 21, 1925. Norbeck MS.
25 Gutzon Borglum to Doane Robinson, January 26, 1925. Norbeck MS.
26 Mount Rushmore was named after Charles E. Rushmore of New York City. It is believed that an old prospector named it after Rushmore when he was in the Black Hills on a business trip several years before 1920. Later Rushmore gave $5,000 for the memorial's development.

October 1 a ceremony was held on the mountain, dedicating it as a national memorial.

Norbeck, the well-driller, and Borglum, the artist, soon became close friends. Norbeck's knowledge and appreciation of art surprised and pleased Borglum, and the fact that Borglum was a significant artist was sufficient to win Norbeck's friendship and respect. They made a good working team. Both were men of tremendous energy and ambition, each with high respect for the talents and abilities of the other. The fact that Norbeck dealt on a friendly basis for about ten years with Borglum was an achievement that testified to his success in personal relations. Borglum was a man of undoubted artistic ability, but with little business judgment, a temperamental disposition, and an absolute inability to work in harmony with others. In a fit of anger he had broken his Stone Mountain models to bits.

Although the plans had been completed and the mountain dedicated, no actual carving yet had been done. Large sums of money were needed even to start the work, and it was here that Norbeck played his most important role.

The solution to the financial problem consumed most of the period from September, 1925, to August, 1927, when the first carving began. It soon became apparent that funds must come from private sources, since the South Dakota legislature refused in 1925 even to appropriate $10,000 for a preliminary survey. Borglum, Robinson, and a few Rapid City citizens solicited funds, appealing to South Dakota business men on the grounds that completion of the memorial would materially increase tourist trade. To wealthy persons elsewhere, their appeal was based on patriotism. Norbeck also helped to raise funds. He solicited $5,000 from the Homestake Gold Mine, and he got similar sums elsewhere. His greatest contribution in this respect, however, came later.

By 1927 approximately $55,000 had been raised and preparations were made to begin the work. In January of that year, the Mount Harney Memorial Association, consisting of Norbeck, Robinson, and Governor Bulow, was formed and charged with supervising the carving. Norbeck then conceived the idea that if he could get the president to speak at a formal opening ceremony, it would give just the needed impetus to the infant project.

He made daily trips to the White House during the first part of May to present the wonders of the Black Hills. He suggested that the presidential party might easily be cared for at the state game lodge, generally used for a tourist hotel, and that executive offices could be established at Rapid City, some thirty miles away. Climate, trout fishing, and the distance from heavily populated centers were all stressed in his attempt to win Coolidge's assent. His efforts were aided by those of Senator McMaster, the South Dakota congressmen, particularly Williamson, and Governor Bulow.[27]

27 William J. Bulow, "My Days With Gutzon Borglum," *Saturday Evening Post*, 219:24 (January 11, 1947).

Late in May Coolidge announced his intention of making the game lodge his summer home. "My understanding of his visit," Norbeck wrote, "is that, outside of rest and recreation, he is coming open-mindedly to study the agricultural problem."[28] Hiram Johnson, however, believed Coolidge had political motives.[29]

The president's special train arrived on June 15. Norbeck boarded it at Lake Preston near the eastern border of the state. The farm problem was uppermost in his mind and as the train sped westward he and Coolidge discussed the agricultural situation in the president's club car. Norbeck told Coolidge that while the recent rains had created a psychological effect on the farmers, there was still an insistent demand for federal farm relief.[30]

Norbeck declared a moratorium on partisan politics during Coolidge's stay in South Dakota. Few would have realized that the two men had often experienced sharp differences. He spent practically his entire time making the presidential party comfortable. He and his family moved into a cabin a few miles west of the game lodge and from there he directed many of the activities. Personally very hospitable, Norbeck wanted to introduce President and Mrs. Coolidge to genuine western hospitality, and he succeeded admirably. To some extent he guided Coolidge's conference appointments and no detail was too small for his attention. He even had to refute newspaper stories about mosquitoes at the game lodge.

Grave doubts soon arose as to whether Norbeck's technique of getting Coolidge to spend the summer in the West was the proper approach for converting him to surplus-control legislation. The first day that Coolidge appeared at his temporary offices in the Rapid City high school he met State Senator J. L. Robbins, a Rapid City conservative, who warmly grasped his hand and said: "Mr. President, I wish to congratulate you for your courage and wisdom in vetoing the McNary-Haugen bill."[31] Norbeck, standing a few feet away, was obviously chagrined!

This was only the beginning. As prominent individuals from the Northwest called on Coolidge, praise for his veto increased. Frederick E. Murphy, publisher of the powerful Minneapolis *Tribune*, was a house guest of the president in July, and he emphasized the belief that the McNary-Haugen bill was vicious legislation. He told Coolidge that the northwestern farmers had been led astray by political rather than by genuine dirt farmers.[32] From Norbeck's point of view injury was added to insult when a delegation from North Dakota informed Coolidge that a farm bill less "radical" than the surplus-control measure would satisfy the farmers in that state."[33]

28   Norbeck to George A. Starring, June 1, 1927. Norbeck MS.
29   Hiram Johnson to Norbeck, May 27, 1927. Norbeck MS.
30   New York *Times*, June 16, 1927, p. 11.
31   Rapid City *Daily Journal*, June 17, 1927.
32   *Ibid.*, July 19, 1927.
33   New York *Times*, July 12, 1927, p. 10.

Even Senator Capper, supposedly a militant farm leader, said he would support "something just as good" as the McNary-Haugen bill.[34]

On the whole, the president's trip seemingly convinced him that his veto was more popular in the Northwest than some of the more vocal friends of the farmer would have led him to believe. This caused Norbeck no little embarrassment, as he had been assuring Coolidge that the farmers would be satisfied with nothing less than legislation that would put agriculture on a definite equality with industry.

Norbeck should have arranged to have a number of leading farm representatives call on Coolidge, who, from his point of view, were considered "sound" on farm relief. Obviously, those in the Northwest who opposed the McNary-Haugen bill did everything possible to curry favor with the president and convince him of the wisdom of his action in vetoing the measure.

While it seemed as though Norbeck was making scant progress in convincing Coolidge of the desirability of surplus-control legislation, he gained presidential support for the Rushmore project. On August 10 he presided at a formal ceremony at which time he introduced the president to a crowd of several thousand proud Dakotans. In speaking of the work Coolidge more than fulfilled Norbeck's expectations. He declared that the memorial was entitled to the "support of private beneficence and the national government."[35] After completion of his short talk, Coolidge presented the drills to Borglum and the actual carving on the country's great shrine to democracy began.

That was a great day for Norbeck. His heart swelled with pride as the drill's staccato bark told that the rock was being carved away. In his mind he could vision the monument's completion, including the figure of his beloved Theodore Roosevelt. As he sat with Coolidge on the improvised platform of rough hewed native pine, his face reflected a look of solid contentment and achievement.

The Fourth of July found Norbeck and Coolidge attending the Belle Fourche rodeo, one of the largest of its kind in the West. As the two men sat together in a special box decked in red, white, and blue, watching the bucking broncos, bulldogging, and other attractions, their contrasting physical appearances hinted at the fundamental differences which separated them. The look of restrained enjoyment which Coolidge wore beneath his ten gallon hat seemed to reflect his Vermont-Amherst background. Norbeck's broad bronzed face, holding a look of intense interest, characterized his close identity with the Great Plains area and his western heritage.[36]

To the surprise of most people, and to the disappointment of many, Coolidge announced in August that he did not choose to run for another

34 Rapid City *Daily Journal*, August 1, 1927.
35 "Address by Calvin Coolidge," *The Black Hills Engineer*, 18:334-35 (November 30, 1930).
36 See the portrait in the New York *Times*, July 10, 1927, p. 3.

term. In spite of Norbeck's close association with the president during the summer, he was taken completely by surprise. Speculative rumors and guesses as to just what the president meant were soon widespread. One of Coolidge's biographers concludes that he meant just what he said,[37] but many contemporaries believed the statement was purposely phrased so that he could accept the nomination if drafted. It is unlikely that Norbeck would have supported Coolidge for the nomination in 1928. Some observers expressed the belief that the summer's association drew the two men closer together on policies. But Norbeck's announcement soon after Coolidge left the state that he would return to Washington and fight for repassage of the McNary-Haugen bill scotched these speculations.[38]

37 Claude M. Fuess, *Calvin Coolidge, The Man From Vermont* (Boston, 1940), p. 393.
38 Mitchell *Evening Republican,* November 5, 1927.

CHAPTER XIII

DEFEAT FOR THE NORTHWEST

During the autumn and winter of 1927-28, emotions again ran high as the farm pressure groups urged Congress to pass another surplus-control bill. The principal farm lobbyists, including Peek, Davis, and Murphy were still in Washington more active than ever. In April, 1928, another McNary-Haugen bill, slightly revised, passed the Senate by a vote of fifty-three to twenty-three,[1] and about two weeks later it was approved by the House 204 to 122.[2]

While these majorities seemed overwhelming, Norbeck observed that "everybody is voting for the bill at the present time on the theory that the President is going to veto it."[3] Because of this factor, it is certain that the recorded votes did not reflect the true opinion. In any event, his observation was correct and on May 23, Coolidge sent a veto message to Congress couched in much sharper terms than the one of fifteen months before. Norbeck paired to override the veto, but the bill's proponents lacked four votes of success in the Senate.

Coolidge's veto was the signal for midwestern farm representatives to unloose an unrestrained volley of threats at the administration. Governor Adam McMullen of Nebraska called for 100,000 farmers to march on the approaching Republican convention in Kansas City. Henry A. Wallace predicted that the Republican party might find its death in the Midwest,[4] and Frank Lowden, with an eye on the presidential nomination, declared that he was still for the entire bill.[5] Norbeck remained silent. For seven years he had heard the farmers and their accredited representatives menacingly declare for aggressive action, but he knew it was only a threat and nothing more.

Actually, the more responsible McNary-Haugenites were deeply demoralized. Some of the leading lobbyists were ready to return home. It was in a discouraged tone that Frank Murphy wrote to Norbeck recapitulating his efforts in behalf of surplus-control legislation during the preceding fifteen months. "It was seriously intended to solve the farm problem," he said of the McNary-Haugen bill, "and it would have done so if it had not been for that smart New Englander who thought he knew more than all the rest of us." Then after thanking Norbeck for his "counsel and assistance," he added: "you took a very important part in the campaign for this legislation, and the farmers of the United States owe you a great debt of gratitude."[6]

1 *Cong. Rec.,* 70 Cong., 1 Sess., April 12, 1928, p. 6283.
2 *Ibid.,* May 3, 1928, pp. 7771-2.
3 Norbeck to Ben Fischback, April 24, 1928. Norbeck MS.
4 New York *Times,* May 24, 1928, p. 1.
5 *Ibid.,* p. 20.
6 Frank Murphy to Norbeck, April 14, 1928. See also Murphy to Norbeck, April 6, 1929. Norbeck MS.

Soon after Coolidge's statement indicating that he did not wish re-nomination, the name of Herbert Hoover loomed high among Republican presidential possibilities. In order to curb the Hoover boom, some of the progressives in Washington, including Senators Borah and Nye, proposed the candidacy of Senator Norris. Norbeck fully realized, as did Borah, Nye, and Norris, that the Nebraska senator had absolutely no chance to obtain the Republican nomination. To push his cause would handicap efforts to nominate someone friendly to surplus-control legislation who might have a chance to win. Norbeck felt that he should take the lead in scotching this abortive move. He announced on October 31, 1927, that he would support Lowden. This was a clarion call to the Midwest progressives and the farm leaders to rally behind a single candidate and carry the battle to the Kansas City convention.[7]

This was not an easy decision. In 1920 he had fought and defeated Lowden in one of South Dakota's most bitter presidential primaries. Since that time the two men had not been on particularly friendly terms, although Lowden had warmly congratulated him on his fight for the McNary-Haugen bill. But Norbeck said it "was the logic of the situation" to support the former Illinois governor. "I have never been a Lowden admirer," he wrote, "but I am not going to let my personal likes and dislikes influence my judgment in a matter as important as this one."[8] Lowden was probably the only man holding views similar to his own on the farm question who had any chance of receiving the nomination.

Norbeck's opposition to Hoover was not based on personal grounds. "It has not been a pleasant task to criticize Hoover," he said. "I don't dislike him personally. I have done it as a matter of duty, in an effort to warn party leaders against making a serious blunder.[9] Their economic and political philosophies, of course, were in sharp contrast. Hoover stood for what he termed "rugged individualism," while Norbeck favored the extension of governmental powers. Norbeck was moving further toward the political left. Hoover was staging a stanch defense of an older order.

Norbeck promoted Lowden's candidacy in his usual vigorous manner, and the first task was to help line up a strong Lowden delegation from his own state. In this he was successful.[10] Other Midwest states also came to Lowden's support and by national convention time he appeared to be a poor second choice, as Hoover was far out in front.

The South Dakota senator did everything possible to thwart the Hoover boom. He created something of a sensation early in 1928, when he inserted a statement in the *Congressional Record* by George N. Peek, part of which stated that Hoover was the "arch-enemy of a square deal for agriculture."[11] Senator Frederick M. Sackett of Kentucky made a

7 New York *Times*, November 1, 1927, p. 1.
8 Norbeck to O. W. Coursey, January 18. 1928. Norbeck MS.
9 Norbeck to L. E. Camfield, June 5, 1928. Norbeck MS.
10 New York *Times*, March 7, 1928, p. 3.
11 *Cong. Rec.*, 70 Cong., 1 Sess., April 5, 1928, pp. 5927-32.

vigorous reply to Peek's statement, after which Norbeck arose and dryly remarked that he knew of nothing that Hoover had done for the American farmer and that he was the most "vulnerable candidate the Republican party had."[12]

His effectiveness both as a legislator and as a Hoover opponent was limited during 1928 because of ill health. For about the first time in his life, his rugged physique failed to support the fast pace which he set for himself. Part of the trouble came from overwork and nervous exhaustion, and he suffered from heart irregularities, chills, bad tonsils, and intense nervousness. In May he went to Rochester, Minnesota, for a complete physical check up. The doctors found nothing seriously wrong, but they kept him there for rest and observation until June 7, when he left for the Republican national convention.

In spite of the efforts of many midwesterners, the nomination of Hoover was practically assured when the Republican convention met on June 12. Norbeck headed his state delegation and arrived in Kansas City in a fighting mood. The only spirited battle came when the resolutions committee refused to incorporate the equalization-fee principle in the farm plank. Norbeck fought as hard as his health permitted to get this adopted, but on the final vote in the sub-committee only fifteen states supported it. Having lost in committee, he announced that the minority would carry the fight to the convention floor. As a practical politician, he realized that this could do nothing more than dramatize the farmers' position.

But the farmers' spirits were not completely chilled by this apparent defeat. Some of those who represented the left wing of agricultural revolt prepared to stage a giant demonstration in the hope of influencing the convention on the farm issue. Governor McMullen of Nebraska had called for 100,000 militant farmers to march on the convention carrying the banners of agrarian unrest. While the number fell far short of this, between 400 and 500 individuals gathered for a climactic demonstration and marched through the streets, hotel lobbies, and to the convention hall, shouting, "We Don't Want Hoover." Upon being denied entrance into the hall, they met on the west side of the auditorium and chanted "We Don't Want Hoover." As William Allen White observed, these marchers did not represent the lunatic fringe of the farm movement, but those who were obsessed with the idea that only surplus-control legislation of the McNary-Haugen type could save the farmers.[13] Norbeck was not among the demonstrators, but like them, he was convinced that there was only one way to be saved!

No demonstration, however, could change the cut and dried pattern of the convention. When the farm forces endeavored to obtain a plank incorporating the McNary-Haugen principle, they were defeated by the decisive vote of 807 to 277. Only three states, North and South Dakota and Illinois, voted unanimously for the minority farm plank. Iowa, Indiana,

12 New York *Times,* April 21, 1928, p. 4.
13 The *Daily Emporia Gazette,* June 14, 1928.

and South Carolina, however, gave it very heavy support.[14] Lowden then withdrew his candidacy and from all appearances McNary-Haugenism was completely routed. But even after Lowden withdrew and the Illinois delegates were supporting Hoover, Norbeck refused to vote for the Secretary of Commerce.

Would he support Hoover? Norbeck and other progressive Republicans must make this decision. The Midwest progressives all knew Hoover's position on the farm question. He believed that the tariff on farm products must be revised and that a Federal Farm Board should be established to assist in farm marketing.[15] By no stretch of the imagination could these ideas be reconciled with what the farm groups had been demanding for five or six years. Norbeck hoped that the Democrats would come out boldly for the McNary-Haugen principle, but they proved to be somewhat evasive on the subject. Although Smith, the Democratic candidate, did not commit himself outright to the equalization fee, his stand was satisfactory to many farm leaders, including Murphy, Peek, and Davis.

Senator Norris also supported Smith. But Norbeck said: "I am not going to bolt the Republican ticket this year. There is no place to go."[16] John J. Raskob asked him whether, after reading Smith's acceptance speech, he could not support the Democratic nominee.[17] To this Norbeck gave no reply. He may have actually distrusted Smith's stand on the farm question, but his attitude leads one to conclude that his main reason for not supporting the New Yorker was because he was a Democrat and favored the repeal of prohibition! And it cannot be overlooked that to have supported Smith would have indirectly strengthened the conservative Republicans in his state.

While he did not favor Smith, neither would he participate in the Hoover campaign. The condition of his health made it necessary to return to Rochester soon after the national convention. Thus he found himself conveniently removed from active politics.

The actions of many of the Northwest's progressives in 1928 adequately illustrates why they were never a greater force in Washington and why, while they made a great deal of noise, their demands received little consideration. For instance, the day after the convention adjourned, Senator McNary announced that he would support Hoover's candidacy and that agricultural conditions could be improved without the equalization fee. McMullen was supporting him actively before the election, and Brookhart, the supposed radical, described Hoover as a great friend of the farmer; "knowing more about handling farm surpluses than any other man in the world."[18] Haugen, Nye, and others soon climbed on the bandwagon. Only

14 New York *Times,* June 15, 1928, p. 4.
15 R. L. Wilbur and A. M. Hyde, *The Hoover Policies* (New York, 1937), p. 50.
16 Norbeck newspaper interview, August 10, 1928. Norbeck MS.
17 John J. Raskob to Norbeck, August 16, 1928. Norbeck MS.
18 New York *Times,* October 27, 1928, p. 10.

a short while before, these same men had been threatening conservative Republicans. But members of the "Old Guard," smart politicians that they were, knew that much of this talk was merely bluster and that when the time came they would "vote right."

Perhaps Norbeck was less guilty than some of his progressive colleagues, but only slightly so. He never endorsed the Hoover farm plan, as did many of the other progressives, but after considerable pressure from South Dakota Republicans, he declared: "Hoover is the next man for President."[19] Although he disliked his party's nominee, his Republicanism was too strong to permit him to oppose Hoover actively.

It must be admitted, however, that those who favored the equalization fee and who disliked Hoover were in a difficult position. The progressives in the spring wheat belt could not have carried their states for Smith even if they had believed that his stand on the farm question was satisfactory. This is well illustrated by the fact that Hoover carried Nebraska, in spite of Senator Norris' opposition. But there was little excuse for their blatant praise of his farm program, when they knew that his stand was exactly opposite that for which most of them had been fighting for seven years. Senator Brookhart furnished one of the best illustrations. Of him Norbeck wrote: "[he] firmly believes that the millenium on earth will start on the fourth day of March [1929] at high noon. . . ."[20] The conservatives would have been less than astute if they had taken the progressive threats seriously.

Norbeck's belief that no substantial aid for agriculture would come from the Hoover administration proved to be nearly correct. He believed that Hoover had no disposition to deal with the problem on its merits and added that the "great concern of the Republican leaders now is not to embarrass Hoover."[21] He had scarcely returned to Washington after the holiday season when Senator McNary and others asked him to support enactment of the McNary-Haugen bill without the equalization fee. His reply was "no." When he expressed his unwillingness to support such a measure, he was informed that it was the "Hoover plan and that big emphasis was going to be placed on cooperative marketing."[22]

President Hoover called a special session of Congress to deal with the agricultural and tariff problems. In addressing the lawmakers on April 16, he made his position crystal clear on the farm problem. "There should be no fee or tax imposed upon the farmer," he said. "No government agency should engage in buying or selling and price fixing of products. . . . The most progressive movement in all agriculture has been the upbuilding of the farmers' own marketing organization. . . ."[23]

19   Huron *Evening Huronite,* October 5, 1928.
20   Norbeck to Willis Cook, November 12, 1928. Norbeck MS.
21   Norbeck to Mrs. Lester Wegner, December 27, 1928. Norbeck MS.
22   Norbeck to Harold Gundvordahl, February 25, 1929. Norbeck MS.
23   Wilbur and Hyde, *The Hoover Policies,* p. 150.

This message dashed any remaining hope of the McNary-Haugenites. Some of them, including McNary, fell in step with the president. The uselessness of reviving the old surplus-control bill was too apparent. The representatives of the farm pressure groups had all but ceased to work for the equalization fee and Peek and Murphy did not even appear in Washington. The attitude was to let the president proceed with his own plan.[24] About the last hope of the surplus-control supporters was to seek the passage of the export-debenture scheme.

The underlying philosophy of this idea was not materially different from that embodied in the McNary-Haugen bill. It was designed to raise the price of farm products by making the tariff effective, or partially so, on the crops of which there was an exportable surplus. The objective was to be achieved by offering an export bounty on a given list of debenturable products. It was believed that the amount of the bounty would be reflected back to the farmers on the entire marketed crop, thus making the tariff effective in some degree. Exporters of debenturable products would receive export debentures or certificates from the United States Treasury, which could be used in turn to pay import duties.[25]

The Senate Agriculture Committee developed a bill along the lines recommended by Hoover, but including the export debenture provision of which he was a bitter enemy. The bill provided for establishing a Federal Farm Board, endowed with broad powers, and placing at its disposal a revolving fund of $500,000,000. This board was directed to encourage orderly marketing through cooperative associations, and to establish stabilization corporations empowered to hold, handle, and market farm commodities in order to prevent losses to producers through fluctuations in agricultural prices.[26]

On April 12 Senators McNary, Norbeck and other members of the Agriculture Committee called on the president seeking his definite commitment on the export-debenture section of the bill. After conferring with his advisers, Hoover wrote to Senator McNary that he opposed that particular section. McNary immediately summoned the committee to vote on whether to report the bill favorably with the debenture feature in spite of the president's opposition. Norbeck argued furiously against adhering to Hoover's wishes. He told the committee members that the entire Agricultural Marketing Act would be worthless without the debenture amendment. But McNary opposed it on the grounds that it would be useless to send another bill to the White House and have it vetoed. The committee

24 Alice M. Christensen, "Agricultural Pressure and Governmental Response in the United States," p. 274.

25 Joseph S. Davis, *The Farm Export Debenture Plan* (Palo Alto, 1929), chap. I.

26 Elmer A. Lewis, *Farm Relief and the Agricultural Adjustment Acts* (Washington, 1938), pp. 1-10.

finally voted eight to six to include the disputed section, and it was reported to the Senate in that form.[27]

Having regained his strength, Norbeck took the Senate floor a few days later in support of the debenture plan. He gave a detailed discussion of the causes of the farm depression and argued that increased production was not the principal difficulty. He declared that production had not kept pace with population advances and that it would be impossible for the farmer to restrict production of wheat, for instance, only to domestic consumption, as was being advocated in some quarters. Farmers, he said, needed a better price and not more advice from city editors! He insisted that the debenture scheme would not give the farmer equality, but that it was a move in the right direction. The nature of his address was more political than economic. He discussed the Kansas City convention and the defeat suffered by the farmers there. Finally, he stated that he would oppose Hoover's farm plan even if he had to stand alone.[28]

He did not answer the principal economic objections to the debenture and equalization-fee schemes; namely, that they would tend to stimulate production and aggravate the surplus problem. His statement that production was not increasing as fast as population was true in some respects, but did not meet the argument. He did not consider the fact that people were eating less grain products, that our export market was steadily shrinking, that in the past increased prices had stimulated production, and that foreign nations might react unfavorably to the United States "dumping" agricultural products on the world markets. The speech reflected the feelings of a man who realized that he was hopelessly defeated. He did little but fling charges and warn of disastrous consequences.

Although the Senate reported the bill with the debenture, the president managed to get it eliminated in the House, and the Senate finally agreed. Just before the vote was taken on the conference report, Norbeck made his last remarks on the measure.

He asserted first that the bill did not originate with the farmers and that they did not want it. The folly of giving a government board half a billion dollars with which to gamble in the grain markets was obvious. Lending money to oppose a speculative market, he said, could not succeed. But he did not make a lengthy argument because he knew it would be useless, and when the vote was taken a few minutes later, the Agricultural Marketing Act received an overwhelming endorsement.[29]

Norbeck and LaFollette were the only Republican senators present who voted against Hoover's farm bill. It took real courage to stand out

27 *Cong. Rec.*, 71 Cong., 1 Sess., April 23, 1929, p. 370.
28 *Ibid.*, May 2, 1929, pp. 774-84.
29 *Ibid.*, June 14, 1929, pp. 2876-77. The vote was seventy-four to eight.

against the administration on a bill that might bring some farm relief. He had the courage of his convictions and was unlike one eastern senator who told him just before the vote was recorded that he would support the measure because there "was nothing to it—except a chance for the government to lose some money. . . ."[30]

Confirmation of members of the Federal Farm Board aroused some heated discussion in the Senate. Considerable objection was raised to some of Hoover's appointees by Norris, Brookhart and other progressive midwesterners. But Norbeck, who had voted against the bill, was willing to let the president proceed and urged the Senate to give Hoover a free hand. "Having started on this impossible scheme of helping the farmer by lending more money and suggesting impossible plans of cooperation," he told his colleagues, "we must await the final result. We know what it is going to be, but it may take a year or two or three. . . . I have done everything I could to keep agriculture out of this experimental whim. . . . The sooner they [Farm Board members] are confirmed, the sooner they can go ahead and demonstrate their uselessness, while their activities are limited to the present law."[31]

He went on to say that the Farm Board could not loan money successfully to cooperatives to stabilize the market. Although the Board planned only to buy seasonal surpluses and help smooth out seasonal price fluctuations, carry-overs almost always existed in such staples as wheat and cotton. Since the price of these commodities was determined largely by the world market, it meant that when the Farm Board bought wheat, for instance, the only way it could keep from losing money was to have a rise in the world market, where the surpluses or carry-over must be sold. In other words, he argued, the Board was not trying to stabilize the market for the amount domestically consumed, as was planned under the equalization-fee scheme, but that it hinted at stabilizing the world market, which was impossible.

Voluntary cooperation, he continued, was unsuccessful because those outside the cooperative, as well as the members, would receive the benefit of the higher price, and this, he claimed, would destroy the system. He pointed to the failure of the Canadian wheat pool and the unsuccessful attempts at bringing all the tobacco growers into one cooperative and the cotton producers into a single organization. Citing the milk and fruit cooperatives as examples, he further insisted there was no need for additional cooperatives, because strong organizations already existed in the fields where they had proved successful.

Although there are two sides to the argument, Norbeck showed an un-

30 *Ibid.*, p. 2886.
31 *Ibid.*, October 16, 1929, p. 4604.

usual grasp of this particular plan and his prediction of disastrous failure was prophetic. Norbeck did not seem to realize, however, that the same factors which were to plague the Federal Farm Board probably would have caused the McNary-Haugen bill to fail; that is, declining world prices and increasing agricultural surpluses in the United States.

Norbeck was not alone in his harsh indictment of the Hoover farm plan. Murphy, chairman of the legislative committee of the Corn Belt Federation, was also bitter against it. Under his leadership, the Corn Belt Federation unanimously adopted a resolution on March 18, saying: "Farmers do not want a political federal farm board that will be all dressed up legislatively but with no place to go. We have no use for stabilization corporations. They cannot meet the surplus problem in any way and would but add additional machinery of a political nature to be carried by an already distressed industry."[32] Very few of the old-time McNary-Haugenites were genuinely converted.

Having disposed of the farm legislation, Congress next turned to tariff revision. Norbeck had voted the party line on this question in both 1921 and 1922, but when he observed that industry and a few specialized farm crops reaped most of the benefits, he began to oppose higher rates. His section, he perceived, was definitely harmed by the protective tariff as long as prices for the products sold were determined by the world market and purchases were made in a protected market. Realizing this, he had begun to work for the McNary-Haugen bill, thinking that both industry and agriculture could receive tariff benefits. But with the defeat of the equalization-fee plan, his attitude changed. Whether he recognized it or not he had been strongly urging the economic nationalism so popular in the twenties.

The Hawley-Smoot tariff bill was first introduced, debated, and passed in the House. There were early indications that only limited revision, as desired by Hoover, would be accomplished, but by the time it passed the House many amendments had been added and protection favors were liberally distributed among the House members.[33]

When the bill reached the Senate, there was a definite move to block higher industrial duties. Norbeck joined a coalition of Insurgent Republicans and Democrats to oppose vigorously a general revision. The first real fight between this coalition and the high protectionists took place in June, 1929, and centered around the Borah resolution, which would have limited "hearings, deliberations, and recommendations . . . to the agricultural and directly related schedules." Norbeck voted for this resolution, which was defeated by the very close vote of 38 to 39, as did most of the Midwest senators along with a number of Democrats.[34] This started months of

32   Frank Murphy to Norbeck, April 6, 1929. Norbeck MS.
33   F. W. Taussig, *The Tariff History of the United States* (New York, 1931), pp. 489-98.
34   *Cong. Rec.*, 71 Cong., 1 Sess., June 17, 1929, p. 2947.

sparring between the Insurgent-Democratic coalition and the protectionist Republicans, aided by some Democrats, particularly the "Sugarcrats."

Considering the tariff as a whole, the coalition was able to block many of the tariff raises demanded by certain eastern senators. The patience of satirical Senator Moses finally snapped. In a speech before the New England Manufacturers Association in Washington on November 7, he declared that he could not promise his constituents much tariff relief in light of the fact that the "sons of the Wild Jackass" were opposing higher duties.[35]

Norbeck was one of the "sons" to whom he referred. There were probably few, if any, who remembered a similar charge by another New Englander, Thomas B. Reed, against another Dakotan. In the 1890's, Reed, whose mastery of sarcasm was second to none, was Speaker of the House. He was frequently annoyed at Congressman John A. Pickler of South Dakota, who was continually insisting that the House take a roll call on the prohibition issue. After having endeavored to avoid such embarrassing votes to the Republicans on numerous occasions, Reed burst out: "I never fully understood the Biblical term 'the wild ass's foal' until I saw Pickler."[36] Moses' well-known admiration for Reed makes it easy to imagine where he secured his label for the disturbing wild men from the West, as it is only a short step from Reed's terminology.

While this clever phraseology proved popular in the Northeast, it was resented, at least outwardly, by those who fell under the label, and it spurred them to greater efforts against the tariff changes desired by the East.

Some of the Midwest senators finally concluded that the new tariff bill might be of some value for agriculture if it was amended to include the export-debenture plan. On October 19, 1929, the Norris amendment passed the Senate, permitting the Federal Farm Board to use the debenture plan on certain basic agricultural commodities if the Board found it could not otherwise accomplish its objective.[37] When the Senate passed the tariff bill on March 24, 1930, by a vote of 53 to 31, it still included the debenture provision. But Norbeck voted against it. He had lost his enthusiasm for this kind of farm relief. To William Hirth he wrote that its passage would lead some to believe that the farm relief issue was settled, and without giving agricultural equality.[38] He felt that the cause of agriculture would be harmed if another act was passed which did not even aim at solving the fundamental problems. While it might be argued that this was not a constructive attitude, time actually proved him correct, as evidenced by the fact that some senators believed that if the Farm Board could not solve

35 New York *Times,* November 9, 1929, p. 1.
36 Arthur W. Dunn, *From Harrison to Harding,* 2 vols. (New York, 1922), I, p. 303.
37 *Cong. Rec.,* 71 Cong., 1 Sess., October 19, 1929, p. 4694.
38 Norbeck to William Hirth, November 29, 1929. Norbeck MS.

the agricultural problem, no legislation could do so. Norbeck hoped to avoid that situation.

His general opposition to the entire tariff bill continued throughout most of the fourteen month period during which it was considered, and on the final vote he was paired against it. On both the farm and tariff legislation Norbeck's position had been one of ineffectual protest.

While he was vigorously opposing the administration's agricultural and tariff policies, he again agreed on foreign policy. Late in 1928 and early in 1929 the question of keeping United States Marines in the little Latin American republic of Nicaragua was served up to an already agitated Senate. The sending of marines there in 1926, after a temporary withdrawal, brought a storm of public protest. In spite of this the State Department went ahead and supervised elections in Nicaragua in November, 1928.

Meanwhile Senate debate over the administration's policy became very heated. Senators Borah, Norris, LaFollette and others bitterly opposed United States intervention. In closing an especially fervent speech, Norris declared that "if we do not call a halt, we eventually will bring down the structure of our government upon our heads."

Norbeck was immediately upon his feet to defend the administration's program. "Mr. President," he said, "no country in the world is so far away that its welfare is not our concern to some degree, but the happenings on this continent are either in our house or in our dooryard. We must frankly take their part in dealing with any trouble that arises between the Arctic Ocean to the North and the Panama Canal to the South." This was necessary, he argued, because Latin Americans were not the same "steady, self-reliant" people as those coming from northern Europe. And he added: "they lack the stability and patience of the northern Europeans"— the ruling classes coming from those Mediterranean countries that "periodically prefer a dictator." In concluding he insisted that the United States could not avoid the responsibility of maintaining order between Canada and Panama, and that this country should announce to its citizens "that in case of trouble it will not be necessary to use any such false pretenses as to run up the British flag and claim protection under same. Give them to understand that our flag will be their protection today, tomorrow, now and in the future, and as long as our Republic endures."[39] This was Norbeck's first speech on foreign affairs and it sounded like an echo from the grave of Theodore Roosevelt.

When an amendment providing for withdrawal of the marines was before the Senate in February, 1929, he opposed it. But many of his midwestern Republican colleagues, including Blaine, Brookhart, Capper, Frazier, McMaster, and Norris voted for it.[40]

It was not that Norbeck was less isolationist than others in his section.

39 *Cong. Rec.*, 70 Cong., 1 Sess., April 29, 1928, pp. 6975-77.
40 The *United States Daily*, February 23, 1929.

It was simply a matter of personal dislike for all Latin American peoples, an aversion that dated back to his first trip to Mexico in 1910. To see the "Nordics" retreating from their advanced position in Nicaragua, even though the marines may have had no right there, was more than he could approve.

Of all the problems relating to foreign affairs, he showed his keenest interest in immigration. And here again he found himself in conflict with the administration. Norbeck, like many others of foreign ancestry, favored keeping other Europeans from coming to American shores. In keeping with this idea he voted for both of the immigration laws of 1921 and 1924. But he objected to the national origins provision, included in the act of 1924. Under this, the combined number of immigrants from all countries included in the quotas was arbitrarily set at about 150,000 a year. It happened, however, that the number of immigrants from Germany, the Scandinavian countries, and Ireland would be slightly reduced. On the other hand, quotas from northern Ireland, England, including some of the English West Indian colonies, were slightly increased, as were those from Greece and Italy.

Shortly before the national origins provision was to become effective, Senate debate reached a high pitch with some of the northwestern senators forming the opposition's vanguard. Norbeck was again active in the debate and this was a subject on which it was hard for him to remain calm. With his face slightly flushed, and with his accent broadened by momentary excitement, he charged that it was bad national policy to allow the "agents of Mussolini" and the "friends of Capone" to come to the United States, while fewer northern Europeans would be admitted. This country, he asserted, should not keep out peoples who had mastered the art of self-government, and allow those who were "unstable" to come in added numbers.[41] But his protests, as well as those of Senator Nye and others, were entirely unavailing.

Although the results of the Seventieth and Seventy-first Congresses were disappointing, there was a brighter side. The passage of his Migratory Bird bill, and his success in obtaining national aid for carving at Mount Rushmore, added sweetening to the bitter doses handed to him by the administration in the Agricultural Marketing Act, the tariff, and the national origins provision.

41 *Cong. Rec.,* 71 Cong., 1 Sess., June 3, 1929, p. 2242.

CHAPTER XIV

A NATIONAL LEADER IN CONSERVATION

Norbeck's life-long interest in wild-life conservation and park development naturally brought him into prominence in these fields after he arrived in Washington. Before 1921 his efforts had been largely circumscribed by state boundaries, but upon his election to the Senate he found the opportunities for the development of his hobby almost unlimited. And it did not take him long to assume a position of commanding importance. Writing about Norbeck's conservation work after his death, Horace Albright, Director of the National Park Service, declared: "We are not likely to see soon another leader arise who will have such a broad knowledge of the conservation problems of the country and the courage, power and legislative skill in drafting and guiding through Congress the laws necessary to provide permanent solutions to these problems."[1] This was a common feeling among many of the nation's top conservationists.

His leadership came in part because of his intense devotion to the cause. There was seldom a time when he was not working on some conservation measure. Furthermore, he had an extensive knowledge of the nation's conservation needs, gained through years of study and actual experience. Perhaps also it was less difficult to achieve leadership in this field because relatively few senators seemed to care anything about conservation legislation.

He had been in Washington only a short time when those interested in preserving the national resources came to depend on him to get their bills through Congress. When the National Park Service, the United States Biological Survey, or some other administrative agency had a bill for introduction, more frequently than not they sent it over to "Pete." The fact that he could often get their bills passed made him popular among the conservationists. This was generally not easy because of the lack of interest. Seldom did these measures gain a high place on the legislative calendars. Lack of interest probably had defeated as much conservation legislation as outright opposition, therefore it was important to put it in the hands of men with extraordinary legislative skill and who were held in high regard by their colleagues. Much conservation legislation had to pass by unanimous consent!

As a member of the committees on Agriculture and Forestry and Public Lands, he was in a position to aid in the passage of many important laws relating to conservation. He also became a director of the National Conference on State Parks, a member of the Executive Board of the American Civic Association, and a member of the Advisory Board of the American Planning and Civic Association. He also served on the Migratory

1 Horace Albright, "Obituary of Senator Norbeck," *American Planning and Civic Comment,* 3:39-40 (January-March, 1937).

Bird Commission and the Special Senate Committee on Wild Life Resources. An interest, stimulated by his idol Theodore Roosevelt some twenty-five years before, was expanded to include all of the forty-eight states and Alaska after he went to Washington.

Many of the country's outstanding conservationists were among his closest friends. But of all his friends interested in this field, Albright was probably the most intimate. Together they traveled thousands of miles in the West, and they worked together in Washington seeking the solutions to national park needs.

His first few years in the Senate were spent with minor conservation and park measures, and those which affected primarily his own state or section. At the same time he prepared to deal with broader problems. In 1924 he was busy obtaining an extension of Custer State Park, which reputedly made it the largest state park in the nation, and in establishing an antelope preserve in northwestern South Dakota. His work on Mount Rushmore, begun in 1925, gradually demanded more and more attention.

In the light of his interest, it could not be expected that Norbeck would be content for long to deal only with local problems. By 1926 he had taken the lead in a vigorous fight for passage of the Migratory Bird Act, one of the most far-reaching wild-life measures passed during his terms in the Senate.

The demand for migratory-bird protection received impetus when, in 1916, a treaty was made between the United States, Canada, and Great Britain for the purpose of protecting migratory birds crossing the international border. Article eight of that treaty pledged the contracting powers to recommend legislation to their respective lawmaking bodies to insure execution of the treaty provisions. Accordingly, the United States passed a law in 1918 prohibiting the killing, capturing, or selling of certain specified migratory birds except in accordance with regulations determined by the Secretary of Agriculture.[2]

While this was an important step in the right direction, this country was still far behind Canada in providing protection for migratory birds. The act of 1918 helped protect them, but did nothing to insure their propagation. The Canadian government, on the other hand, had taken direct steps to increase the number of birds by establishing inviolate sanctuaries where the flocks of ducks and geese might rest, mate, and raise their young. To many this seemed even more necessary in the United States where there were more hunters and relatively fewer natural refuges.

The conservationists pointed out that the state laws were conflicting and inadequate, and that in many cases the best nesting grounds were being drained and put to other uses. It was the fear of gradual bird extinction

2 The law was declared constitutional by the Supreme Court in *Missouri* v. *Holland.*

which prompted the conservationists to advocate that the United States go further in implementing the treaty with Canada.

Consequently, in 1921 Senator Harry S. New introduced a bill providing for the purchase of land to be designated as inviolate bird sanctuaries. In order to carry out this program, it was suggested that a federal hunting license of one dollar be levied on those who wished to hunt migratory birds. It was this federal license feature which produced much of the opposition and most of the bitterness in the subsequent Senate debate. The New bill passed the Senate in December, 1922, but the House defeated it some two months later.[3]

Senator Norbeck had been a strong supporter of the defeated bill, and upon his suggestion, Senator Brookhart introduced a similar measure in 1924.[4] Both Brookhart and Norbeck fought hard for their bill, but when the Iowa senator lost his seat in April, 1926, Norbeck was left alone to push the measure.

During the following weeks, he carried on a single-handed battle with Senator James Reed of Missouri, the bill's chief opponent and an effective adversary. Reed was ably assisted by Democratic senators C. C. Dill of Washington and William H. King of Utah. Reed especially opposed the provision requiring hunters to buy a federal license, and also the section calling for a greater number of federal game wardens to enforce the act. He said that logically the bill should be entitled: "a bill to raise a large sum of money annually to hire some additional sneaks to interfere with the rights and privileges of the states to regulate their own business." With caustic sarcasm he added that it would be equally sensible to establish sanctuaries for jack rabbits![5] Dill and King echoed those sentiments with almost equal bitterness. When no Republican senators would come to his support, Norbeck finally had to admit defeat in the face of such formidable Democratic opposition. The bill was laid aside on June 1.

But his Norwegian stubbornness and tenacity were intensified by his loss of the first round and he meant to finish what he had started.

Late in 1927 he introduced another bill, very much like the one Brookhart had proposed. It provided for the purchase of bird sanctuaries from funds raised by selling federal hunting licenses. It also permitted the establishment of so-called public shooting grounds near the sanctuaries. His first objective was to secure game refuges where the birds could rest, breed, and raise their young unmolested. Since land purchases would require enormous sums of money, he believed the best way to raise the necessary amount was to make each hunter of migratory birds purchase a federal license at one dollar. He estimated that in this manner approximately one million dollars a year would be made available for land purchases and law enforcement.

---

3 "Game Refuge Bill Becomes a Law," *American Game*, 18:27-30 (March, 1929).

4 Norbeck to J. A. McGuire, April 9, 1928. Norbeck MS.

5 *Cong. Rec.*, 69 Cong., 1 Sess., May 15, 1926, p. 9413.

Some sincere conservationists believed that direct government appropriations would be a better method of raising money, but Norbeck argued that in all probability only a few pork barrel appropriations could be obtained in light of the general lack of interest. Also this would allow politics to infest the program. But a federal license was abhorrent to men like Senator Reed, a crusader against extending powers of the national government.

Although Norbeck was not as insistent on the public shooting grounds feature, he believed this also had its advantages. In this way everyone could hunt on an equal basis during specified seasons. He believed that if public hunting grounds were not provided, wealthy sportsmen would buy up the land near the sanctuaries and monopolize the hunting during the open seasons.[6] This already had occurred in some areas where private individuals had purchased land near the best duck runs.

Very few senators showed any interest in Norbeck's migratory bird measure. The inertia, and the opposition of Reed, Dill, King, and later Blaine of Wisconsin, made it an uphill fight. While the conservation organizations gave him strong support, it was disheartening when they could not agree on the kind of a bill that should be enacted and when the Izaak Walton League in his own state opposed his measure. Some conservationists favored the federal license provision, while others opposed it. The same difference of opinion was registered on the public hunting grounds feature.[7] All the conservation agencies wanted game refuges, but they had no unified plan to obtain them. There was nothing for Norbeck to do under these circumstances but to proceed in the best possible way.

He asked to have his measure considered in February, 1928, but Senator Dill opposed taking it up at that time. Dill finally agreed not to filibuster against it if consideration was postponed and hearings held. Norbeck agreed to this procedure, much to his dismay later.[8] Meanwhile, his bird bill became the laughing stock of Congress. "To Congress," he wrote, "the whole bird conservation matter is a joke."[9]

Two months later, however, he succeeded in getting the Senate to take up the measure. The debate became extremely bitter. Senator Dill did not filibuster but he did everything else to delay and destroy it, including attempts to add crippling amendments. But Blaine of Wisconsin was even more obdurate. Norbeck expected Democratic opposition, but his wrath knew no bounds when members of his own party gave solace and strength to the enemy! Blaine argued that the license fee was most dangerous. "There is no reason," he stormed, "why the little boy in blue jeans should pay a dollar toward a fund out of which will be created an army of game wardens. . . . Here is a bill in which it is proposed to extend the

---

6　Norbeck to J. A. McGuire, April 9, 1928. Norbeck MS.
7　Keith McCanse, "The Migratory Bird Refuge and Public Shooting Grounds Bill," *The Game Breeder,* 38:230-31 (December, 1927).
8　Norbeck to Senator Lawrence C. Phipps, March 14, 1928. Norbeck MS.
9　Norbeck to W. T. Hornaday, April 18, 1928. Norbeck MS.

arm of bureaucratic administration. . . . There is a constant attempt . . . to extend this arm of centralized government over states and over the people. . . ."

Then Dill took up the cudgel. Glaring at Norbeck, he said: "The Senator will agree to almost any kind of an amendment as long as we do not interfere with charging everybody a license." And the Dakotan fired back: "As long as we do not get any money to do business, the Senator is willing to agree to any kind of a bill we want."

Blaine then charged that the federal game wardens provided for in the bill might become active politically in the various states. Norbeck had been waiting for just such an opening. No longer was he angry and a mischievous twinkle filled his eyes. He told Blaine that in all of his political experience it had never occurred to him that game wardens might be used to a good advantage politically. "The Senator from Wisconsin is quite enlightening to me," he added. "He has been governor of his state for six years, and I presume he understands what he is talking about— this army of sixty-odd game wardens traveling over Wisconsin in a political campaign."[10] In spite of Blaine's angry protest at this obvious inference, Norbeck held his ground and Blaine said nothing more about game wardens in politics!

Here again Norbeck was finding himself in conflict with those to whom the extension of federal powers was anathema. To him a federal license and federal game wardens were means of bringing about efficiency and progress, while to others they represented outside control, bureaucracy, and a decline in "states rights."

Frayed feelings, lost patiences, and sharp words continued to characterize the debate. Usually Norbeck had no difficulty getting on with people with whom he honestly differed on principle. But as the arguments wore on in an almost empty Senate chamber, he wrote: "I think I am getting some of this poison in my own system. I am developing a distinct aversion to certain fellows in this fight who claim to be conservationists and are helping Jim Reed carry on the destructive work."[11]

The bill finally passed on a voice vote of sixteen to twelve, which alone shows the lack of general interest. His opponents finally defeated the federal license feature, but he countered successfully with an amendment authorizing appropriations from the federal treasury. A matter of less importance, that of public shooting grounds, was also stricken out. But he got the most important thing; the bill provided for establishing game sanctuaries—if Congress would appropriate the authorizations.

The conservation forces hailed the bill's passage with enthusiasm. No praise seemed too high to heap upon Norbeck and his work. Typical was that found in the magazine *American Game*. It declared that the measure

10 *Cong. Rec.*, 70 Cong., 1 Sess., March 26, 1928, pp. 5355-76.
11 Norbeck to W. T. Hornaday, April 21, 1928. Norbeck MS.

was the most important event in migratory bird conservation since the enactment of the original law ten years before, and added: "Senator Norbeck earned the everlasting gratitude of all friends of conservation by his tireless and persistent efforts for this legislation."[12]

The House passed a revised Norbeck bill the following February, under the leadership of Representative Andresen of Minnesota.[13]

Norbeck was actually disappointed in the law because he realized there was a great deal of difference between having appropriations "authorized" and finally obtaining them. Without large sums of money no game refuges could be created, and unless someone put up an annual fight to obtain the necessary funds, he believed they would not be appropriated. "I am discouraged because of my inability to impress on you people," he wrote to Edmund Seymour, President of the American Bison Association, "that appropriations can not be picked from branches just like fruit, and that the . . . Norbeck bill means nothing without [sic] it."[14]

Unfortunately, his prediction that Congress would be slow in appropriating money for the purchase and development of bird sanctuaries was correct. During the first four years of the law's operation, only about half of the authorizations were appropriated, totaling altogether less than a million dollars—the amount he had hoped for each year if the federal license had been provided. A good beginning had been made, however, and in spite of inadequate funds twenty-two refuges were established by 1933, comprising 1,084,683 acres.[15]

There were a few senators who never gave up the idea of the federal license. Norbeck, Hawes and others continued to agitate for it. As a member of the Migratory Bird Commission and the Special Senate Committee on Wild Life Resources, Norbeck was in a position to wield great influence. Finally in 1934 his act of 1929 was amended to provide for the federal license. The measure which many members of Congress five years earlier believed to be of such little significance that they neglected to register their votes proved to be a conservation law of great importance.

While Norbeck was busy with migratory bird legislation, he was also working toward the completion of Mount Rushmore. No other legislation could completely divert him from this project.

Work on the figure of Washington proceeded at a good pace during the summer and late fall of 1927. Major Jesse G. Tucker, a former associate of Borglum at Stone Mountain, was in charge. But by the end of the drilling season, funds were exhausted and the project came to a standstill. The enthusiasm generated by President Coolidge's visit in August had run

---

12 "Game Refuge Bill Becomes Law," p. 28.
13 *Cong. Rec.*, 70 Cong., 2 Sess., February 11, 1929, pp. 3190-1. See also "The Migratory Bird Conservation Act," *Bird-Lore*, 31:152-59 (March-April, 1929).
14 Norbeck to Edmund Seymour, March 24, 1929. Norbeck MS.
15 *Report of the Migratory Bird Conservation Commission*, 1933, p. 1.

its course and throughout 1928 practically nothing was done toward the carving.

Borglum continued to assure the Mount Rushmore Association that he could raise the necessary funds among his wealthy friends, but this belief, growing from his unbounded enthusiasm, proved to be illusory. Norbeck's acceptance for a time of Borglum's optimistic promises at their face value slowed the work considerably. When the sculptor kept promising that he could raise the money, others did not work with as much zeal to find a suitable financial plan. Soon, however, Norbeck realized that Borglum's faith exceeded his works. Consequently, a plan was developed whereby federal aid might be secured.

Borglum apparently was the originator of the idea, but after he first suggested soliciting national support he changed his mind several times before the South Dakota congressional delegation succeeded in obtaining it. As the bill was introduced it provided that the federal government would supply $250,000 on a matching basis for the memorial's completion. Borglum estimated that $500,000 would be sufficient.

After out-maneuvering the opposition, Norbeck and McMaster succeeded in getting favorable Senate action on May 16, 1928.[16] Returning to his office late at night, Norbeck wrote to an old friend: "That was the hardest day's work I have done since I came to Washington."[17]

After employing every parliamentary tactic he knew to get the measure passed, he received a wire from Borglum the following day which read: "have a disposition not to help if federal government takes charge. Believe a million dollars can be raised for that entire development if not turned over to U. S. Government."[18] Borglum changed his mind so frequently that Norbeck was not surprised by this telegram. But he was thoroughly disgusted. Although Borglum had raised several thousand dollars, he had demonstrated his inability to raise sufficient amounts. Norbeck knew that federal aid furnished about the last hope. The next day he wrote to Doane Robinson: "He does not want the $250,000 from Congress now. He wants to go to New York, London, Jerusalem, or Heaven and get a million dollars. He is quite certain that a million is more than $250,000—that is the only thing he is sure about."[19]

In the House Congressman William Williamson guided the bill. He had drawn up the original measure and Norbeck depended heavily on his broad legal knowledge and sound common sense. He managed to get the House to pass the measure in a slightly different form a few days later, but because of the rush of business at the close of the session, the Senate had no opportunity to agree to the House amendments. There was nothing to do but mark time until Congress reconvened.

16 *Cong. Rec.*, 70 Cong., 1 Sess., May 16, 1928, p. 8867.
17 Norbeck to Doane Robinson, May 18, 1928. Norbeck MS.
18 Gutzon Borglum to Norbeck, May 17, 1928. Norbeck MS.
19 Norbeck to Doane Robinson, May 17, 1928. Norbeck MS.

In the meantime, with no action in Washington, no private subscriptions, and no carving on the mountain, the whole project seemed dead. "Everything is flat in South Dakota," Norbeck wrote to Borglum. "The fact that neither you nor I were able to scare up a few dollars for work during the summer of 1928 has led people to believe that we were just talking hot air. . . . Very few people in South Dakota take the matter seriously anymore. . . . Most people . . . figure that Stone Mountain is dead and that Rushmore is in the same class."[20]

By continuous work, however, Representative Louis Cramton of Michigan, aided by Williamson and a few others, got the bill passed in the House on February 22, 1929. It provided for a Mount Rushmore Memorial Commission and authorized the use of $250,000 on a matching basis.[21]

While the senator had carried much of the load up to that time, he had no desire to act on the Commission. Writing to Robinson, he declared that he had one main thought: to put people on the Commission "that can get the money and build the Monument, regardless of who is entitled to credit for the onerous burden that has been carried for four long years.[22] Consequently, he was not appointed, but President Hoover tendered him an invitation to the Commission's first meeting at the White House. There, J. C. Cullinan, wealthy Texas oil man was elected chairman. John Boland, a Rapid City business man, was made chairman of the Executive Committee, which had the real responsibility for completing the carving.

The first critical stage of the memorial's completion was past. Presidential support had been secured and the federal government had pledged to furnish one-half of the funds. Indeed, 1929 was a banner year in the Rushmore development and the work progressed comparatively rapidly.

Norbeck now turned his attention to road construction in the park—particularly roads which would lead to the memorial. He hoped to construct a highway from near the game lodge, where Coolidge had spent the summer, northwest over Iron Mountain to Rushmore. His ambition was to make it possible for tourists to approach the memorial over a picturesque road from which the carved figures would be viewed at many points. In order to lay out the most artistic trail, he walked and rode over Iron Mountain more than twenty times. Outwardly as rough as the northern pine of Norway, Norbeck had the soul of an artist. He wanted to picture nature's unsurpassed artistic beauty for the thousands who would visit the Black Hills. As previously pointed out, his artistic objectives brought him in conflict with the engineers who built roads according to mathematical and engineering principles. He insisted that none of the natural beauty be destroyed. When it appeared that a roadside tree was in danger of destruction from heavy machinery, he instructed the workmen to surround

20 Norbeck to Gutzon Borglum, January 25, 1929. Norbeck MS.
21 *Cong. Rec.*, 70 Cong., 2 Sess., February 22, 1929, pp. 4011-2.
22 Norbeck to Doane Robinson, February 27, 1929. Norbeck MS.

it with heavy planks for protection. Since he was chairman of the Custer State Park Board, little was done without his approval.

In 1932 the Iron Mountain road was completed and stands as another monument to his artistic instincts. It passes through three solid rock tunnels, each framing a spectacular view of Mount Rushmore several miles away.

The Huron *Evening Huronite,* which had a tendency to be critical of Norbeck, asserted editorially that he "has been a leader in the development of a new form of art. . . . In laying out these magnificiently beautiful roads, he pioneered in the framing of natural scenery for the public. He found great pictures in nature and gave them to the world by building roads to them."[23] And Borglum was equally flattering. In his characteristic exuberant manner, he asserted: "Senator Norbeck's Iron Mountain road promises to be an indispensable part of the Memorial itself, a part of the sculptured art."[24] "I can't recollect anything I have ever seen of your road work that I would change," he remarked on another occasion.[25] Although Norbeck accepted such comments modestly, he was very proud of his work. There would have been no Needles highway or Iron Mountain road, he said, "if I had listened to the 'diploma boys' [engineers]."[26]

His park activities in 1929 were not confined to the Black Hills. Norbeck's planning and vigorous support were also largely responsible for the passage of the so-called Kendrick bill establishing Grand Teton National Park, which took in that beautiful and almost inaccessible area around Jackson Hole. He also initiated a measure extending the boundaries of Yellowstone Park. Altogether it was a banner year for the conservationists.

---

23 Huron *Evening Huronite,* February 23, 1934.
24 Gutzon Borglum to J. C. Cullinan, September 4, 1931. Norbeck MS.
25 Gutzon Borglum to Norbeck, December 16, 1930. Norbeck MS.
26 Norbeck to Harry L. Gandy, October 17, 1935. Norbeck MS.

CHAPTER XV

A TRIP TO EUROPE

At the end of a decade in the Senate, Norbeck occupied a leading place. His aversion to personal publicity and flamboyant debate, so typical of many senators, made him a poor subject for columnists and headline-hunting newsmen. Consequently, he was not so widely known as many of his associates.

Norbeck's personal standing with his colleagues and his influence coming from committee assignments grew steadily. Always a leader on the Agriculture and Forestry Committee, he stood fourth from the chairmanship in 1930. He still played an important role in the Pensions Committee, although he had asked to be relieved of the chairmanship in 1926. On the Public Lands and Survey Committee he was the third ranking member. But most of all his power and influence had been enhanced with appointment late in 1927 to the chairmanship of the powerful Banking and Currency Committee. After receiving this assignment he resigned from several other committee posts, the most important being that of Naval Affairs. Because he ran with the herd of the "sons of the Wild Jackass," however, his name was seldom connected with the more important administration legislation. But by 1930 only twenty-six senators outranked him in continuous service.

He now occupied one of the most desirable seats in the Senate chamber. It was the fourth seat to the right of the aisle on the front row, almost directly in front of the vice president. His friend Hiram Johnson sat on his immediate left with McNary occupying the next seat. Senators Oddie, Keyes, and Capper sat on his right. He had an office in room 303 of the Senate Office Building, which was connected with the Banking and Currency Committee room. The many pictures on the walls revealed his intense interest in conservation. A large picture of the head of George Washington being carved on Mount Rushmore was the most conspicuous. Also scenes of his Black Hills highways, of Teton National Park, and of a group of four musk-oxen, part of the herd of thirty-three which he had had moved from Greenland to Alaska, all immediately caught a visitor's eye.

Sitting behind a big mahogany desk with his usual cigar clinched between his teeth, the sixty year old senator appeared little changed after ten years in Washington. As one writer had said of Brookhart: tenure in the Senate had changed neither his pants nor his philosophy.[1] This could have been said of Norbeck with perhaps even more accuracy.

Ray Tucker, writing in the *North American Review* in 1930, described him as a man with "no suppressed pride of place . . . [one who] makes no attempt to conceal his broad Scandinavian accent, which with his plain dress, gives him the cast of a prosperous butcher. . . . Seemingly a naive

1 Ray Tucker and Frederick R. Barkley, *Sons of the Wild Jackass,* (Boston, 1932), p. 346.

and childlike spirit, 'Pete' as he is known, is . . . one of the smartest politicians in the Senate; his naivete is an affection and armament."[2] What appeared to an Easterner as a "prosperous butcher" closely approximated Norbeck's general appearance. His six foot, 230 pound stature gave the impression of rugged strength and power. He wore his thick, bristling, iron-grey hair clipped short, and a heavy, full mustache completely covered his upper lip. His ruddy, Scandinavian complexion identified him with the rural life he loved so well. He dressed respectably but not extravagantly. He usually wore a dark grey or blue suit, high topped walking shoes, a striped or plain patterned shirt with a detachable collar, complemented by a conservative appearing cravat. A few wrinkles in his suit did not detract from his appearance, and his long, swinging stride was typical of the broad open spaces from which he came.

The Norbecks lived comfortably at The Riverside apartment in Washington. Two of the children, Harold and Selma, were with them. Harold worked part-time in his father's office. As the family responsibilities diminished, Mrs. Norbeck found time to entertain many of her South Dakota friends, some of whom always seemed to be in Washington. Her Sunday evening suppers were eagerly anticipated by the guests from back home. It was not uncommon for the senator to spend much of Sunday, as well as three or four evenings a week, at his office, but he usually dropped in at these Sunday night gatherings before the evening had passed.

Mrs. Norbeck was a devoted church worker in Washington as she had been in Redfield and Pierre. But she regretted her husband's lack of interest. He attended Sunday services somewhat irregularly, but took no active part. He took pride, however, in his membership in the Norwegian Lutheran church and several of the church's high officials were his close friends. When a constituent wrote for information on a rumor that he had left the church, he quickly replied that such a thing could never be!

Senator and Mrs. Norbeck did not dance or play cards, and an evening at a night club was unthinkable. Golf was also out. It was not that they objected to these recreations; Norbeck simply considered them a waste of time, and his wife did not urge anything that might stand in the way of her husband's work. Most of his relaxation was found in walking, visiting art galleries and museums, or, when time permitted, traveling through the nation's state and national parks. The family frequently made summer trips to Colorado, Wyoming, Utah, Montana, Idaho, and sometimes to Canada. He never learned to relax completely, and he worked like one who believed that the nation's welfare depended upon his efforts.

In 1927 the old family home in Redfield was sold. Thereafter, when the senator and his wife visited Redfield, they stayed with his brother George. The same year they started to build a comfortable cabin, named Valhalla, on the Needles highway not far from Mount Rushmore. This

2 Ray Tucker, "Those Sons of the Wild Jackasses," *The North American Review*, 229:231-39 (February, 1929).

not only provided a restful and healthful place to spend the summers, but it was possible for Norbeck to supervise more closely the developments in Custer State Park.

Norbeck's fraternal associations almost completely lapsed during his tenure in Washington. He showed somewhat more interest in his Norwegian-American Historical Association membership and the American-Scandinavian Foundation. He read avidly all types of Scandinavian literature. Frithiof's saga or works by reputable Scandinavian historians were read with equal enjoyment. His constant exploring and digging into his ancestors' past served to inflate his ideas of their greatness. His opinions on immigration and his attitude toward Latin Americans were some of the practical manifestations of this.

There is little doubt that by 1930 he was the outstanding Scandinavian-American in Washington. And he had a wide knowledge and understanding of the people which he represented.

It was not surprising then that in November, 1929, President Hoover appointed him to head a five-man commission to represent the United States at the Icelandic millennial celebration commemorating the founding of the Althing, the Icelandic national parliament. The celebration was scheduled for the following June. Although he had tentatively planned to attend this outstanding gathering as a private citizen, he was more than pleased with his official appointment. President Hoover could not have granted him a more acceptable personal favor.

His study of Scandinavian legends and history had not omitted Iceland. "I have read nearly everything available in the English language on Iceland," he once wrote.[3] To him the settlement and progress of this little Scandinavian outpost had been one of real romance.

For many years the Senator and Mrs. Norbeck had looked forward to visiting their parents' old homes in Norway and Sweden. Here seemed to be an opportunity to combine pleasure with official duty. Congressman O. B. Burtness of North Dakota was also appointed to the official commission and Burtness and Norbeck soon worked out a plan whereby, after attending the Icelandic celebration, they, with their wives, would make an extended European trip. Burtness agreed to take his car, a Franklin model whose performance did not always measure up to his expectations, in which they planned leisurely to tour the continent. As the Norbecks prepared to leave Washington, even the bitter debate over the Hawley-Smoot tariff bill seemed less significant.

On June 14 the two couples boarded their ship at Montreal, and after a voyage of six days they arrived near Reykjavik, the capital of Iceland. The formal three day celebration was held about thirty miles from Reykjavik at Thingvellir, the seat of the original Althing and a mecca for Icelanders. Many distinguished visitors were present. Among them were

3 Peter Norbeck to O. J. Bogstad, November 8, 1929. Norbeck MS.

the king and queen of Denmark and Iceland, as well as high government and ecclesiastical officials from Europe, Canada, and the United States. The festivities opened on June 26 at which time Norbeck made a short address. He praised the courageous pioneers who had left their homes and ventured to Iceland hundreds of years before. "It mattered not to them that the road was hard," he said, "but they were insistent that the course should be right. They lived the simple life and well knew that strength came from toil, fortitude, and self-denial, and wisdom from experience."[4] When it came to speech making, the gospel of hard work was his stock in trade! Needless to say, he felt highly flattered to sit on the same platform and participate in a program with the king of Denmark.

The senator appeared at his best, thanks to his wife's efforts. Although he would have been satisfied to wear an ordinary business suit on all occasions, Mrs. Norbeck had other plans. For morning wear, she saw that her husband wore an impeccable cutaway and striped trousers, and in the afternoon and evenings she insisted that he wear equally appropriate clothes. This constant changing slightly annoyed Norbeck who only infrequently wore what he called "store clothes."

Between the various formal meetings and for one day after the celebration, he made a cursory study of Iceland's economic life. For a long time he had urged the United States government to maintain a consul or trade agent in that country. He now wanted to investigate the economic life at first hand in an effort to gather evidence that a United States consul was really necessary. He noted that while cultivation was difficult, grazing was a profitable industry and that creameries and cheese factories were operating. In a newspaper interview he told reporters that he wished to correct the impression that Iceland was "bleak, cold, and backward."[5] His week's stay on the North Atlantic island was even more enjoyable than he had anticipated.

On June 30 the Norbecks and their friends continued on to Glasgow. From there they motored to London. During their stay there they called at the American embassy and spent an afternoon with Ambassador Charles G. Dawes. But they could not linger long in London. One of their main objectives was to attend the great celebration at Trondheim commemorating the 900th year of the death of King Olav of Norway and the introduction of Christianity into that country. So they crossed the channel to Calais and motored to Brussels, Antwerp, Bremen, and Hamburg. At Brussels they stopped long enough for Norbeck to satisfy his long standing desire to visit a famous European art gallery. For years he had been a frequent patron at the principal art galleries in the United States, but he had always hoped to visit some of those abroad. His knowledge of Rembrandt, VanDyck, and Rubens was extensive and it was with deep pleasure that he now looked

4 A copy of the Norbeck speech is filed in the Norbeck MS.
5 Sioux Falls *Daily Argus Leader,* August 2, 1930.

upon some of the originals of those master artists. Proceeding from Brussels, the party stopped over in Antwerp to visit the National Fair and then passed on to Bremen and Hamburg. At the latter place the party visited the famous Hagenbeck zoo. It was almost impossible for Norbeck to pass up an art gallery, museum, or zoo.

After touring Denmark they arrived in Oslo, where Norbeck had a one-half hour audience with the king. He left no accounts of this experience, but it must have been solid enjoyment to converse with the king of the country about which his parents had told him so much.

The party then hurried on to attend the great celebration at Trondheim. Other loyal Norwegians from South and North Dakota were present to greet them. After spending two days enjoying the gala festivities, the Norbecks spent the better part of two weeks visiting relatives in that vicinity. Then they motored to Sweden where Norbeck visited his father's boyhood home in Jemtland. He found it a prosperous and well settled province and not much like his father had described it. There was something sentimental about this rough well-driller, and as he walked over the old farm he thought again of the stories his father had related to him back on the Clay county homestead.

They were detained in Stockholm when Burtness' Franklin developed motor trouble. But they were soon on their way to Berlin, Potsdam, Dresden, and other German cities. The art gallery was the chief attraction at Dresden.

Norbeck took a distinct liking to the German people who he observed were all very busy. The effects of the war were scarcely noticeable, he said. This was in sharp contrast to his impression of the French who appeared tired, weary, and somewhat listless. Anyone not moving at top speed and exerting full energy, or anyone who appeared to live leisurely as the French did, probably seemed lazy or listless to him. He showed only a faint interest in current political and economic developments. He never even mentioned Hitler or Mussolini in any of the accounts of his trip and he seemed oblivious to the important economic and political forces which were sweeping Europe. This may have been because he thought those to whom he wrote would have no interest in European politics. But even so, this seems strange for a man who watched political developments in his own country with such keen interest. His few casual observations concerned routine matters such as farming. During the entire trip, his chief attention was drawn to Europe's cultural life.

Other cities visited included Wittenberg, Prague, Munich, and Oberammergau, where he viewed the Passion Play. Paris was the last major European stop and, after spending only a few days there, the travelers left for Cherbourg. They arrived in the United States early in September after a ten week's absence.

After Norbeck's return home the king of Denmark and Iceland conferred membership in the Order of the Falcons upon him. This honor made the trip a complete success. The Icelandic member of the Danish cabinet provided him with the appropriate medals and papers, objects held in trust for him by the State Department until such time as he no longer held an official position in the United States government.[6]

6 The factual information concerning Norbeck's trip abroad has been derived from letters written by Senator and Mrs. Norbeck. Peter Norbeck to Mrs. Nellie Wegner, August 6, 1930, and Mrs. Peter Norbeck to The Family at Home, September 1, 1930.

CHAPTER XVI

A FINAL DRIVE FOR AGRICULTURAL EQUALITY

Upon Norbeck's return from Europe, he found the agricultural situation rapidly becoming worse. After the panic in October and November, 1929, the Federal Farm Board had loaned so extensively to cooperatives that by May of the next year it held eight per cent of the wheat and ten per cent of the cotton crop.[1] The production and marketing of the 1930 yields brought another crisis in November, when the Board found it necessary to make additional loans. Also the government accumulated supplies of wheat and cotton through its stabilization corporations.

The supply continued large, and it was becoming obvious that the Board could not continue to put an artificial price under certain farm products whose price was determined in the world market, while making no forced reduction of production; that is, of course, unless Congress wished to appropriate much more money for that purpose. It was clear that prices would remain higher than the world market only as long as the Board had funds to buy and hold part of the crop, thereby keeping the surplus off the market. Actually the Board was speculating in futures and could succeed financially only if the world price of the purchased crops advanced.[2] Norbeck's prediction of failure for this scheme was proving distressingly correct.

While resting in Redfield and attending to many neglected business matters, he received an urgent request from Senator McNary to return to Washington at once to consider new agricultural legislation. McNary, chairman of the Agriculture and Forestry Committee, desired immediate hearings in order to have some measure ready for presentation when Congress met in December. Norbeck agreed to leave for Washington as soon as possible, but condemned the existing farm relief law as "inadequate or worse" and as simply "delaying solving the problem on sound economic grounds."[3] He was willing to support the debenture plan, although he did not think it was nearly as good as the equalization fee, by which the farmer would pay for part of the benefits. He concluded by telling the Oregon senator that it would be better to do nothing than disappoint the farmers again.[4]

The Congress which met in December of 1930 did little or nothing of a constructive nature for agriculture, despite the pleas of the major farm organizations. During 1931 the Farm Board continued to flounder through the slough of increasing surpluses and an intensified farm depression. Here and there little stabs were taken at the farm problem, but there was little serious disposition to meet it with a head-on attack. Norbeck flirted with

1 R. L. Wilbur and A. M. Hyde, *The Hoover Policies*, p. 154-55.
2 C. A. and Mary Beard, *America in Mid-passage* (New York, 1939), p. 41. The Beards maintain that millions of dollars fell into the hands of speculators.
3 Norbeck to C. L. McNary, November 19, 1930. Norbeck MS.
4 *Ibid.*

the idea of re-introducing the McNary-Haugen bill, but he was only rattling the dry bones of a dead carcass, and somewhat sheepishly admitted that the surplus-control measure was an "old shoe" and had no chance to pass.[5] So far as Congress was concerned, the farm problem seemed insoluble, and 1931 passed without worth-while legislation. At the same time, the purchasing power of the farm dollar was steadily declining until in February, 1933, it was worth only fifty per cent of the pre-war average.[6]

Congress still showed little desire to tackle this thorny problem when it met in December, 1931. Almost immediately, however, Norbeck introduced a bill allocating $125,000,000 as a revolving fund upon which the Federal Farm Land Banks could draw needed reserves. The Norbeck-Steagall bill also allowed the Land Banks to extend time up to five years on the payment of farm mortgages, if it would help the farmer and be safe for the bank.[7]

He next piloted a measure through Congress making the debentures of the Intermediate Credits Banks discountable with the Federal Reserve System. This law made it possible for the Intermediate Credits Banks to secure additional funds and to enlarge their loaning operations.[8]

At the same time he was dealing with the problem of seed loans. His work made it possible for farmers who actually needed seed loans in 1932 to secure them through the Department of Agriculture from funds provided in the Reconstruction Finance Corporation Act. Senator E. D. Smith offered a rider to the RFC bill providing $50,000,000 for this purpose from the $2,000,000,000 Reconstruction Finance Corporation fund. Norbeck objected to the form of Smith's rider because it did not specify more definitely which farmers would receive government aid. When the bill came to conference committee, he was prepared to have it changed so as "to give preference to those sections of the country [this meant primarily the Northwest] that have suffered from crop failures in 1931." For political reasons he induced Senator Wheeler to offer his amendment. "The Democrats [in the House] did not catch on," he wrote, "because they were not suspicious of Wheeler. If I had done this, there would have been a rough house."[9]

During the winter of 1931-32, conditions among the "drouth-grasshopper-snow-ridden farmers" of the Northwest were extremely critical. The demands for food, fuel, and clothing, as well as livestock feed, taxed local relief agencies far beyond their capacities. The people's plight became so desperate in some areas that officials took up collections from private sources

5 Norbeck to W. R. Ronald, April 18, 1932. Norbeck MS.
6 Chester C. Davis, "The Development of Agricultural Policy Since the End of the World War," p. 313.
7 *Cong. Rec.,* 72 Cong., 1 Sess., January 12, 1932, p. 1775.
8 *Ibid.,* April 25, 1932, p. 8860. The bill passed the Senate in April and the House approved it soon afterwards.
9 Norbeck to H. S. Hedrick, February 1, 1932. Norbeck MS.

in order to raise a fund to purchase feed for starving livestock.[10] Late in 1931 Senator Capper introduced a joint resolution providing for the distribution of 40,000,000 bushels of government wheat to the needy through the American Red Cross. While his resolution passed the Senate, it was sidetracked in the House. When the Capper bill became stalled, Norbeck went to work with his usual vigor. Early in 1932, he introduced another joint resolution which authorized the Federal Farm Board to distribute 5,000,000 bushels of wheat through the Red Cross.[11] He believed it would be more politic not to ask for too much, at least at that particular time.

After perfunctory debate the measure passed the Senate and was on its way to the House, where changes had been prepared by his South Dakota colleagues. There it was amended to allow the distribution of 40,000,000 bushels, the amount originally asked for by Capper, and on March 3 the bill passed.[12] In about a week he had secured action on a measure of vital importance to his state and to the Northwest. He was also responsible for obtaining funds for grasshopper eradication and control, and an amendment which allowed the Joint-Stock Land Banks to do business in more than two states.[13]

Norbeck's leadership in agricultural legislation during the first session of the Seventy-second Congress stemmed from his chairmanship of the influential Banking and Currency Committee. Most of his emergency farm relief measures were not handled by the Agriculture Committee, but rather went to the Banking and Currency group. There he commanded attention and was especially committed to handling the farm legislation.

The Northwest heaped high praise on South Dakota's senior senator because of his work for farm relief. The Sioux City *Tribune* in his neighboring state was the most flattering. "What a whaling record Norbeck has piled up," said editor Kelly. "And what have the other western and midwestern senators done beyond voting 'yes' on measures Norbeck initiated? Peter Norbeck today is the outstanding spokesman for agriculture in the American Congress. He not only speaks, but he acts, and he supplies a type of leadership that is sadly lacking in Washington."[14] James Shillay of the Minneapolis *Tribune* wrote: "you are the 'favorite son' around this office because of your successful fight for the seed loan item."[15] And George Authier filled several daily columns with praise for Norbeck.

Actually, however, Norbeck has accomplished very little, and he realized this even if some of his supporters did not. The quantity of the legislation far exceeded its quality. It was only ameliorative. The solution to the Northwest's basic farm problems was as far away as ever. In attempting

10 Huron *Evening Huronite*, February 23, 1932.
11 *Cong. Rec.*, 72 Cong., 1 Sess., February 24, 1932, p. 4631.
12 *Ibid.*, March 3, 1932, p. 5221.
13 *Ibid.*, 71 Cong., 3 Sess., March 3, 1931, p. 6949.
14 Sioux City *Tribune*, February 4, 1932.
15 James Shillay to Norbeck, January 23, 1932. Norbeck MS.

to relieve the most acute distress, Norbeck was doing the very thing he had formerly opposed; that is, extending more credit to already debt-burdened farmers.

In the light of lower agricultural income, increase in mortgages and farm tendency, extensive bank failures in rural areas, price depressing surpluses, and other maladies in the farm industry, almost everyone interested in agriculture, both in and out of Washington, was seeking a remedy. Between 1928 and 1933, when the first Agricultural Adjustment Act was passed, there was a growing doubt by some students of the farm problem whether the principles involved in either the equalization-fee scheme or the export-debenture plan would work under new world conditions. For that matter, many economists, as well as political leaders, had always doubted if the principles embodied in the McNary-Haugen bills would work, at least for any length of time. In any event, foreign demands for American farm produce were gradually declining and it appeared doubtful whether the United States could export its now large surplus without bringing retaliatory measures from European and other countries. After 1929 greater attention was given to the so-called domestic allotment plan of farm relief, which ultimately came to include acreage restriction as one of its basic features.

For a number of years some of those interested in the farm question had believed that the best way to solve the problem created by agricultural surpluses was to restrict production through acreage control. One of the leaders of this movement was Harry N. Owen, publisher of the *Farm, Stock and Home* at St. Paul. Early in 1922 he wrote to Norbeck expressing the opinion that acreage restriction would be the best method of eliminating the surplus. He asserted that most manufacturers limited their production to conform with the probable market, and added that the failure of the farmers to adopt this same principle was the main reason why they found themselves in an unfavored economic position.[16] Owen also hammered at this idea in the columns of his magazine.

His argument evidently impressed South Dakota's then new senator, because about a year later he wrote to a friend that the much discussed stabilization of farm prices would be sure to increase the output and that it would be necessary to adopt some plan of restricted production. "If we could reduce our acreage a little on wheat," he stated, "we would need no stabilization laws; the price increase would be automatic."[17] In other words, the tariff would become effective on this exportable crop.

The idea of acreage regulation received relatively little attention in Congress during most of the 1920's. The heated and emotional campaign centering around surplus-control overshadowed any other plan of farm relief. Norbeck, however, was among those who gave it some thought.

16 Harry N. Owen to Norbeck, January 18, 1922. Norbeck MS.
17 Norbeck to H. A .Fromke, March 26, 1923. Norbeck MS.

"I have long believed that it would be a slow process to eliminate the surplus," he wrote in 1926, "except by a strong organized effort on the part of the farmers, supported by governmental force of some kind." But he added that Congress was unwilling to empower any body to limit agricultural acreage.[18] The following year, when the first McNary-Haugen bill was passed, he had privately expressed the opinion that the measure would be materially improved if there was some provision for acreage restriction.[19] He did not attempt, however, to add such an amendment to the bill. He was evidently not fully convinced of the idea's practicality.

In its first form the voluntary domestic allotment plan did not contain any provision for acreage restriction. It was believed, however, that it would not stimulate acreage expansion, as was almost inevitable under the McNary-Haugen and export-debenture plans. Chester C. Davis has lucidly described this somewhat complicated idea by saying:

> . . . it involved raising the price the farmers would receive on the domestically consumed portion of their export crops by limiting sales of such crops in the domestic market. The part of the crop which farmers could sell in the domestic market was called the domestic allotment, and they were given certificates covering that allotment. In order to move a commodity into domestic consumption, processors had to cover the quantities offered for sale with certificates purchased from farmers. The increased return on each farmer's domestic allotment was to result from the fact that he received not only the world price, but also the proceeds from the sale of his certificates. No certificates were issued on production in excess of the domestic allotment, and on this quantity the farmers received only the prevailing world prices.[20]

Since farmers would not receive a higher price for their production above the domestic allotment, the plan's promoters believed that many farmers would voluntarily limit their production to their allotment.

The plan seems to have been first worked out by W. J. Spillman of the Department of Agriculture and published in his book *Balancing the Farm Output* in 1927. It later underwent successive modifications by John D. Black of Harvard University and M. L. Wilson of Montana State College.

During 1931 and the early part of 1932, Wilson traveled extensively in Montana discussing with farmers and business men the possible plans of agricultural relief; the equalization-fee plan, the export-debenture, a method of government stabilization, and finally the voluntary domestic allotment plan. Many farmers, as well as other citizens, showed an immediate and intense interest in the latter idea and its popularity soon became widespread.[21]

18 Norbeck to H. E. Beebe, May 10, 1926. Norbeck MS.
19 Norbeck to Charles A. Howard, January 29, 1927. Norbeck MS.
20 Davis, "The Development of Agricultural Policy Since the End of the World War," p. 316. John D. Black presented this plan in 1929 during Congressional hearings on the Agricultural Marketing Act.
21 W. R. Ronald, "The Origin of the Domestic Allotment Plan," *Cong. Digest*, 12:37-38 (February, 1933).

By that time Wilson had modified the scheme considerably. In contrast with earlier forms, an excise tax would be levied on the processors of basic agricultural commodities and no benefits would be given to farmers who did not agree to sign contracts limiting acreage. The tax receipts would be distributed to producers of basic crops on a pro rata basis on the part of the crop domestically consumed. The benefits were to correspond roughly to the amount of the tariff, or an amount sufficient to give the designated product pre-war purchasing power.[22] The essential idea was to obtain a favorable balance between production and consumption. The plan dealt primarily with production and not marketing, as did the McNary-Haugen idea. It did not imply that only enough farm produce would be raised to meet home demands, but the domestic allotment system was designed to regulate production to United States' needs, plus that which could be sold profitably abroad; an amount which was steadily declining.

While Wilson may be considered the leader in pushing this new plan, others were simultaneously thinking along the same line. As early as June, 1931, Robert Lusk, editor of the Huron *Evening Huronite,* had advocated a production control plan which was reprinted in several newspapers throughout the Northwest.[23] The thought was gradually growing that the best way to handle the surplus problem was to limit production. But the idea spread slowly. Farm organizations looked upon it with skepticism and, in some instances, positive hostility. Leaders of the Farmers' Union and the Farm Bureau Federation were not quickly convinced that the new scheme would solve the farm problem. Officers of the Farm Bureau Federation emphatically stated that they were still for the McNary-Haugen bill.[24]

Moreover, the agricultural leaders in Congress were in no mood to accept such a measure. Norbeck, a tireless worker for federal farm aid, was typical of that group. Although he had seemed to favor acreage restriction at several times during the 1920's, he gave no indication now that he even considered it as a remote solution. "It is absolutely impossible to reduce the United States farming production to the U. S. consumption," he wrote.[25] He, like many others who had worked six or eight years for the McNary-Haugen principle, was so imbued with that idea that he could see little value in any other plan.

Adherents of the domestic allotment plan, however, could not be discouraged and by April, 1932, they were making plans to introduce a bill in Congress. Early in that month W. L. Stockton, vice-president of the Montana Farm Bureau, asked those interested in the proposal to meet in Chicago on the 19th. "I am inviting a few agricultural economists, business

22 M. L. Wilson, "The Domestic Allotment Plan," *Day and Hour Series,* University of Minnesota, 1933, pp. 27-29.
23 Huron *Evening Huronite,* June 11, 1931.
24 W. R. Ronald, "Memorandum," This is a forty-eight page typewritten memorandum concerning the drive for the domestic allotment plan.
25 Norbeck to M. J. Christopher, January 30, 1931. Norbeck MS.

men, agricultural editors, and representatives of farm organizations," he wrote to Lusk.[26] Since Lusk had been active in promoting crop control schemes in South Dakota, he was anxious to attend the gathering. But more than that, he hoped to induce Norbeck to attend, so that the South Dakota senator might be converted to the idea's feasibility. Accordingly, he wrote to Norbeck urging him to go to Chicago and participate in the approaching conference.[27] The senator agreed to go, but upon learning that the conference date conflicted with the first Senate hearings of the Stock Exchange investigation, he was forced to change his plans only the day before the meeting opened.[28]

In any event, the domestic allotment gathering went off as scheduled. Lusk was unable to attend, but editor W. R. Ronald of the Mitchell *Evening Republican* was present upon his request. The principal work of the meeting was the appointment of a promotion committee, including Wilson, Louis S. Clarke, an Omaha investment banker, Henry A. Wallace, R. R. Rodgers, a Prudential Life Insurance Company executive, and Ronald, who was selected as publicity director for the committee of five.[29]

Lusk and Ronald were both effective promoters and they immediately began urging Norbeck to lead the fight in Congress for this plan. While Norbeck had never been allergic to novel ideas, his strength was not in originality of thought. Rather it lay in his ability to actuate the plans of others through tenacious fighting and political skill. In this case his conversion to the domestic allotment proposal came slowly and with reluctance. After making a thorough study of the plan, he finally pronounced its underlying principles as sound; but he was still skeptical of its administrative features.[30] Later events reveal that Norbeck never believed that the domestic allotment idea came up to the McNary-Haugen standard. By April 20, however, Ronald was able to write: "Senator Norbeck is known to be friendly to it." And then he added: "He has demonstrated that when he leads a fight for a farm measure, he gets the respect of the Senate."[31]

A few days later, Norbeck made it possible for Wilson to outline the plan before the Senate Agriculture Committee, after which the Montanan reported that he expected the South Dakota senator to introduce a bill soon incorporating the domestic allotment principle.

Norbeck's introduction of a domestic allotment bill was delayed, however, because of the priority held by pending farm legislation, the most important measure being the so-called three-way farm relief bill, which authorized, but did not require, the Federal Farm Board to invoke any one of three plans: (1) the export-debenture, (2) the equalization-fee, (3) a diluted ver-

26 W. L. Stockton to Robert Lusk, April 7, 1932. Lusk MS.
27 Robert Lusk to Norbeck, April 9, 1932. Lusk MS.
28 Norbeck to Robert Lusk, April 18, 1932. Lusk MS.
29 Huron *Evening Huronite,* April 20, 1932.
30 Norbeck to Robert Lusk, April 1, 1932. Norbeck MS.
31 Mitchell *Evening Republican,* April 20, 1932.

sion of the allotment plan sponsored by the Farmers' Union.[32] This measure represented an entire winter's work by the three major farm organizations, and while it was pending, there was no chance to obtain action on other farm legislation. The way was not cleared until June 15, when the Senate recommitted the three-way bill to committee.[33]

Late in the evening of June 29, Norbeck introduced a modified form of the domestic allotment plan. It was admittedly an emergency measure, but the leaders knew that no permanent plan could be enacted in that Congress because of Hoover's opposition and because the Democratic House was not anxious to help a Republican administration add lustre to its record just before a presidential election. Therefore, pending the development of some more permanent plan, this measure was to be effective for one year only.

It provided for immediate and direct payments to farmers on the portion of their wheat, cotton, and hogs used in domestic consumption during the current year. Forty-two cents a bushel on wheat, which equalled the tariff, five cents a pound on cotton, and two cents a pound on hogs would be paid for the amount domestically consumed. The Secretary of Agriculture was authorized to determine the percentage of the 1932 crop which was required for home consumption. The farmer would then be given a certificate redeemable by any government fiscal agency designated by the Secretary of Agriculture for the above adjustment payments, minus a small administrative cost. The adjustment charges were to be met by taxing the processors. Since the bill was designed to go into effect fifteen days after enactment, some temporary advances might be required from the treasury to be returned when the processing tax was collected. The crops were already planted, therefore it was not thought necessary to provide for acreage restriction.[34]

Norbeck succeeding in getting the Senate to consider his bill on July 13. He spoke briefly in its favor, pointing out that the farmers would obtain the benefit of the tariff, while at the same time production could not be stimulated. He argued that his bill would increase buying power and give hope to people who were hopeless, and "have a stimulating effect all along the line."[35] Following a short speech by Senator Capper, the bill was read a third time and passed without a record vote.[36]

The lack of opposition can best be accounted for by the absence of several administration senators when the bill passed. This was part of Norbeck's plan. A reporter for the Kansas City *Star* called it the "surprise measure of the session."[37]

---

32 *Cong. Rec.*, 72 Cong., 1 Sess., June 13, 1932, pp. 12771-72.
33 *Ibid.*, June 15, p. 13000.
34 *Senate Report*, No. 973, Serial No. 9488, 72 Cong., 1 Sess.
35 *Cong. Rec.*, 72 Cong., 1 Sess., July 13, 1932, p. 15190.
36 *Ibid.*, p. 15194.
37 Kansas City *Star*, July 14, 1932.

To the surprise of many, the bill immediately found favor in the House, where a similar proposal sponsored by Congressman Rainey of Illinois was pending. In an unusually hasty session the House Agriculture Committee rushed through a favorable report on the Norbeck bill and sent it to the Rules Committee in an effort to get prompt action.[38] On the evening of July 13 there was a strong belief around the Capitol that the bill would pass the House if it could obtain the "green light" from the Rules Committee.[39]

But opponents quickly rallied their forces in an effort to block its passage. Senators William H. King and Hiram Bingham, Democrat and Republican respectively, announced their intention of asking for the measure's reconsideration the following day.[40] When the Senate met the next morning, Bingham asked to make a motion to recall the bill from the House. Senator Norris, who had the floor, refused to yield for such a motion and tried heroically to sidetrack Bingham's motion. Senator LaFollette also came to the bill's support asking that Norbeck be called before any further action be taken. But Bingham was finally successful in obtaining recognition. These unexpected developments brought Norbeck storming to the Senate chamber. He asked if the Bingham motion was debatable and was informed by the presiding officer that it was not. This dashed his hope of being able to stall long enough for the House to take action. A few minutes later a vote was taken to recall the papers from the House, and it carried by thirty to twenty-five.[41] This killed any chance of getting agricultural relief, as Congress adjourned two days later.

Norbeck did not permit adjournment without a protest. "During this long session," he told his colleagues, "Congress has passed measures to relieve bankers and to relieve railroads [he referred to the RFC]. The big fellows have been relieved. . . . The agricultural question, which I think is the key to the whole situation, has had scant consideration. . . I protest . . . against going home. We should remain in session another month and pass necessary farm legislation."[42]

There were several reasons why Norbeck's measure was defeated. The high probability that Hoover would veto any such legislation caused some senators to oppose it. There were rumors that the Democratic House did not want to pass any substantial legislation, preferring to continue embarrassing the Hoover administration. Therefore, the Rules Committee did not give the bill the right of way before it could be recalled. Norbeck believed that Senator Dickinson of Iowa was largely responsible for the result, and that an agreement had been reached between "Republican and Democratic

38 New York *Times*, July 14, 1932, p. 1.
39 *Ibid.*
40 *Ibid.*
41 *Cong. Rec.*, 72 Cong., 1 Sess., July 14, 1932, p. 15338.
42 *Ibid.*, July 16, p. 15631.

leaders to ditch it."[43] The fact that King and Bingham were equally active in their opposition gives some credence to his charge.

Also it is not without significance that Republican critics of the plan were becoming legion. Even William Allen White, in the heart of a distressed agricultural region, called it "largely nonsense,"[44] and a few months later the Chicago *Daily Tribune* said in a bitter editorial: "To call the scheme utter madness is to flatter it." Concerning the feature which gave the Secretary of Agriculture the power to determine the domestic allotment for each farmer, the caustic editor added: "A man who combined the integrity of George Washington, the energy of Theodore Roosevelt, and the administrative ability of Alexander Hamilton couldn't handle so prodigious a task."[45]

The chief significance of Norbeck's efforts was that it publicized the new plan of farm relief and served to convert some of the leading political figures. This was also the turning point away from McNary-Haugenism for some of the farm organizations, particularly the American Farm Bureau Federation.[46] Furthermore, as soon as it was defeated, Norbeck introduced another domestic allotment bill and Congressman Clifford Hope of Kansas prepared a companion measure for the House. Although the Hope-Norbeck bills did not receive any consideration in that session, they pointed the direction which agricultural relief legislaton was to take. These developments, plus the efforts of Rexford Tugwell, were largely responsble for Governor Roosevelt's acceptance of the basic tenets of the domestic allotment plan in his speech at Topeka, Kansas, on September 14. Several weeks later Edward O'Neal, President of the Farm Bureau Federation, threw his support behind the principle.[47] The plan to balance farm production with probable consumption was well developed before Roosevelt's New Deal.

It took Norbeck several weeks to clear his desk, which was piled high with unanswered correspondence, farm relief plans, and data on the Stock Exchange investigation. It was with a feeling of relief that he left Washington late in July. But in South Dakota he found unbelievably low farm prices. Wheat was selling at from twenty-five to thirty cents a bushel, oats were eight cents and corn fourteen cents. He purchased hogs for one of his farms for only one dollar and seventy-five cents a hundred weight! Conditions were reminiscent of the days spent on his Charles Mix county farm during the Panic of 1893. These conditions made further legislative procrastination extremely dangerous. Norbeck found his usually composed neighbors already turning to direct action. The spirit of Daniel Shays was running rampant over the Plains.

43 Huron *Evening Huronite,* July 14, 1932. See also Norbeck to E. F. Lusk, July 28, 1932. Norbeck MS.

44 The *Daily Emporia Gazette,* July 19, 1932.

45 Chicago *Daily Tribune,* January 9, 1933.

46 Edwin G. Nourse, J. S. Davis, and J. D. Black, *Three Years of the Agricultural Adjustment Administration* (Washington, 1937), p. 14.

47 New York *Times,* December 6, 1932, p. 38. See also Ronald, "Memorandum."

CHAPTER XVII

THE WELL-DRILLER AND WALL STREET

Although Norbeck spent a great deal of time dealing with farm problems during the Seventy-second session, his most important work was connected with supervising and directing the New York Stock Exchange investigation. This responsibility grew out of his chairmanship of the Banking and Currency Committee. It was a task for which he was hardly prepared, but one which subsequent events demonstrated to be part of his most significant and lasting work.

The reason for his original appointment to the important Banking and Currency Committee in 1921 is not entirely clear. When he arrived in Washington, he discussed committee assignments with his friend, Congressman Williamson, who was very anxious to obtain membership on the House Banking Committee. He urged Norbeck to seek a similar post in the Senate. If they succeeded, said Williamson, they would be in a position to work together on prospective banking legislation affording aid to agriculture.[1] Norbeck's correspondence indicates that he made no strong bid for the assignment. His appointment may have resulted from chairman George P. McLean's earnest desire to have all points of view represented on the committee. Certainly the Plains senator's political and economic views did not correspond with those of most members.

In any event, he had few qualifications for his committee work. He had dealt with banks in South Dakota, but did not have any clear or concise ideas on national banking and currency problems. His knowledge was general rather than technical or specific, and came from business experience and dealing with credit problems in his home state. He frankly admitted his unpreparedness for the assignment to one of the most important Senate committees.

From 1921 to 1926 Norbeck displayed only meager interest in this committee. He attended the meetings regularly, but made no speeches on banking problems, and his correspondence is almost completely devoid of any reference to his committee activities. After serving four years he was perfectly willing to be replaced by his colleague McMaster, who was a banker and very desirous of this appointment. Norbeck even appeared before the committee with McMaster and offered to withdraw if his colleague would then get the assignment. But when the appointments were made in 1925, he was again included.[2]

In a surprisingly short time, Norbeck became the third ranking Republican member. In 1926 Senator O. E. Weller failed of re-election and so only chairman McLean outranked Norbeck. When Congress assembled the following year, McLean expressed his desire to retire because of the heavy

1 William Williamson to Author, February 26, 1945.
2 Norbeck to Editor of *Colliers*, January 21, 1928. Norbeck MS.

responsibility and poor health. Since Norbeck's primary interests had been in other fields, particularly agriculture, the Republican members of the committee did not expect that he would demand his seniority rights,[3] and they prepared to give him another chairmanship. Norbeck was uncertain as to whether he should assent. As was often the case, he asked Williamson about the advisability of accepting the chairmanship. Williamson told him that he would lose considerable prestige if he did not accept. After considering this counsel, Norbeck went before the committee and stated that he felt it was an honor to himself and to his state which he should not waive.[4]

In the meantime there had been a move to sidetrack him to the chairmanship of the Public Lands Committee. It was not that his colleagues doubted his integrity of purpose, but rather they had a feeling that he had not displayed sufficient interest and had not given a great deal of thought to matters pending before the committee.[5] Some senators thought he was too progressive and independent and hoped he would be content with a lesser appointment. One Democrat later expressed the opinion that if the Republicans resented Norbeck's advancement "it was simply because he was an old Teddy Roosevelt 'Bull Mooser' and not because they had anyone better for the job."[6] Although Senator Edge, the next ranking Republican, would have been much more acceptable to the administration, there was no serious attempt to block Norbeck's preference after he made the request. He expressed the belief, however, that if the Republican majority for organizing the Senate had been greater, he "would probably have had to be content with some other chairmanship."[7]

After his appointment in December, 1927, Norbeck read more widely in the field of banking and currency, but he never acquired a technical knowledge of the subjects. He often consulted Williamson when faced with some difficult problem relating to his committee work. It also became his habit to turn the more thorny problems over to Senator Glass. The fact that he allowed the Virginian, one of the framers of the Federal Reserve System, a relatively free hand, indicates his good judgment as well as a recognition of his own inadequacy. He sometimes jokingly remarked that "as an authority on banking and currency he was the ablest well-driller in Congress!"[8]

Ultimately he acquired a surprisingly broad knowledge of banking, especially as it related to agriculture. He was aware of speculative Wall Street practices, a knowledge gained perhaps from such books as Louis

3   Walter E. Edge to Author, February 21, 1945.
4   William Williamson to Author, February 26, 1945.
5   Walter E. Edge to Author, February 21, 1945; and George Wharton Pepper to Author, February 23, 1945.
6   Secretary to Senator Carter Glass to Author, March 13, 1945.
7   Norbeck to Casper Nohner, February 14, 1928. Norbeck MS.
8   Sioux City *Journal*, January 4, 1931.

Brandeis' *Other People's Money,* with which he was familiar. He was not one of the "lambs" of the 1920's, and he understood the relation between the average investor and the stock market. Writing to Harry King, who was seeking advice about certain investments, he asserted: "It is not impossible for outsiders to make money on the market, but they do it by taking much larger chances than those who are on the inside. Therefore, in the long run, the outsiders lose and the insiders win."[9]

Less than six months after his appointment as chairman, he warned against the uncontrolled and excessive speculation. He threw his support behind the LaFollette resolution which looked toward checking speculative abuses by admonishing the Federal Reserve Board to discourage lending money for this purpose. "The situation is and continues to grow more dangerous," he said.[10] Although he sounded occasional warnings, he did not play a conspicuous role in endeavoring to curb the wild gambling in Wall Street.

It was only about a month before the Wall Street crash that he gave out a strong warning on what was likely to happen. After charging that the Senate had not passed the LaFollette resolution because of opposition from the conservatives, he declared: "I think Wall Street has gone crazy. Prices are badly inflated. What goes up must come down. A boom always bursts. The innocent people are the sufferers. There was a time when business was organized and conducted for a business profit. It is now organized for a promotion profit. The new motto is to sell stock to suckers and take up a new line."[11] He expressed the hope that changes in the banking laws might be made so as to prevent that sort of "wild speculation." Ray Tucker later wrote in a sarcastic vein that Norbeck had amply demonstrated his qualifications for his Banking and Currency chairmanship when he said: "Vell, vot goes up must come down."[12]

His warning was treated critically even in his own state. The Huron *Evening Huronite* said editorially:

> Persons here in South Dakota who are familiar with Senator Norbeck's record as an economist will not be so heartily in favor of the Senator's taking apart the machinery of the nation's business to see what makes it tick, and hammer around among the gadgets to make it tick, more quietly. . . . One hardly feels that the 'Father of the Rural Credits' is the man to straighten out the financial tangles of the nation's business.[13]

The depression thrust new and serious problems on the chairman and his committee. In retrospect, some of Norbeck's colleagues believed that it would have been better for the entire nation if during the critical years

9   Norbeck to Harry King, January 8, 1927.
10   New York *Times,* May 13, 1928, p. 10. See also *Senate Report,* No. 1124, 70 Cong., 1 Sess.
11   Mitchell *Evening Republican,* September 20, 1929.
12   Ray Tucker, "Those Sons of Wild Jackasses," *North American Review,* 229:231-39 (February, 1930).
13   Huron *Evening Huronite,* September 21, 1929.

following 1929 the committee could have been headed by a man with a greater interest in banking and a wider and more intelligent grasp of its problems.[14] On the other hand, there is something to be said for a man of Norbeck's type. His common sense proved a genuine asset in handling general problems. He placed the technical work in the hands of those more highly trained and experienced, since he had no exaggerated notions of his own ability in this field. His willingness to be fair and impartial with all groups, his probity of character and legislative ability, made him an able, constructive, and independent chairman.

The unprecedented speculation of the 1920's and the subsequent collapse led to a demand for radical reforms in the nation's banking laws. Norbeck almost automatically turned those problems over to Senator Glass, who in 1931 headed a five-man committee responsible for investigating the operation of the national banking system. The two leaders were in substantial agreement that the misuse of credit must be prevented, that commercial and investment banking should be separated, and that a more efficient system of bank receiverships should be developed. But they disagreed sharply over the extension of branch, group, and chain banking. While Glass favored greater development of centralized banking, Norbeck argued that the control of credit by a few was dangerous.

As the hearings progressed during January and February, 1931, Norbeck was the most active defender of the unit banking system. In this respect he was reflecting his sectional viewpoint. His attitude is understandable when it is considered that one of the largest bank holding companies, the Northwest Bancorporation of Chicago and Minneapolis, was rapidly reaching its tenacles into his section of the country.[15] Norbeck was frankly prejudiced against this development, partly, no doubt, because the small banks had always been generous in lending him money, but also because he believed that the local banker had contributed greatly to "building up the country." He was still heavily in debt, but he refused to stop his opposition to chain banking even when one firm offered to loan him sufficient money to pay his obligations.[16]

After extensive hearings the first Glass banking bill was introduced in January, 1932, only to be put aside immediately for administration legislation designed to cope with the depression. A flood of proposals for solving the nation's economic ills continually deluged Norbeck and the committee. Somewhat flabbergasted by the pleas, suggestions, and criticisms, he wrote: "I really begin to think I am fortunate in the fact that part of the stuff goes over my head—I do not understand it all. If I did, maybe I wouldn't sleep."[17] This was the expression of a sincere public servant who was terribly bewildered and muddled by a feeling of his

14 George Wharton Pepper to Author, February 23, 1945.
15 Horace White, *Money and Banking* (New York, 1935), p. 679.
16 Norbeck to H. A. Sturgis, January 12, 1931. Norbeck MS.
17 Norbeck to John Hirning, January 27, 1932. Norbeck MS.

own inadequacy. He had no definite plan for solving the depession, except for his belief that a basic step would be restoration of the farmers' purchasing power through government aid.

Norbeck played no prominent part in framing the Reconstruction Finance Corporation Act, although he was chairman of the committee in the Senate which considered it. His chief interest appeared in making available $50,000,000 from the fund for farm seed loans. He had little faith in lending money to big business as a means of restoring prosperity. Besides, he resented the fact that representatives of banks, railroads, and other businesses, who had worked so diligently against the McNary-Haugen bill, because it entailed putting the "government in business," were now unblushingly clamoring for government relief! Anyway, he said, "credit relief at best is a temporary expedient."[18]

Of all the matters to come before the Banking and Currency Committee in 1932, the New York Stock Exchange investigation was of singular importance. Throughout 1931 and the early part of the next year, it was charged that a large amount of short selling was destroying public confidence and retarding recovery. Although the Stock Exchange officials had taken some steps to curb this practice, President Hoover decided to initiate government action when he learned that a "big bear raid" was in the offing. In February, 1932, he requested Senator Frederic Walcott, who had been formerly connected with the Stock Exchange and his favorite on the Banking and Currency committee, and Senator Norbeck to take active and immediate steps to investigate short selling.[19] Hoover had no thought of investigating the whole Wall Street structure, and it was clear from his actions that he wished the Connecticut senator to handle any investigation.[20]

But three months before Hoover decided to urge definite action, a resolution had been introduced in the Senate calling for an investigation of short selling. On March 3 Norbeck reported the resolution favorably, but in a much revised form. The preamble, specifically directing the Senate to investigate short selling, had been stricken out. As amended, it authorized an inquiry into the buying, selling, borrowing, and lending of listed securities, and the effect such practices had upon interstate and foreign commerce, "upon the operation of the national banking system and the Federal Reserve System, and upon the market for securities of the United States government. . . ."[21] The authorized expense account had been raised from $3,000 to $50,000. It is impossible to determine just what influence Norbeck exerted in broadening the resolution and increasing the available funds, but it was considerable if any inference can be drawn from his later activities.

18   Quoted by Charles P. Stewart in the Sioux City *Journal*, January 13, 1932.
19   R. L. Wilbur and A. M. Hyde, *The Hoover Policies*, p. 345.
20   John T. Flynn to Author, November 29, 1944.
21   *Cong. Rec.*, 72 Cong., 1 Sess., March 3, 1932. p. 5182.

The investigation was scheduled to begin on March 8. On that date, however, Norbeck announced that it would be necessary to delay "three or four days" because the Glass banking bill had first call on the committee's time. "The bulls and the bears may rest a few days more," he commented.[22] But Norbeck was going about his new task enthusiastically. When he was asked what effect the inquiry might have on the stock market, he almost shouted: "I don't know and I don't care."[23] He had already determined that a sweeping investigation must be made regardless of the consequences.

Not three or four days, but a month elapsed, and still there was no inquiry. On April 5 Norbeck again announced that the Glass bill had precedence in the committee, and that the opening date for the investigation was uncertain.[24] Rumors were beginning to circulate that further delay would probably mean the virtual death of the investigation; but Norbeck was reluctant to begin hearings until he had acquired more information on the supposed speculative abuses. He disliked considering public questions without the facts. To call witnesses without being able to check their testimony would avail little.

On Friday afternoon, April 8, the Banking and Currency Committee met in an unusual session. Without previous announcement and unknown to Norbeck, who was temporarily out of Washington, the committee voted to begin the inquiry the following Monday. Senator Brookhart, acting chairman, was authorized to subpoena Richard Whitney, president of the New York Stock Exchange, for questioning and to require him to bring information to Washington that might bear on short selling.[25] Reports that a big bear raid was to take place the following day was the reason given for proceeding immediately.

Upon being informed of this, Norbeck left Chicago and rushed back to Washington to assume active charge. He knew that Brookhart would not intentionally white-wash Wall Street, but he feared that those opposing an investigation would use him as a tool to probe into the activities of a few short sellers and then call off the whole affair. He had once said that Brookhart was the most easily fooled man in Washington. And what was worse, Norbeck claimed, the Iowa senator did not know it afterwards![26]

Furthermore, he believed there was something sinister in the committee's hasty action, taken in his absence. "Last Friday," he wrote, "I was absent in Chicago . . . and something happened—a special meeting of the Banking and Currency Committee without my knowledge or consent, to carry out a well laid scheme—which fortunately I will be able to thwart. Confidentially, the purpose of the meeting was to get a Wall Street attorney

22 New York *Times*, March 8, 1932, p. 31.
23 *Time*, 19:47 (March 14, 1932).
24 New York *Times*, April 5, 1932, p. 18.
25 *Ibid.*, April 9, 1932, p. 1.
26 Norbeck to James E. Stewart, March 25, 1932. Norbeck MS.

to do the investigation of Wall Street."[27] John T. Flynn, a contemporary Wall Street critic and a supporter of a thorough inquiry, has given a similar interpretation, declaring, "The plan was to hold a few hurried meetings, bring a few of the big traders and others to Washington, adjourn the hearing in a few days, start the drums and trumpets again, and resume our upward march to the old prosperity of Coolidge and Mellon."[28] He added on another occasion that the plan was well timed during the absence of Senator Norbeck.[29]

When Norbeck returned to Washington he told Flynn that the investigation must not be limited to short selling, but that the entire Wall Street structure should be probed. He added that the Stock Exchange had been responsible "not merely for the current sinking of the market, but for the general sharpening of the depression and, perhaps, for precipitating it." Norbeck expressed the idea that a full inquiry was long overdue and that this was the chance "to have a real one."[30]

The senator was fully convinced that the administration did not want a complete investigation, so he thrust Walcott, who had taken the lead up to that time, aside and took active charge himself. President Hoover, on the other hand, later asserted that when Norbeck called at the White House on the afternoon of April 12 he urged him "to leave no stone unturned to get at the truth."[31] Perhaps the committee chairman was over-suspicious of the administration's motives, but the subsequent actions of those close to the president tended to substantiate his convictions.

Richard Whitney faced Norbeck across the mahogany conference table on Monday morning, April 11. It might be said that the well-driller and the Stock Exchange president, with their different backgrounds and interests, personalized the cleavage between rural and urban America of which short selling was only one aspect.

For four days chief counsel Claude Branch and assistant counsel, William A. Gray, aided by the more inquisitive senators, questioned the evasive Whitney. The Stock Exchange president displayed an amazing ignorance of stock market practices, and his poise and self-assurance plainly needled the less clever and inadequately informed senators, as well as the counsel. Whitney admitted the practice of short selling and defended it as being necessary to the market. He made a distinction between speculation and gambling, disclaimed any knowledge of current bear raids, and insisted that he was unfamiliar with any large operators using dummy names in the stock market. He declared that he had never even heard of a floor pool!

27 Norbeck to J. D. Coon, April 11, 1932. Norbeck MS.
28 John T. Flynn, "The Marines Land in Wall Street," *Harper's*, 169:149-50 (July, 1934).
29 The Washington *Daily News*, October 24, 1934. Norbeck asked Flynn to outline the course which he thought the investigation should take, and Flynn presented several proposals to the Senator.
30 John T. Flynn to Author, November 29, 1944.
31 Herbert Hoover to M. B. Ronald, August 29, 1936. Norbeck MS.

Whitney obviously enjoyed showing how little the senators and their lawyers knew about the intricacies of the Stock Exchange. When attorney Gray asked him near the close of the afternoon session on April 21, if he would like to finish so he could return to New York, Whitney replied: "I do not particularly care, Mr. Gray. I will say that I am very happy here."[32]

By the end of the fourth day, Norbeck could not conceal his deep irritation. The discussion of pools and rigging the market produced a brisk exchange between the chairman and Whitney. Norbeck accused Whitney of refusing to admit that anything on the Exchange was improper or illegal and that many of the rules were not actually enforced. When Whitney asked for proof, the senator replied: "You attend these hearings for a while and we will give you some proof," to which Whitney replied: "I have. (laughter)."[33]

The Stock Exchange president plainly won the first round. All attempts to obtain admission of illicit or improper actions were entirely unavailing. The committee's unpreparedness presented a sorry picture. Whitney's evasiveness aroused Norbeck's anger, but he had to admit that the committee had been proceeding with "pretty punk" information.[34] The Whitney testimony confirmed Norbeck's belief that the inquiry would be useless unless the committee obtained a capable counsel who had the facts. A case could not be built upon rumor, gossip, and preconceived suspicions. Whitney had adequately demonstrated that he would not admit wrongdoing until he was forced to do so by positive evidence held by the investigators.

The committee's experience with Whitney had a chilling effect on the investigating ardor of many senators. Walcott showed no interest in anything except short selling and one Democratic senator termed the whole inquiry a joke.[35] Glass made no secret of his displeasure over the hearings. Fully aware of these attitudes, Norbeck stuck by his earlier decision to make a thorough and complete investigation. The decision as to what course to follow brought a sharp split among committee members. Walcott, speaking for the conservative members, and probably for the president, strongly favored abandoning the investigation. But Norbeck, supported by Blaine and Brookhart, insisted on a complete probe. After a very stormy committee meeting on April 20, Norbeck stalked out of the committee room. His flushed face gave evidence of the difficulties inside and he thundered to newspaper reporters: "We are going to carry this investigation through to the end. It will not be dropped in the middle or soft-pedaled."[36]

---

32 *Hearings Before the Committee on Banking and Currency, United States Senate, Stock Exchange Practices*, 72 Cong., 1 Sess., Pt. 1, pp. 276 ff.

33 *Ibid.*

34 New York *Times*, April 26, 1932, p. 2.

35 *Ibid.*, April 14, and April 26, 1932.

36 New York *Times*, April 22, 1932, p. 1; St. Louis *Post-Dispatch*, April 22, 1932; *Christian Science Monitor*, April 21, 1932.

It is likely that his stubborn determination at this point prevented the investigation from fizzling out before it actually got started.

Although Norbeck insisted on carrying the inquiry to the limit, he announced that politics would have no part and that the committee would not seek sensationalism. Legitimate business, he said, had nothing to fear. He wished only to expose and correct existing abuses in the securities market. Although he was not a Wall Street hater, he possessed the natural western prejudice against the money capital and held the traditional view that Wall Street was the farmers' enemy.

On April 21-22 the committee heard the testimony of Percy A. Rockefeller, Thomas E. Bragg, Ben Smith, and Matthew C. Brush—all large traders. They displayed an utter frankness by admitting the existence of pools and syndicates. These had been created for the benefit of "insiders" and stocks had been manipulated for the same purpose. But even these men did not reveal anything that was not generally known by those familiar with the Stock Exchange; at least the techniques were common knowledge.

Three days later Norbeck appointed a steering committee of Glass, Fletcher, Couzens, and himself as chairman. A few days later Townsend was added. He asserted that the committee was going to determine whether or not the American "buyer and seller has a fair market." Investigators would be sent "wherever it is necessary, whether to New York or San Francisco, or anyplace," he declared.[37] The absence of Senator Walcott from the steering committee caused considerable comment in the press. But it should not have been surprising in light of his and Norbeck's contrasting ideas on the object and extent of the investigation.

The selection of a satisfactory counsel was Norbeck's next problem. Both Branch and Gray left much to be desired. The choice of a satisfactory attorney, however, was not an easy one: first, because of the large number of applicants, approximately 1000, and secondly, because the legal fee of $200 a month was too small. Consequently he continued to employ Gray while searching for a better qualified man.

Meanwhile, Norbeck took the problem to the people *via* the radio. In two broadcasts he declared that owners of stock must be protected by law, and he predicted that confidence could not be restored and prosperity returned until some of the abuses in the business world had been abolished. "The lambs have been sheared," he said, "and it takes time to grow more wool." Some Wall Street practices, he asserted, led him to agree with a Chicago banker who said: "it was the worst crap game [sic] in the country."

He continued by saying that a drastic revision of the Stock Exchange practices was needed and that the "buying public was entitled to full information." Cunning manipulators and centralized wealth in general came in for their full share of criticism from the Plains senator. His tone and phrases were reminiscent of the days of Andrew Jackson![38]

37 New York *Times*, April 26, 1932, p. 1.
38 His speeches were delivered on April 22 and May 9, 1932. Norbeck MS.

His addresses, however, were delivered poorly. The ether waves only magnified his broad accent, described by one correspondent as that of a Scandinavian servant girl. Sport was made of his pronunciation of "manipulate" as "maniperlate." But he made a sincere effort to describe conditions as he saw them.

Criticism poured in with his next mail. One incensed business man wrote: "I wish to protest to you in connection with your address over the radio last night, which displayed such lamentable ignorance of the topic you were endeavoring to discuss. The broadcasting of your ignorant and uneducated ideas is tending to prolong the deplorable depression. . . ."[39] He was accused of being a "vote-grabbing demagogue . . . and a disgrace to representative government," and one listener declared, "The net result of Mr. Norbeck's speech was probably to constitute in the minds of his hearers a serious indictment of the judgment of voters in certain parts of the country."[40]

Many letters of congratulations, however, were also received. But they were not written on engraved stationery. A steel worker wrote: "I am sure glad to know there is some one that isn't afraid of big business and big money," while a Columbus, Ohio, realtor declared the address had the ring "of one who thinks true."[41]

Public hearings were resumed on May 19. Meanwhile, the investigators had been busy obtaining material on the next cases to be brought before the committee. With the aid of subpoenas they pried into the files of the traders and secured the desired data. But just when it looked as though worth-while information was about to be revealed, some senators expressed the fear that the inquiry was not having the effect which they had originally anticipated. It had been thought by some that the market could be stabilized if the bear raiders were driven to cover. Actually, the market was weaker. A demand now arose from within the subcommittee to abandon the investigation.[42] Writing on May 23, Norbeck said: "Confidentially, this investigation is getting to be a great care for me. The other members of the committee pay so little attention to it. . . . Yesterday Senator Couzens wanted to bring it to a close quickly, [and] Senator Glass objected to exposing the Warner Co. without exposing other movie picture corporations. . . ." "Two months ago," he wrote, "Senator Walcott favored the preventing of short-selling. Today he says that it is too late to prevent the things that might have been prevented, and his view is that it does not matter much what is done now."[43]

39 Harlow C. Vorhees to Norbeck, May 10, 1932. Norbeck MS.
40 A. K. Taylor to Norbeck, undated, 1932; P. M. Cushing to the New York *Evening Post*, May 12, 1932.
41 James Blecher to Norbeck, May 9, 1932; E. F. Fassig to Norbeck, May 10, 1932. Norbeck MS.
42 New York *Times*, May 19, 1932, p. 31.
43 Norbeck to Harry King, May 23, 1932; Norbeck to John H. Kelly, June 8, 1932. Norbeck MS.

His difficulties were increased when he became the center of a violent personal attack. On April 23 the New York *Herald Tribune* accused Norbeck of destroying business confidence and added that "as between Matthew Brush and Senator Peter Norbeck, the latter is incomparably the greater bear."[44] The New York *Daily Investment News* came out with an article on Norbeck and the South Dakota rural credits venture, quoting long passages from a highly critical report by M. Q. Sharpe, South Dakota's politically ambitious attorney-general. It also quoted Senator Glass as saying that "enough has been shown to indicate a degree of crookedness that requires legislative correction," and Senator Couzens was quoted as asserting that sufficient information had been disclosed, that more would be only "duplication and repetition of what has already been shown."[45]

Everything possible was done to make the readers believe that an investigation was unnecessary and that Norbeck was totally unfit to conduct one if it was required. Flynn referred to these tactics as Wall Street terror.[46] Even strong pressure to end the investigation came from South Dakota.[47]

When the committee resumed hearings, it pried into the affairs of M. J. Meehan and Company, General Asphalt, Goldman-Sachs Trading Corporation, Warner Brothers, Fox Theatres and Fox Films, copper pools, and others. In general it was discovered that the operation of stock pools for the benefit of "insiders" was common, that corporation affairs were often manipulated for the benefit of those in control, and that officers and directors of corporations often dealt in their own stock. Also it was found that the market was frequently "pegged" to keep the price of stock from going below a certain level while an issue was sold to the public, and that publicity was improperly used to induce prople to buy stocks of questionable value.[48] The revelations were far more important than in any of the previous hearings.

In order to continue the investigation, it became necessary for Norbeck to obtain additional power and funds from Congress. On June 17 he introduced a resolution providing for an extension of the committee's powers under the original act until the end of the Seventy-second Congress, March 4, 1933. He also asked for another $50,000.[49] After a hard Senate fight his requests were granted.

After Congress adjourned, the chairman announced that the work of the investigation would be handled throughout the summer by a subcommittee consisting of Glass, Townsend, and himself. The plans were to gather information preparatory to the opening of Congress in December when the hearings would be resumed. James E. Stewart, one of the senator's

44 New York *Herald Tribune*, April 23, 1932.
45 New York *Daily Investment News*, May 24, 1932.
46 Washington *Daily News*, May 24, 1932.
47 R. E. Driscoll, in interview with Author, July 15, 1944.
48 *Hearings, Stock Exchange Investigation*, Pt., 2.
49 *Cong. Rec.*, 72 Cong., 1 Sess., June 17, 1932, p. 13235.

South Dakota friends, supervised the program during the summer and autumn. He was aided by the chief investigator, D. A. Olson.

During the summer months, a group of investigators pried into the Insull Utilities collapse and gathered material on the Kruger and Toll financial debacle, which had involved thousands of American stockholders. The committee proceeded slowly, as it wanted to hold down expenses and avoid becoming involved in any political controversies. The fact that Stewart and Olson did not work well together retarded progress. According to Stewart, Olson wanted to handle the investigation in such a way that it would be impossible for anyone else to present the evidence to the committee. Furthermore, he "suggested that certain things might be done which would have quite a bearing on the campaign and on your [Norbeck's] fortunes politically."[50] Just prior to the November election, a representative of a brokerage firm, which had been exposed as having participated in stock pools, approached Stewart with the impossible suggestion that Norbeck accept a $1,000 campaign contribution.[51]

Although Norbeck planned to hold hearings in December on the crash of the Insull Utilities Empire, one delay followed another. On December 31 he wrote: "I am having a dickens of a time here to get my Wall Street investigation started. There is so much 'inertia'; I find it in the most unexpected places, even among those from whom I expected much help."[52] Again the main difficulty was disagreement within the committee. Some senators urged calling off the whole affair and declared that they did not actually have authority to investigate the Insull debacle. Norbeck, however, insisted that the inquiry must continue and that the Senate's $50,000 grant of the previous July gave sufficient authority to proceed.[53] On December 26, he wrote: "Strictly confidentially will state there are members of the Banking Committee that do not have any relish for this work."[54]

In spite of these obstacles, the Kruger and Toll manipulations were investigated early in January with John Marrinan, economic adviser for the committee, doing the questioning. But as the committee was slow in proceeding to other cases, numerous newspapers began attacking Norbeck and his aids for procrastination and a desire to white-wash Wall Street. While six months earlier, many papers had assailed him for destroying confidence by continuing the inquiry, they now flayed him for not working more rapidly. These unsubstantiated charges seemed to be confirmed when Irving Ben Cooper, newly hired counsel, resigned on January 17, after having been employed only a week. Cooper asserted that Marrinan had been instructed to "keep the lid" on the investigation. Norbeck explained that Cooper had

50 James E. Stewart to Norbeck, October 4, 1932. Norbeck MS.
51 James E. Stewart to S. X. Way, November 1, 1932. Norbeck MS.
52 Norbeck to E. E. Gelheus, December 31, 1932. Norbeck MS.
53 New York *Times,* January 1, 1933, p. 9.
54 Norbeck to Harold L. Ickes, December 26, 1932. Ickes was being considered as an attorney for the committee, but he refused.

TACK HAMMER TACTICS!

Used by permission of the New York *World-Telegram*

demanded 500 blank subpoenas, when only twenty-seven had been issued up to that time. "I, as chairman of the Committee," he said, "declined to delegate to him [Cooper] powers of the Senate, which I, as a Senator, would think it dangerous and unsound to delegate to anyone."[55]

The senator did not regret Cooper's resignation, because at that time he was negotiating with Ferdinand Pecora, who on January 24 was appointed chief counsel. Norbeck hired him upon the recommendation of Bainbridge Colby, former Secretary of State under President Wilson.[56] Pecora proved to be the man for whom Norbeck had been searching for almost a year, and he announced that the new attorney would "have all the authority necessary to make a comprehensive investigation."[57]

Pecora's public announcement that the investigation was going to be a fact-finding and not a "head-hunting" exploration did not inspire confidence. Critics interpreted this to mean that a genuine investigation would never materialize. Typical of the comments was that in the New York *World-Telegram.* "It now appears clear," said the editor, "that the Senate Committee does not intend to make a real investigation of the great frauds inflicted upon the American people by stock manipulators and speculators in the boom days. For real investigative action the American people can only wait until the next meeting of Congress, when the Committee on Banking and Currency may be made up of more courageous men."[58] It agreed with Cooper that Marrinan's job was to "sit on the lid." James McMullin said in his syndicated column that "the impression grows here that the stock market investigation will finish spending its $50,000 as rapidly as possible and shut up shop."[59]

These accusations gained credence when D. A. Olson resigned early in February. He levelled a bombastic barrage against Norbeck, asserting that the chairman had refused to allow him to proceed when he tried to expose certain income tax dodgers, and that he had been "handicapped at every step." He complained that he had been forced to "conform to a standard of incompetence and procrastination" which was entirely new in his experience, and added that the "apparent objective of the investigation was to whitewash Wall Street.[60]

The falsity of Olson's charges, as well as other anti-investigation propaganda, became apparent within a few days, when the Insull hearings began, followed only a short time later by the National City Bank exposure. What had appeared to be procrastination had been necessary delay. With the aid of a large staff of accountants, statisticians, lawyers, and clerks, Pecora had been gathering the necessary data. Norbeck was determined not to begin

55 New York *Times,* January 19, 1933, p. 1.
56 Norbeck to O. L. Brownlee, August 23, 1934. Norbeck MS.
57 New York *Times,* January 23, 1933, p. 23.
58 New York *World-Telegram,* February 2, 1933.
59 Sioux City *Tribune,* January 25, 1933.
60 D. A. Olson to Peter Norbeck, February 8, 1933. Norbeck MS.

additional public hearings until the committee had complete evidence. He would rather take abuse and criticism than proceed without proper evidence as he had done in the Whitney case. The results amply justified the delay.

As the manipulations of Insull and the National City Bank began to unfold, the Democrats began to show a revived interest. This was especially true after President-elect Roosevelt announced in February that he intended to carry the investigation to the limit. Upon reading Roosevelt's statement, Norbeck declared: "He is right. I am with him, even though the chairmanship of the Committee will pass from me on March 4."[61]

With the organization of the new Congress, Senator Fletcher became chairman of the committee. The investigation proceeded under his direction, with the aid of Pecora. One after another the Wall Street manipulators were brought under the fire of Pecora's questioning, which is well summarized in his book *Wall Street Under Oath.*

By the time Norbeck turned over the chairmanship to Fletcher, it was apparent that regulatory legislation was necessary and desirable. He was one of the earliest and strongest advocates of federal legislation to control and regulate the Stock Exchange. On May 11 he told the Senate: "we have got to break down every crooked organization so that we can throw the fear of God into them and let them know there is law in the land." He declared that more simple corporate structures were necessary and that more straightforward accounting and auditing systems were needed. He further explained that directors and officials of the stock market should be held responsible for fraud and deceptions, and that a federal license to sell securities in interstate commerce would be desirable.[62]

Congress moved rapidly to enact laws to correct many of the abuses revealed by the investigation. The Securities Act of 1933, the Securities and Exchange Act of 1934, and the Public Utilities Holding Company Act of 1935 were all facilitated by the committee's revelations.

John T. Flynn in appraising Norbeck's contributions has described how the well-driller foiled the plans of those who opposed a complete probe.

> But, alas, fate had planted one of its minions on the track in the person of Senator Peter Norbeck of South Dakota. . . . Norbeck is one of those prairie Republicans—half Democrat, half other ingredients, but less than one-half of one per cent Republican. He too thought Wall Street had wicked bears. But he was convinced there was plenty more wrong there and that this was a grand chance to have a look at it. It was Norbeck, big, honest, calm, filled with common sense, who made this an investigation of Wall Street, who kept doggedly at the probe, who finally engaged Ferdinand Pecora . . . and who more than any other man gave the investigation its tone, its character, and direction. He must come first in any distribution of awards for the results.[63]

61 New York *Times,* February 7, 1933, p. 25.
62 *Cong. Rec.,* 73 Cong., 1 Sess., May 11, 1933, pp. 2223-33.
63 Flynn, "The Marines Land in Wall Street," pp. 149-50.

The fact that most of the credit went to others did not particularly concern Norbeck. He told an old friend that he had learned "from long experience it is more important to get results than to get credit for results."[64]

64 Norbeck to George Anderson, April 4, 1934. Norbeck MS.

CHAPTER XVIII

THE ELECTION OF 1932

Norbeck's strength and influence in the Senate reached its highest peak during the Seventy-second Congress. His direction of the Stock Exchange investigation and his leadership in seeking farm relief gave him prestige hitherto withheld. Despite his antipathy to personal publicity, the matters with which he dealt naturally brought him into the national limelight. At the same time, however, he was faced with the most serious election threat of his twenty-eight year public career.

The South Dakota Republicans were still sharply divided between the Norbeck faction and the so-called conservatives who rallied around Hoover and the national administration. Leaders of this group had become increasingly antagonistic toward Norbeck, not only because of his progressiveness, but because they held him responsible for the defeat of Governor Gunderson six years before. For four years a Democratic governor had directed the state's administration, while the Republicans languished for patronage. Norbeck's opponents charged that he could have prevented this. It is true that he had been partly responsible for Gunderson's defeat. As previously shown, while Norbeck did not actively oppose Gunderson, many of his friends did.

In 1930 a Republican, Warren E. Green, was elected governor. He was personally friendly to the senator, but most of his supporters were anti-Norbeck men and very little of the state patronage went to Norbeck's friends. Although not all of the "old line" Republicans opposed Norbeck, most of those in control of the state administration at that time did.

Norbeck's opponents began as early as the autumn of 1931 to lay the groundwork for his defeat. In spite of the fact that a conservative Republican could hardly be optimistic about victory in 1932, the anti-Norbeck faction of the party worked harder than ever before to eliminate him in the primaries. The leader of the move to block his renomination was S. W. Clark of Redfield. The friendship between Clark and Norbeck which had been shattered in 1924 when Norbeck helped to defeat Sterling, Clark's law partner, had never been mended.

While Clark's opposition had been very intense in 1926, the passing of six years had made it even more violent. Throughout the entire autumn and winter of 1931-32 he wrote long public letters to Norbeck, accusing him of all sorts of shortcomings. Norbeck's friends answered these charges in "an eye for an eye and a tooth for a tooth" manner. Sometimes the senator wrote public letters in his own defense. The chief weakness in Clark's attack was that it centered around Norbeck's relation to the rural credits fiasco. To most voters these charges were "old stuff." This issue had been thrashed out before the electorate in every election since 1926, whenever a Norbeck supporter was running for office. The people were losing interest in what many had come to consider a personal quarrel between Clark and Norbeck. But Clark continued his blistering attack, hoping to develop more anti-Norbeck sentiment among Republicans.

On January 15 Herbert F. Brownell of Sioux Falls announced that he would seek Norbeck's position. Brownell was a successful business man and fairly well known throughout the state. Compared to the well-driller he was a novice at campaigning, but he did have a limited schooling in political affairs. He was a party "regular."

Brownell launched an intensive and well-financed campaign in which he repeated many of the Clark charges. In an address at Huron, he reminded the voters that when Norbeck became governor in 1917, South Dakota had been debt free, but Norbeck's unbusinesslike administration had put the state in the "red" by millions of dollars. He concluded that his opponent had "been weighed in the balance and found wanting."[1] As had been true in the 1926 campaign, most of the charges centered around Norbeck's gubernatorial record. Brownell's reluctance to attack Norbeck's senatorial service led the senator's supporters to declare that his opponents were tacitly admitting his effectiveness in Washington. Ronald emphasized this point through the columns of his Mitchell *Evening Republican*.[2]

Brownell's attack was sharpened by the usual bitter comments of the Pierre *Daily Dakotan*. This paper charged that the Democrats in the state were all for Norbeck "because in a pinch down at Washington when the Democrats need a vote, he always responds."[3] One citizen, who described himself as a "rock-ribbed, dyed-in-the-wool Republican," asserted in an open letter to the Sioux Falls *Daily Argus Leader*: "I say give us a Democrat anytime in preference to those half-breeds who delight in being elected Republicans and then crippling the efforts of a Republican President."[4] Clark amused some of his listeners by suggesting that the bust which sculptor Gutzon Borglum was making of Norbeck be placed in a conspicuous location in the state with the inscription: "The Man Who Busted South Dakota."[5]

To meet this attack, Norbeck had every cog in his political machine well oiled and operating at full speed, although he never seriously doubted but that he would be renominated. For instance, a county bank cashier used the following technique. "In filling out an application for a feed loan," he wrote, "we always call attention to the prospective borrower to the part played by Senator Norbeck in making it possible for him to save his livestock from starvation."[6] The president of a large wholesale fruit and vegetable company offered to put an organization of thirty salesmen in

1   Huron *Evening Huronite*, March 29, 1932.
2   Mitchell *Evening Republican*, April 9, 1932.
3   Pierre *Daily Dakotan*, May 2, 1932.
4   Sioux Falls *Daily Argus Leader*, January 7, 1931.
5   George Norbeck to Norbeck, April 16, 1932. Norbeck MS.
6   Unnamed correspondent to Norbeck, February 23, 1932. Norbeck MS.

western South Dakota at Norbeck's service.[7] And one of his farm friends, upon hearing that Norbeck was scheduled to speak over the radio on the Stock Exchange investigation, rushed to town and gave out a general telephone announcement to fifty-one rural lines and villages![8] His organization might well have been the envy of a New York Tammany Hall boss. "Brother George" and James E. Stewart were at the controls and nothing productive of a vote was left undone.

In spite of this, Norbeck did not realize the tremendous victory which he was about to win. When the votes were counted, Brownell was overwhelmingly defeated by a vote of 95,494 to 27,777.[9] Brownell had discovered what his neighbor Danforth had learned six years before; you could not gun for Norbeck with a cap pistol and expect to slay him. The Sioux City *Journal*, a conservative paper and one never particularly friendly to Norbeck, asserted: "South Dakotans are to be congratulated on two things, the availability of Peter Norbeck and the good sense to recognize him as an ideal man to represent them in the United States Senate."[10]

Norbeck's striking primary victory did not lull him into overconfidence. He well realized that the November election would not fall into its previous pattern. Formerly, the nomination had almost assured election in South Dakota. But conditions were not normal. The economic crisis was creating a wave of political discontent which might reach overwhelming proportions. The fact that his colleague Senator McMaster suffered a surprising defeat two years earlier at the hands of Democratic Governor Bulow, held an obvious significance.

He had defeated his Democratic opponent, U. S. G. Cherry, in 1920, but Cherry was a much stronger candidate than he had been twelve years before. Democratic strength throughout the nation was sweeping along like a whirlwind. The very psychology of the situation was to Norbeck's disadvantage. People were simply against the "ins." Norbeck, however, had never flinched before a lively political battle. In fact, outside of the expense incurred, he enjoyed it. And the approaching one had all the earmarks of a good one. No doubt it would be the political fight of his life.

As was true of most Democratic candidates that year, Cherry based his campaign on the issues growing out of the depression. He advocated some constructive policies, however, including making the tariff effective on farm products, granting loans at low rates of interest to farmers, mild inflation, readjustment of the tariff, and the abolition of the Federal Farm Board.[11] He flayed the Hoover administration in bitterest tones and accused Norbeck of having done nothing to get real farm relief.

Norbeck recognized that the national Republican party was seriously

---

7 Unnamed correspondent to Norbeck, February 1, 1932. Norbeck MS.
8 Ernest E. Gelheus to Norbeck, May 3, 1932. Norbeck MS.
9 *South Dakota Legislative Manual*, 1937, p. 369.
10 Sioux City *Journal*, May 6, 1932.
11 Mitchell *Evening Republican*, November 7, 1932.

handicapped by the depression. Furthermore, he realized that if he tried to defend the administration, and particularly Hoover, his chance of re-election would be indeed dim. He decided to steer a middle-of-the-road course, neither condemning nor praising Hoover. He did not want to alienate Hoover Republicans unnecessarily, and yet he wanted to hold the support of the farmers, whose principal pastime was criticizing Hoover. He decided to fight his own campaign and let Hoover do the same.

This policy, of course, was anathema to the Hoover Republicans. While they did not like Norbeck, they recognized his vote-getting qualities and planned to build the campaign around him. But when George Wright, state chairman, asked him for aid in the presidential contest, he replied that he was going to devote his attention exclusively to the senatorial race.[12] The Hoover forces in the state interpreted this as a breach of party faith. But Norbeck sensed the approaching Democratic victory and believed that under no

Keep Norbeck On The Job!

12   Norbeck to George W. Wright, February 4, 1932. Norbeck MS.

circumstances could Hoover carry South Dakota. Therefore, he reasoned, it would be political suicide to team up with a candidate whose defeat was predetermined. Besides, he owed nothing to the national Republican party. He had always fought and financed his own campaigns. So he took his campaign away from state headquarters and directed it from Redfield.

The newspapers in the state did everything possible to induce him to commit himself on Hoover, but he refused to do so. During the summer, he refused to make any public pronouncement other than a promise to support the Republican party; a statement which meant little to the Hoover supporters, as it might be interpreted in several ways. Newspaper editors speculated on just what the statement might imply. The Webster *Journal* admitted that Norbeck would be a stronger candidate if he did not try to carry Hoover and Green [Republican candidate for governor], but added: "If the Senator continues to devote his time and attention to unearthing the scalawags of Wall Street and the banking magnates who are responsible for destruction of farm welfare, he need not worry about making any public statements regarding Hoover and Green."[13]

The president's manager hoped that Norbeck would make a statement friendly to Hoover at the state fair which was held in September at Huron. Secretary of War Patrick J. Hurley was sent to sing administration praises to a throng of about 30,000 depression-ridden farmers and townspeople. Norbeck had a splendid opportunity to give Hoover some support when he introduced Hurley, but as one reporter expressed it: "They got the well-digging Senator right up to the water, but they couldn't make him drink."[14] At a dinner party given the same night, Norbeck again avoided endorsing Hoover and merely said the candidates ought to support their own party tickets. Then he added: "I still insist I have the right to try to reform my party from within."[15]

Although he did not support Hoover, he was not friendly to Roosevelt's candidacy. He would not follow Norris, Borah, Hiram Johnson, and "Young Bob" LaFollette who actively campaigned for Roosevelt. Excepting Norris, who had supported the Democrats in 1928, these senators might have followed a different course if they had been running for re-election in their various states. Of Roosevelt, Norbeck wrote in July: "I have absolutely no confidence in him or his party, and I know the Party and its leaders thoroughly."[16] He may have viewed Roosevelt's candidacy in a more friendly light after the New York governor said at Topeka, when referring to the agricultural problem: "This nation cannot endure if it is half 'boom' and half 'broke.' "[17] Norbeck had been preaching that theme for twelve years

13 Webster *Journal*, August 19, 1932.
14 Chicago *Daily Tribune*, September 30, 1932.
15 *Ibid.*
16 Norbeck to W. R. Ronald, July 11, 1932. Norbeck MS.
17 New York *Times*, September 15, 1932, p. 14.

and it must have given him satisfaction to hear it coming from the man who would probably be the next president. Norbeck pledged that, if Roosevelt should be elected, he would work with his administration to develop a constructive agricultural program. He argued that his fight for farm parity had been above party lines for twelve years, and that it would continue to be so.

When Norbeck's friends saw they could not elect Hoover, the slogan in many communities came to be "elect Norbeck and Roosevelt." One political wheelhorse wrote: "those of us that are interested in the Senator's election have abandoned any hope of electing Hoover and we are concentrating on the ticket from the Senator down."[18] "The slogan here was to elect Norbeck and Roosevelt," wrote another worker. Editor Ronald came out boldly for this combination and justified his position by saying: "Governor Roosevelt is a progressive, Senator Norbeck is a progressive; therefore, this paper supports them both."[19]

A substantial number of Democrats also aided the senator. In fact, this had been the case in every November election in which he had been a candidate. "Pete," wrote one Democrat, "I think you are a big asset to this state . . . and I am for you bigger than a house. . . ."[20]

Norbeck personally directed his campaign. Never had he put forth a more strenuous effort. He traveled over 10,000 miles, making 150 speeches before that many different audiences, and he gave three major radio addresses. His friends worked with equal vigor. Even the state president of the W. C. T. U. wrote to her "Dear Sisters:" "DO NOT, UNDER ANY CONSIDERATION, FAIL TO VOTE FOR HIM."[21] As the contest became hotter, his friends labored with increasing fury. One loyal lieutenant frantically tried to get people to write public letters endorsing the senator. When the response became slow, he simply wrote the letters himself and attached what he called "fake names." "We have been out day and night working for you Senator," wrote another supporter, adding: "It has been a hell of a fight."[22] The campaign could hardly have been described more accurately.

The election returns showed that there had been no basis for his unusual anxiety. Although Roosevelt carried this normally heavy Republican state by a majority of 84,000, Norbeck defeated Cherry by over 26,000 votes. This was a singular victory. All other major Republican office-seekers in the state were roughly thrust aside by an aroused electorate. And with the exception of Senator Nye of North Dakota, Norbeck was the only Republican to win in the entire Midwest. The pillars of the Coolidge-Hoover days had fallen before the voters' wrath and when the smoke had cleared,

18   F. M. Scobic to James E. Stewart, October 11, 1932. Norbeck MS.
19   Mitchell *Evening Republican,* October 31, 1932.
20   W. W. White to Norbeck, June 20, 1932. Norbeck MS.
21   Flora A. Mitchell to Members of the W. C. T. U., Form Letter, November 4, 1932. Norbeck MS.
22   Charles Weller to Norbeck, November 12, 1932, and J. P. Tschetter to Norbeck, November 7, 1932. Norbeck MS.

Bingham, Smoot, Moses, Watson, Blaine and other leaders of contemporary Republicanism were crushed in ignominious defeat. Even Senator Capper, whose political organization was one of the most formidable in the country, wrote to Norbeck: "Frankly, I am glad I was not running this year."[23] Besides South and North Dakota, only Oregon, Vermont, New Jersey, and Pennsylvania elected a Republican senator. Norbeck's demand that his party liberalize its policies and get in tune with the times could no longer be brushed off as the meaningless clatter of a midwestern malcontent.

The election demonstrated that the voters had confidence in the integrity and ability of "the big Norwegian from Spink county." In the final analysis, it was his personal standing with the voters that saved him. He later pictured this in a letter to an old friend and political adviser. "During the campaign," he wrote, "I found in every precinct that there was somebody boosting for me, someone who had served with me in the legislature, someone for whom I had drilled a well and gotten acquainted, or someone who had worked on some of my well rigs, or someone who believed strongly in my political creed—and Party lines did not seem to enter into that support very much."[24] Here was the secret of his success.

Many stories circulated concerning his political prowess, but one was especially apt. A visitor in a Norwegian home, so the story went, observed two pictures hanging on the wall of the living room. One was a print of Christ and the other a photograph of Norbeck. The visitor commented on this fact, and the farmer replied: "ay tell you how it is, ay look to Pete as far as he can go an' than ay look to the Lord. Between 'em ay manage to get through somehow."

The editor of the Sioux City *Journal* expressed a widespread attitude when he said: "Pete Norbeck's greatest charm is his willingness to be himself. He puts on no airs and makes no pretension of being something he is not. . . . He talks with an accent but thinks without one. At times his party regularity has been brought into question, but this much can be said for Pete Norbeck—he always can be found fighting the battle of his own people. He never forgets that he hails from South Dakota and the Middle West."[25]

Shortly after the election, he left for Rochester for another periodic physical check-up. His visits to the clinic were becoming more and more frequent as a result of chronic mouth sores. While it was not generally known, these ulcerated areas were malignant. Radium treatments, X-ray therapy, and minor surgery were only partially effective in controlling these growths. They were not particularly painful, but they were very annoying and were beginning to interfere slightly with his speech. Also the meager chance of finding a permanent cure was depressing.

23 Arthur Capper to Norbeck, November 15, 1932. Norbeck MS.
24 Norbeck to John Sutherland, December 15, 1932. Norbeck MS.
25 Sioux City *Journal*, May 6, 1932.

At Rochester he gave out his first post-election interview. When asked if the recent landslide had finished his party, he bluntly replied: "The Republican party isn't through by a damn sight!"[26] But he added a word of caution and advice. According to him, the chances of his party's comeback depended on two things: the success of the Democrats in dealing with the economic situation, and whether the Republicans would adopt policies which would inspire confidence in all parts of the country.

During the campaign, he had again affirmed his devotion to the independent Republicanism of the first Roosevelt. The *Congressional Directory* had continually carried the label of "Roosevelt Republican" for the Dakotan. Now newsmen jokingly asked him whether "Roosevelt Republican" referred to Theodore or Franklin Roosevelt! Norbeck was quick to inform them that he meant the Bull Mooser. The meaning of this brand of Republicanism may have been dubious to some, but to Norbeck it simply meant that he would follow the same middle-of-the-road progressivism which had characterized his entire public career. He would work to get the Republican leaders to accept more liberal and progressive policies. This was absolutely necessary, he said, if his party hoped to again control the government. "Theodore Roosevelt reversed Mark Hanna's policy," he asserted. "We need another Theodore Roosevelt in the Party; he is not in sight."[27]

26 Rochester (Minnesota) *Post-Bulletin*, November 15, 1932.
27 Norbeck to Wright Tarbell, January 21, 1933. Norbeck MS.

CHAPTER XIX

A "THEODORE ROOSEVELT REPUBLICAN" AND THE NEW DEAL

No one expected that Norbeck would play a very significant role in the formulation and execution of the New Deal. Unlike some of his Republican colleagues, he had refused to support Roosevelt's candidacy, and thus he found himself aligned with a minority party that had been thoroughly repudiated by the voters and with whose philosophy he was in disagreement. In spite of his progressive record and support of the idea that the federal government should take the lead in combatting the depression, the Democrats made no effort to bring him into their program. With sixty Democratic senators, it was unnecessary to look outside the party for support.

On March 4, 1933, he sat in the depleted Republican ranks and watched Roosevelt and his administration sweep into power amidst a national feeling of hopeful anticipation. As the New Deal machine gained momentum, veteran legislators of the tranquil Harding and Coolidge days stood somewhat aghast as the president and his advisers sent a wide variety of hastily drawn measures to Congress where they were quickly passed by the desperate legislators. Only infrequently was a feeble but ineffectual protest heard. One of these came from the Dakotan during the consideration of emergency banking legislation.

On March 9 Senator Fletcher, who replaced Norbeck as chairman of the Banking and Currency Committee, introduced a bill for relieving the banking emergency and moved that it be referred to the committee and reported favorably the same day. Norbeck arose and laconically asked if such an important bill was going to receive less than one day's consideration. Fletcher replied that it was his desire to report it "in an hour if we can." I am not going to object," Norbeck added, "but when we undertake to frame important banking legislation in an hour we are liable to get ourselves in trouble."[1] This was all he said, but it indicated that he was having difficulty in adjusting himself to such rapid fire action. Incidentally, too, as a champion of the small unit bank, he was afraid that hurried legislation might result in favors to the large banking corporations.

The president's expectancy that Congress would almost automatically endorse his proposals, regardless of whether the members fully understood them, caused Norbeck some annoyance. "I chafed a good deal through the month of March because I was not able to find out what was going on nor what the program was," he wrote, "but later I learned that the Democrats knew as little about it as I did."[2] This fact seemed to provide some little consolation!

During 1933 he was aligned with the president much more often than

---

1 *Cong. Rec.*, 73 Cong., 1 Sess., March 9, 1933, p. 46.
2 Norbeck to O. W. Coursey, April 28, 1933. Norbeck MS.

many of his Republican colleagues, or even some conservative Democrats. As a general rule, he said, he preferred the "New Deal" to the "Old Deal." It was Roosevelt's bold attack on the nation's problems, as well as his progressiveness, that appealed to Norbeck. He told one of his old friends that "Roosevelt has turned out so much better than I had dared hope that I occasionally find myself singing faint praises. Yes, I know he is making a mess of a lot of things, but, My God, he is trying. What is more . . . they are introducing a little humanity into government . . . where it had been outlawed for some time."[3]

On basic New Deal legislation affecting agriculture, work relief, currency and monetary matters, regulatory and reform measures, conservation, and reciprocal trade agreements, Norbeck supported the administration wholeheartedly. On at least two occasions, the devaluation of the dollar and the work relief law of 1935, he played a significant behind-the-scenes role. In his opinion, Roosevelt was making a sincere effort to deal intelligently with national problems, especially the farm problem. As a persistent advocate of farm relief, he welcomed the Agricultural Adjustment Act.

He played only a small part in the formation of the AAA, but it is worth noting that this law included at least two principles for which Norbeck had vigorously campaigned in the preceding Congress: the restriction of farm acreage and government benefit payments. His domestic allotment bill had done a great deal in laying the groundwork for this New Deal measure.

But he never completely abandoned his belief in the McNary-Haugen principle. Even after the AAA was framed, he expressed his preference for surplus-control legislation. He believed that paying farmers to let part of their land remain unproductive was too expensive to be a permanent solution to the farm problem. Ultimately he came to support a plan whereby the government would purchase outright some twelve or thirteen per cent of the producing agricultural land and hold it out of production. The acreage, he suggested, might be used for game and wild-life reservations and reforestation.[4]

Nothing aroused the old Norbeck spirit and fire, however, like an attack on the New Deal farm program, especially when it came from a Republican. He bitterly resented harsh Republican criticism of what he considered the only real farm measure passed during his stay in Washington. It was senseless, he argued, to censure the Democrats' farm relief record in light of Republican performance. He believed the Republicans were capable of writing a better farm bill, but added, "they were in power twelve years without doing it."[5]

Senator Dickinson of Iowa was a frequent critic of the AAA. After one of his critical speeches, Norbeck jumped to his feet in defense of the law. Following a bitter verbal exchange, the Iowa Republican would not speak

3 Norbeck to James E. Stewart, May 25, 1933. Norbeck MS.
4 *Cong. Rec.,* 74 Cong., 2 Sess., February 15, 1936, p. 2138 ff.
5 Norbeck to Lars P. Peterson, January 11, 1936. Norbeck MS.

to the Dakotan for "several months." Norbeck wrote to Ronald saying that the "A. A. A. was under too much attack . . . by men who ought to be supporting it."[6] He labelled the Supreme Court's invalidation of the law the "worst setback that South Dakota has had since I came to Washington fifteen years ago."[7]

His defense of the New Deal farm program was consistent and he did not write to dissatisfied constituents condemning it, while supporting it in Washington. To one disgruntled Republican voter he wrote: "The President is doing the best he can in all the red tape that exists here."[8] He had never said as much for Harding, Coolidge, or Hoover!

On the question of dollar devaluation, he was again found supporting Roosevelt. As a young man he had been a strong exponent of the gold standard, but in recent years he had consistently voted for inflationary legislation. In 1933 it was no secret that a number of the more conservative Democrats and some Republicans opposed Roosevelt's scheme to cheapen the dollar. "While several senators, including myself, were out of the [Banking and Currency Committee] room," he explained, "a motion was carried nine to eight to strike out the provision [of the Gold Reserve Act of 1934] giving the president this authority. On my return to the room, I moved to reconsider; we carried that by one vote. Then came the main question again . . . our side won" on a tie vote.[9] Later he declared that he cast the deciding vote after Glass, McAdoo, Fletcher, and Gore had thrown in "with the creditor side."[10]

Despite his general agreement with most New Deal policies, he detested the National Recovery Act. His primary opposition came as a result of the law's monopolistic tendencies, and it increased when prices began to rise in spite of the president's desire to keep them at, or near, the old levels. Since he believed many of the farmers' difficulties arose from the high prices of commodities they had to buy, he reasoned that higher commodity prices would nullify the benefits of the AAA. His opposition to the hours and wage provision stemmed from his inability to adjust his thinking to the forty hour week.

The growing seriousness and complexity of world problems found Norbeck with no consistent policies or well thought out ideas. He believed, along with most representatives of the farm states and the farm organizations, that the Philippines should be freed. Although he was absent when the vote was recorded, it was announced that he would vote "yea" if present. Privately he wrote that to shed the Philippines was "good riddance from an American viewpoint."[11] Although he may not have realized it, and

6 Norbeck to W. R. Ronald, July 31, 1935. Norbeck MS.
7 Norbeck to Mrs. Stella McCart, January 16, 1936. Norbeck MS.
8 Norbeck to C. H. Corey, March 10, 1936. Norbeck MS.
9 Norbeck to W. R. Ronald, April 24, 1933. Norbeck MS.
10 Norbeck to O. P. Engstrom, March 9, 1935. Norbeck MS.
11 Norbeck to Mrs. J. V. Rock, April 1, 1935. Norbeck MS.

probably would not have admitted it, he was motivated by the prevalent economic nationalism and isolation.

On the other hand, his support of the Hull reciprocal trade agreements contrasted sharply with the economic nationalism which he had been supporting, either knowingly or unknowingly, since his arrival in Washington. But his support of the Hull trade pacts was consistent with his opposition to the Hawley-Smoot tariff and his policy of moving away from high protection.

In 1935, when Roosevelt attempted to obtain Senate ratification of the World Court, Norbeck remained as non-committal as possible. His replies to inquiries as to how he stood on the Court issue were usually made in such a fashion that he could later defend his position regardless of how the Senate might vote. This type of hedging on a public question was unusual for Norbeck, who had a reputation among his constitutents for full and direct answers. It is best explained by his confused thinking.[12]

In justifying his vote against adherence to the Court on July 29, 1935, he explained that he wanted to avoid "entangling alliances" as much as possible.[13] Such a statement does not illustrate much interest or thought on the subject and was in marked contrast to his expression, "I am not afraid of the entangling alliance," made sixteen years before!

On the question of neutrality and armament he was even more perplexed. He explained: "We recognize that preparedness creates a military sentiment. We recognize also that history shows that defenseless nations were the victims of selfish neighbors. Eventually we should find the Nation well united on a sensible policy. At the present time we do not know which way to go." [14]

Norbeck's position was rather typical of many leaders in government and business. It is no wonder that President Roosevelt found it difficult to unite the nation on a concerted foreign policy when many national lawmakers were so utterly confused.

After the AAA was passed, Norbeck worked more leisurely than at any time during his stay in Washington. He relaxed more frequently and his daughter, Selma, would sometimes talk him into spending an evening at a night club, something that had been unthinkable in earlier years. He made no effort to help determine policy in an overwhelming Democratic Congress, and devoted much of his attention to such personal interests as conservation. Now and then a small group of "conservation Senators" would go down along the Potomac for a clam bake, and there in the shadow of the campfire's dying embers discuss their mutual interest. On these occasions, questions of politics, unemployment, farm relief, and other vital matters seemed very remote. They were memorable times for Norbeck.

Ill health forced him to spend progressively less time in Washington.

12 Norbeck to Mrs. G. F. Kane, May 16, 1934. Norbeck MS.
13 Norbeck to Mrs. E. W. Freige, April 3, 1935. Norbeck MS.
14 Norbeck to Mrs. William F. Voy, February 3, 1936. Norbeck MS.

During 1934 he was in Minnesota and South Dakota most of the time. In February he returned to Rochester where minor surgery was performed on his tongue. This was only partially successful in checking the spreading malignancy. His weight had fallen off about twenty-five pounds, and a somewhat haggard face with deepening lines gave evidence of a hard-lived sixty-four years. He remained in Rochester until April.

In compliance with his doctor's prescription for more rest and out-of-door exercise, he went to South Dakota. He was in no mood to return to Washington for any length of time. Personally he was respected and liked by his colleagues, but politically he could find no element in which he felt at home. The Republicans thought he was too friendly to the New Deal, and the Democrats had little use for him because of his Republicanism. His standing in his own party was declining because of his unpopular demand that the party leaders follow a more progressive course, and the Democrats did not want him, he said, "except when they get in a pinch for a vote."[15] For the first time since 1921, he exclaimed: "I feel lonesome down here."[16]

When he returned home, the Norbeck company was about to begin drilling a large well at Rapid City. The senator took personal charge of the operations. Every day he could be found dressed in overalls and sweater, superintending the job. He also made preparations to put down another well on the Cheyenne Indian Reservation. His big hands were not so powerful as they had been thirty years before, but his heavily accented profanity was as sharp as ever, as he gave orders to the crew members. It was a real pleasure for him again to supervise a drilling job. His business had always held a certain romance, and he declared: "I enjoyed well-drilling as much as I ever enjoyed politics. [?] I am proud of the twelve thousand artesian wells (and a few oil wells) for I have in that way contributed something to the development and progress of the country."[17]

This short period with the well machine did wonders for his health and upon returning to Washington early in 1935 he looked almost like his former self. He did not throw himself into his work with quite his usual energy, however, and tended to depend more heavily on his son Harold, who handled much of the routine correspondence and departmental work. Through close association with his father in several political campaigns, Harold had come to know most of the leading Norbeck supporters, and had developed much of his father's shrewdness for politics.

Much of Norbeck's attention during 1935 was directed toward resolving the difficulties which surrounded the Mount Rushmore project. After 1929 carving proceeded slowly and little progress was made except on the Washington figure. This was because of inadequate finances, and differences between John Boland, chairman of the Commission's Executive Committee, and Borglum.

15 Norbeck to A. I. Olding, February 19, 1935. Norbeck MS.
16 Norbeck to N. E. Knight, January 18, 1936. Norbeck MS.
17 Norbeck to Cora B. Johnson, December 9, 1927. Norbeck MS.

Boland, who was responsible for handling business matters, attempted to keep Borglum's activities confined to sculpturing. But the sculptor insisted on interfering in business affairs, something for which he was absolutely unfitted. He could or would not understand that there were certain requirements and regulations in the use of federal money, and failed to comprehend other elementary business requirements. This in no way detracted from his great artistic contributions, but it did provide inside difficulties which jeopardized the project's continuation.

Norbeck, who had accepted membership on the memorial's commission in 1931, found that he had to act as mediator between Borglum and Boland, who were at swords points most of the time. Whenever Boland demanded that ordinary business procedures be followed, Borglum accused him of interference and pleaded for Norbeck to use his influence in removing the "petty politicians." The senator almost always sided with Boland, who was a successful business man in his own right, and at the same time attempted to sooth Borglum and keep the work progressing.[18]

Besides this conflict of personalities which was not conducive to the project's progress, financial difficulties were perennial. A crisis in 1932 was weathered successfully when Norbeck, after six conferences with Governor Warren E. Green, obtained $50,000 from federal relief funds allocated to South Dakota.[19]

But the difficulty with Borglum continued and by 1933 the relationship among the memorial's leading sponsors had become critical. On September 13 Norbeck, along with William Williamson and Roland, went to Borglum's studio at the foot of Mount Rushmore for a "showdown." Norbeck admittedly lost his temper and flayed Borglum for trying to assume business duties for which he was unsuited and incapable of executing. In language more applicable to an inefficient well-drilling crew, he attacked him for endeavoring to assume Boland's duties and warned Borglum to tend strictly to his own responsibilities. Finally, he said that he would no longer tolerate the constant bickering between the sculptor and the Executive Commission.[20]

This unfortunate meeting unquestionably put a severe strain on a close friendship of almost ten years. Borglum was deeply hurt. But a few days later, Norbeck told him that he was sorry for having lost his temper. At the same time, however, he held to the truth of his accusations. Borglum, on the other hand, replied that he would not even let the senator apologize. "I don't blame you," he said, "I do blame others"—meaning Boland.[21]

Borglum accepted criticism that he probably would not have taken from any other person. This was partially due to his realization that Nor-

18 Norbeck to John Boland, May 17, 1929; and to Doane Robinson, June 1, 1929. Norbeck MS.

19 Norbeck to John Boland, August 26, 1935. Norbeck MS.

20 Gutzon Borglum to Norbeck, September 14, 1933.

21 Gutzon Borglum to Norbeck, September 27, 1933. Norbeck MS.

beck was the real promoter of this opportunity, and also because he had faith and confidence in the senator's judgment. Norbeck was always profuse in his praise of Borglum's artistic and sculptural work, but on one occasion he declared: "you are so deficient in business judgment and methods as to be almost blind."[22] In spite of such frankness, Borglum wrote: "Your opinion is the only opinion I care a hoop about on the whole Commission, and you know that's been so from the beginning."[23] It is entirely possible, however, that Borglum might have quit at Rushmore if he had not wanted to vindicate the Stone Mountain debacle.[24]

While the personal differences were temporarily resolved, financial problems continued to plague the commission. By 1934 the money was again exhausted and carving could not proceed. Again Norbeck came to the rescue. After considerable legislative manipulation, he succeeded in pushing through Congress a bill which removed the requirement of immediate dollar for dollar matching to secure federal funds, thus making available about $105,000 for the working season.[25]

These funds, however, were soon depleted. Norbeck now decided to ask for a direct appropriation of $200,000, which Borglum thought would be enough to finish the memorial. Norbeck encouraged his Democratic colleague Bulow to introduce the Rushmore appropriation bill for reasons of politics.

It happened that the Senate was then considering President Roosevelt's request for a $4,800,000,000 work relief appropriation. There was a sharp difference of opinion as to how best to handle the relief problem. Many believed that it would be cheaper to resort to some form of a dole, while others thought work relief was the better method, although admittedly more expensive. An effort was made to cut the appropriation by about $2,000,000,000, and it was supported by most of the Republican members of the Appropriations Committee, except Norbeck, as well as such administration stalwarts as Glass, Copeland, Adams, and McCarran. When the matter came to a vote in committee, Norbeck was the only Republican who favored Roosevelt's plan, which was reported favorably by one vote, and ultimately passed.[26]

The president had made a personal request of Norbeck to support his policy, but the senator told Ronald that "I intended to help him anyway." He admitted that he could not map a better relief program than that presented by Roosevelt. And then he explained: "As a Republican I do not feel like criticizing very severely when I recall the nonsense Hoover handed to Congress and to the country."[27]

22 Norbeck to Gutzon Borglum, December 18, 1934. Norbeck MS.
23 Gutzon Borglum to Norbeck, December 17, 1934. Norbeck MS.
24 Gutzon Borglum to Doane Robinson, May 11, 1925. Norbeck MS.
25 *Cong. Rec.*, 73 Cong., 2 Sess., May 31, 1934, p. 10110.
26 Norbeck to A. G. Granger, February 6, 1935. Norbeck MS.
27 Norbeck to Stewart Sharpe, February 28, 1935. Norbeck MS.

The bill providing for $200,000 for Mount Rushmore, which he and Senator Bulow were pushing, was meeting with very little success. Seemingly, only presidential support could facilitate its passage. After working with Roosevelt on his relief bill, Norbeck did not hesitate to seek White House support for his measure.

As Norbeck presented the problem, Roosevelt showed an obvious interest, but he was noncommittal. Norbeck left the White House discouraged. But within a few days, he received a very heartening communication from the president saying: "your description of the progress of work on the memorial and of its inspirational value to our people in the years to come convinces me of the need for legislation to authorize an additional appropriation of $200,000 for the completion of this project."[28] Presidential blessing was sufficient and the bill became a law a few weeks later.

This assured the memorial's completion. The development was now supervised by the Interior Department. The large number of interested parties and loyal workers makes it difficult to assess Norbeck's role in the completion of this national shrine. While Borglum was responsible for the sculptural masterpiece, it seems highly unlikely that it would ever have been finished without Norbeck's constant attention over a period of ten years. He played the leading role in resolving four different financial crises, any one of which, had it been handled unsuccessfully, could have made a second Stone Mountain in South Dakota. And his success in dealing with Borglum can hardly be over-emphasized.

As time passed, Norbeck found himself more and more in agreement with the New Deal's basic tenets. About the time that Roosevelt helped him with the Rushmore appropriation bill, he declared: "In spite of a deep conviction that a lot of unnecessary blunders are being made, I find myself today more disposed to support Roosevelt than I have had any time during the whole administration. . . ."[29] If Roosevelt's positive and progressive program drew him toward the Democrats, the attitude of his party's self-styled leaders alienated him even further from the Republican fold. Bingham, Watson, Moses, Smoot, and others of similar political and economic philosophies were directing the course of the Grand Old Party—in spite of the fact that most of them had been repudiated at the polls. The pleas of the progressive Republicans for a voice in the party's affairs and repudiation of the conservatism of Harding, Coolidge, and Hoover fell on deaf ears.

Norbeck's strongest blast at Republican leadership and policies came in the summer of 1935 and grew out of the so-called "grass-roots" meeting held in June at Springfield, Illinois. This conference of Republican leaders, supposedly representing people from the grass roots of ten midwestern states, was called to organize the party in that area for the defeat of Roosevelt and the New Deal. Among the important leaders were Harrison E. Spangler

28 Franklin D. Roosevelt to Norbeck, July 3, 1935. Norbeck MS.
29 Norbeck to Herman D. Eilers, July 15, 1935. Norbeck MS.

of Iowa and John D. M. Hamilton of Kansas. The delegates assembled proclaiming "save the constitution" and declaring that Roosevelt should be held personally responsible for the New Deal acts. Fervent applause greeted Spangler, Hamilton, and Frank Lowden as they denounced the New Deal in most bitter and caustic language. The Roosevelt administration was branded "unconstitutional and un-American," and the Republicans called for a campaign based on "strict adherence to the constitution, a sound money policy, and a balanced federal budget."[30] Important resolutions passed at the conference called for the gold standard, abolition of the reciprocal trade agreements, and a return to "individualism."[31] Although no official resolution was passed condemning the AAA, the individual conference leaders criticized it with utmost vigor and apparent pleasure. A few weeks after the Springfield meeting, Spangler was selected as chairman of a permanent organization established in Chicago to oppose the president's re-election.

Norbeck was suspicious of the whole affair. He doubted if the impetus for such denunciations came from the grass roots. He knew from first hand experience that there was no substantial demand for a return to the gold standard, not in the Midwest anyway, and he had heard relatively little denunciation of the president and the New Deal in his state. His suspicions were increased, when he learned that none of South Dakota's progressives had been invited. Nonetheless, S. X. Way, Norbeck's political barometer, attended. He reported that the meeting had neither "grass" nor "roots" and that conservatives dominated the whole affair![32]

Way's description of the Springfield meeting aroused Norbeck's fighting blood, and he bitterly criticized his party's leadership, although he well realized it would have little effect.

The Republican party, he said, must offer something more than eighteen criticisms of the Roosevelt administration and the scare about losing the constitution if it expected to win a national election. He asserted that the party must "sponsor sound economic policies good for every section of the country." Furthermore, it must deal "frankly and honestly with the voters," and must not depend on camouflaging the issues for success. "In looking for a campaign issue," he declared, "we must not depend too much on fault-finding and the failure of the Democrats to keep their promises. The Republicans have shortcomings of this kind to answer for also. We can not win on Democratic mistakes.... We must have a sound, forward-looking constructive policy of our own. The farm program can not be abandoned; it must be improved upon. The New Deal is full of mistakes, but the old deal is no substitute." Then he added what he considered the most important point: "Above all they [Republicans] can not win without

30 New York *Times,* June 8, 1935, p. 1; and June 11, 1935, p. 1.
31 *Ibid.,* June 12, 1935, p. 12.
32 S. X. Way to Norbeck, June 16, 1935. Norbeck MS.

inviting the Progressives into the Party and giving them a voice in party affairs."[33]

Such advice was anathema to conservative Republicans, but to many it sounded like counsel really originating at the "grass roots." The Sioux City *Tribune* declared: "Mr. Norbeck speaks the language of American liberalism of all parties. . . . The . . . Senator's remarks were as timely as sound. . . . It is refreshing to hear the voice of reason occasionally."[34] The liberal Republican newspaper in his own state said that Norbeck presented "political realities."[35] But the conservative Sioux Falls *Daily Argus Leader* termed his suggestions "absurd."[36]

Throughout 1935 his correspondence was filled with complaints against his party's leaders and policies. It even indicated that his party loyalties were becoming strained. He had always preferred to work for progressive principles within the Republican ranks, but the chances of reviving the insurgent progressivism of thirty years earlier now seemed beyond the realm of probability. And as long as the Republicans clung to their conservatism, he scoffed at the idea of them winning in 1936. To his friend Way, he wrote: "We must realize Roosevelt can not be beaten by anybody. He will probably win because there is no organized, unselfish, intelligent opposition to him."[37]

He viewed the Republican presidential timber with deep dismay. The leading contenders, Landon, Knox, and Borah, were to him little more than dead wood. But late in 1935, after Borah's solicitation for assistance, he announced that he would back the Idaho senator. He privately admitted there were many things on which he and Borah did not agree, but added: "he is the nearest of any of the candidates meeting the requirements of our peculiar situation."[38]

Because of ill health, Norbeck was unable to go to South Dakota and campaign actively for a solid Borah delegation to the Republican national convention. His presence was indeed necessary if the Borah delegates were to win, because the conservatives and anti-Norbeck faction in the state were lining up solidly for Landon. A half-hearted primary campaign was waged between the Landon and Borah forces, in which the Landon delegates came out victorious by a small majority.[39]

The anti-Norbeck faction hailed the results with joy, interpreting the vote as a slap at Norbeck who had been friendly to the New Deal. This campaign, however, did not test Norbeck's strength. He was not even

33 New York *Times*, August 11, Pt. IV, p. 8. See also Norbeck to Bertrand Snell, August 8, 1935. Norbeck MS.
34 Sioux City *Tribune*, August 9, 1935.
35 Mitchell *Daily Republic*, August 10, 1935.
36 Sioux Falls *Daily Argus Leader*, August 10, 1935.
37 Norbeck to S. X. Way, November 13, 1935. Norbeck MS.
38 Norbeck to B. K. Bettelheim, February 3, 1936. Norbeck MS.
39 *South Dakota Legislative Manual*, 1937, p. 382.

in the state and, according to one of his friends, the farmers, his chief supporters, did not go to the polls in any substantial numbers.[40]

Norbeck made several bitter attacks on Landon before and after his presidential nomination. And he was then taken to task sharply by the Sioux Falls *Daily Argus Leader,* the state's strongest mouthpiece for the Kansan. Editorially, it said: "In view of his [Norbeck's] attitude throughout the past two or three years, it seems that President Roosevelt should be his ideal candidate and the New Deal his ideal platform. Therefore, placing principle above party, why doesn't the South Dakotan withdraw from the Republican organization and join the Democrats."[41] Actually, Norbeck had drifted much closer to the Democratic party and to a wide acceptance of Roosevelt's whole program than he was willing publicly to admit.

In July he left for his summer home, Valhalla. The question of his stand in the approaching presidential election weighed heavily upon him. To make matters worse the conservatives were gaining strength in South Dakota, and his friend Way, who had been national Republican committeeman for many years, was ousted in the June state convention. The Huron *Evening Huronite* declared before the convention that it would be "mighty poor strategy . . . to affront the Norbeck element of the party by ousting S. X. Way . . . as national committeeman." It added that Way and Norbeck might join the Democrats if that occurred.[42]

As Norbeck relaxed and enjoyed the invigorating climate and beautiful scenery of the Black Hills, it appeared as though he might take no active part in the campaign. This was in keeping with his actions in previous presidential elections when he had not approved of his party's candidate.

He was torn between following his liberal convictions and falling in line with his party. Despite all the criticism of the AAA, he realized that most of the farmers and old time Republican progressives in South Dakota were for Roosevelt, even though the conservatives had come to dominate the party machinery. Should he follow a course that would be politically expedient, or come out boldly in support of his principles.

It is not clear just when Norbeck finally decided to make a public statement in support of Roosevelt's re-election. But by September he had determined to follow that course. Early in the month he was forced to return to Rochester and while resting there Way arrived. There they discussed what kind of a statement they should issue.

The malignancy in Norbeck's mouth and jaw was fast becoming worse, even to the extent of impeding his speech. As his physical condition grew more serious, he wrote: "It makes me tired, I may not put out a statement.

40 Enoch Norbeck to Norbeck, May 6, 1936. Norbeck MS.
41 Sioux Falls *Daily Argus Leader,* February 1, 1936.
42 Huron *Evening Huronite,* May 28, 1936.

I hate the work of making it. But I enclose start at two confidential drafts I hurriedly made."[43] Shortly afterwards he wrote to Enoch:

I have done nothing yet. But it is the old question of doing my duty or taking the easy way out. I feel strongly that the Northwest's agriculture has been saved from ruin by F. D. R.'s philosophy. . . . The Republicans are so controlled by the 'business' view which is so narrow. It reflects the mind of the wealthy class —the investors, the manufacturers and the bankers. The Eastern Republicans control the party and have always been provincial. I think its [sic] time we fight for our own interests and make the party leaders play fair. If they lose once more, they will be better. . . . Can Republicans persuade the farmer that three-cent hogs under Hoover is better than nine-cent hogs under Roosevelt. . . . You might be right that I should save myself by keeping out of the contest but it's hard when South Dakota interests may be in jeopardy.[44]

Nine days later Norbeck and Way released a joint statement endorsing Roosevelt's re-election. They declared that the Republican party was controlled by the "large industrial interest . . . and money scalpers," that Roosevelt had actually lessened the crushing farm debt by devaluing the dollar, and that farm prices were materially better than under Hoover. They charged the Republicans with having no adequate farm program and since "we do not want to vote to set agriculture back to the old unfair level or to retard national recovery, . . . we are going to vote for one Democrat, Franklin D. Roosevelt."[45]

Not since the days of Populism had an event in South Dakota politics been so sensational. The man who had led the Republican party for twenty years was cooperating to elect a Democratic president! As might be expected, the reactions varied from warm praise to violent criticism.

The conservative Republicans were vehement beyond words. They circulated all sorts of fantastic stories, partly in an effort to counteract the statement's influence. Some charged that Way had written it and then practically forced the physically weak senator to sign it. Others declared that Norbeck was mentally ill. Harlan Bushfield, state chairman, accused Norbeck of being a tool for "sinister" New Deal forces operating from Washington.[46]

On the other hand, the progressives and Democrats were jubilant. The Sioux City *Tribune* asserted that Norbeck had been true to his "progressive traditions." It added that "the gulf between the Norbeck progressives and the reactionary Republicans was as deep and as wide as the gulf between Franklin D. Roosevelt and Herbert Hoover. . . . Standing, as he does, four square for human rights over property rights,

43 Norbeck to George Norbeck, September 23, 1936. Norbeck MS.
44 Norbeck to Enoch Norbeck, October 5, 1936. Norbeck MS.
45 *Norbeck, Way Endorse Roosevelt*, October 14, 1936. Copy in Norbeck MS.
46 Sioux Falls *Daily Argus Leader*, October 15, 1936. Norbeck MS.

Norbeck has done and will continue to do the manly thing."[47] "All honor to them for taking that step when it became obvious that there is not now any chance of making the party progressive," said the Mitchell *Daily Republic*. "They have fought a good fight within the Republican party, now their conviction makes it necessary for them to carry the fight under another banner."[48]

The Sioux Falls *Daily Argus Leader*, however, bitterly attacked the senator. It charged that he was imbued with the same evil philosophy embodied in the New Deal, and added that since he had harnessed the state with the ill-fated rural credits system it was only natural that he would align himself with Roosevelt, who was responsible for imposing the greatest debt ever known upon the United States. It continued: "Norbeck and Roosevelt have much in common. They think alike. They act alike. Roosevelt today is doing to the nation what Norbeck did for South Dakota several years ago." The campaign battle today, said the editor, "is not between Republicans and Democrats in the former sense. It is a tussle between two types of government."[49]

This had been a tremendously difficult and important decision, but it should not have occasioned such widespread surprise. To support Roosevelt was the logical consummation of his thirty year fight for progressivism. He could not have followed any other course and been true to his convictions. This was especially true when his only alternative was to support Landon, who was backed by the conservative Republicans.

It is difficult to determine just what effect Norbeck's statement had on the election's outcome in South Dakota. Although Roosevelt's majority was not as large as in 1932, he carried this formerly Republican state by a margin of 35,000 votes. This indicated that many Republicans supported him and no doubt some of them did so because of Norbeck's action.

47 Sioux City *Tribune*, October 15, 1936.
48 Mitchell *Daily Republic*, October 15, 1936.
49 Sioux Falls *Daily Argus Leader*, October 15, 1936.

CHAPTER XX

THE END OF A CAREER

After the November election, Norbeck rested at his brother George's home in Redfield. His tongue and jaw had become so cancerous that he could no longer speak understandably. He spent most of his time reading and writing letters, first scribbling them by hand and then having them transcribed.

As he viewed the bustling little town from a large bay window, it brought back happy memories of earlier days. He remembered so vividly that crisp fall day thirty-five years before, when Norbeck and Nicholson pulled some ten well rigs into town. Thoughts of business expansion, as well as the town fights over prohibition, and the county political battles, all flashed across his mind. He recalled the friendliness with which he and his wife first had been greeted, and the occasional house party or church gathering that helped make their young lives enjoyable and exciting. And then there was the subsequent era of bitterness and strife which had arisen over business and politics. But now again everything was peaceful and everyone seemed friendly. Visitors dropped in, letters cluttered the mails, and the telephone rang frequently, all to learn how the senator was.

As the December sun glistened on a light skiff of snow, a whole career was relived. And he wrote to Mrs. Norbeck, who was away for a few days, of all these things and thoughts.

But all was not reminiscence. He was making plans to return to Washington. Shortly after noon of December 20, however, he quietly died of heart failure; a condition complicated by the growth of cancer. Harold, brother George, a secretary, and Doctor P. R. Scallin were at his bedside.

Although his situation was recognized as serious, even members of the family were unprepared for this sudden development. Mrs. Norbeck, entirely unaware of the immediate danger, was attending church at the time.

Two days later funeral services were held in Our Saviour's Lutheran church in Redfield, the same one he had helped to establish over thirty years before. Reverend Lloyd Strand, pastor, President Lars Boe of St. Olaf College, and President C. M. Granskou of Augustana College in Sioux Falls, officiated.

Senator Norbeck was dead, and as hundreds of people jammed the little church and the churchyard around it, Redfield's business houses closed and the South Dakota legislature temporarily adjourned.

The following day his body was taken back to his boyhood home in Charles Mix county. There in the shadow of the Missouri river hills, the state and nation paid him last tribute. Besides local dignitaries, Senators Frazier, Bulow, McNary, and LaFollette were on hand to pay respect to their old colleague. He was buried beside his parents in the old Bloomington cemetery about seven miles southeast of Platte. Thus ended the career of this plain man from the prairies, who had led his people through such a long and important period. His life had been the very embodiment of the independence and self-reliance of his Norse forebears.

His death left a wide gap in the ranks of Republican progressivism. For almost thirty years he had carried the banner of liberalism in his state with the result that his name flashed clearly across the pages of state and national history. Through peace and war, depression and prosperity, his progressivism represented that of a majority of South Dakota Republicans. In one political campaign after another, he brushed aside his opponents in an enviable way. His unwillingness to conform to accepted political standards of party regularity were no handicap to him. He had his own uncanny method of hitting upon men and measures that would assure his political future and the fortunes of his objectives. He knew the people of his state as no other man had ever known them, and he sensed their desires. Thus he felt confident and secure in his attitude on public questions.

In spite of his flirtation with state socialism while he was governor, he never embraced its basic theories and strongly opposed "radicalism." His progressivism was the middle-of-the-road or moderate kind proclaimed by Theodore Roosevelt. Political maturity did not bring about a greater conservatism, which so often accompanies old age. Looking in the same direction at sixty-six as he had at thirty-six, he accepted many of the policies of another Roosevelt, a Democrat. He was among those few Republicans in the Midwest who came to prominence during the progressive period, who clung to their principles tenaciously and consistently through both Republican and Democratic administrations.

Norbeck's career is chiefly significant because of the ideals which he represented and the political and economic philosophy which he espoused. Actually he was a New Dealer before Franklin D. Roosevelt's era. Much of his progressiveness resulted in the extension of governmental powers which he believed would be beneficial to the average citizen. From the very beginning of his official activities he was a great believer in the welfare and advancement of the "common man." His demand for greater governmental activity came from a strong conviction that the average citizen could best be served in this way.

A state-owned rural credit system, he argued, would relieve debt-burdened farmers. A state coal mine and cement plant could produce cheap coal and cement. And he envisioned South Dakota's farms and villages lighted by electricity produced by government-owned plants on the Missouri river. His object was always the same: to help South Dakota's people. While the means he chose often failed, his motives were always sound. The estimate placed on Norbeck and his work will be gauged by the same yardstick that future historians will apply to the New Deal in general. Philosophically, his program and that of the New Deal were of the same pattern. If posterity should condemn the New Deal, it will hold the Norbeck program in equal disparagement.

His official acts were not free from mistakes, some of them serious. His ill-fated rural credits venture was a complete and costly failure. And his lack of interest and understanding of the momentous world problems with which the United States had to deal was of no credit to him.

But he was responsible for a sizeable amount of constructive legislation in South Dakota. He sponsored railroad legislation, a tax commission law, workmen's compensation legislation, a good roads program, a grain marketing act, and laws to help returning veterans of the First World War. It cannot be overlooked that outside of political accomplishments, he made it possible for thousands of farmers in South Dakota and surrounding states to have artesian wells at a very reasonable cost. Perhaps this was his most outstanding contribution to his state's development.

In Washington his constant work on behalf of farm parity helped bring the problems of agriculture into national focus, and while his name was not attached to important farm legislation, he was always among the advance guard in seeking agricultural relief. His direction of the Stock Exchange investigation entitled him to a place among the leading senators of that period.

Although Norbeck was a rough-and-tumble well-driller and politician, his artistic nature and love of natural beauty caused him to achieve national prominence in the field of park and conservation legislation. The Migratory Bird Act of 1929, the establishment of Custer State Park and the Badlands National Park, along with the Rushmore Memorial are all testimonials to his efforts. He once declared: "I would rather be remembered as an artist than as a United States Senator." As long as the imperishable granite of Mount Rushmore remains, the names of Borglum and Norbeck will be remembered.

Norbeck admitted that he was a sectionalist. His was the same kind of sectionalism, for instance, as that exemplified by Calvin Coolidge or Senator Reed of Pennsylvania. He never forgot that he was from South Dakota and from the Northwest. He never lost the common touch. The glories and glamour of Washington's marble halls did not break that close bond with his rural constituents. A man of rare simplicity, he was natural in all of his relationships. The people of his area were first in his thoughts. His philosophy is well summed up in a statement which he made when he was asked to change his vote on the confirmation of Charles B. Warren for attorney-general. He wrote: "I am firm in my conviction that if I stay by the people of South Dakota, I won't fail; if I stay by these political bosses in order to get a few plums, I will be lost." Herein lies an important aspect of Norbeck's public life. His career, aside from all other factors, is of historical interest and importance because it typifies so well the trend toward pressure group influence and representation in American politics.

Political success was his because he supported the farmers of his area with a singleness of purpose; even though some of the policies which he supported may not have been the best for the country as a whole.

Norbeck was largely a product of his environment, one seething with rural unrest. Many farmers had concluded that government aid was an absolute necessity to bring about "economic equality." Norbeck's career represents in an unusual manner this rural discontent as reflected in a demand for government relief. Few men's careers reflect more clearly the time and place in which they lived than did that of Peter Norbeck.

BIBLIOGRAPHY

MANUSCRIPTS

The Norbeck files have furnished the principal source material for this study. These are controlled by Harold, the Senator's son, and are deposited at the University of South Dakota library. The materials fill sixteen trunk size boxes and can be used only with the permission of Harold Norbeck. The Norbeck correspondence covers the period from 1898 to 1936, with the bulk of it covering the years, 1921 to 1936. Besides letters, Norbeck's files contain pamphlets, state and federal documents, and newspaper clippings.

Other manuscript materials consulted were the William Hirth papers located in the Western Historical Manuscripts Collection at the University of Missouri. Robert Lusk of the Huron *Evening Huronite* and W. R. Ronald of the Mitchell *Evening Republican* gave the author access to their materials relating to the domestic allotment plan of farm relief. The few remaining files of the late Frank Murphy of Wheaton, Minnesota, were also examined, as well as the papers of Chester C. Davis, S. X. Way, and Coe I. Crawford.

UNITED STATES GOVERNMENT DOCUMENTS

Artesian and Underflow Investigation, 52 Cong., 1 Sess. Sen. Ex. Doc., 41, Pt. 2.

Congressional Directory. Government Printing Office, Washington, D. C., 1921.

Congressional Record. Government Printing Office, Washington, D. C., 1920-1936.

Fifteenth Census of the United States, 1930, Agriculture, II, Pt. 1. Government Printing Office, Washington, D. C.

Hearings Before a Subcommittee of the Committee on Banking and Currency, United States Senate, On Operation of the National and Federal Reserve Banking Systems, 71 Cong., 3 Sess. Government Printing Office, Washington, 1931.

Report of the Director of the United States Geological Survey, 1901, Pt. 4. Government Printing Office, Washington, 1902.

Report of the United States Geological Survey, v17, 1896. Government Printing Office, Washington, 1896.

Report of the United States Geological Survey, v18, 1897. Government Printing Office, Washington, 1897.

Report of the Joint Commission of Agricultural Inquiry, 67 Cong., 1 Sess., H. Rept., 408, 4 Pts. Government Printing Office, Washington, 1922.

Report of the Migratory Bird Commission, 1933. Government Printing Office, Washington, 1934.

Senate Report, "Emergency Agricultural Bill," 973, Serial No. 9488, 72 Cong., 1 Sess. Government Printing Office, Washington, 1932.

Senate Report, "The Agricultural Surplus Control Bill," 1304, Serial No. 8629, 69 Cong., 2 Sess. Government Printing Office, Washington, 1927.

Statistical Abstract of the United States. Government Printing Office, Washington, 1930.

Stock Exchange Practices, Hearings Before the Committee on Banking and Currency, United States Senate, 72 Cong., 1 Sess. 1932. Government Printing Office, Washington, 1932.

Stock Exchange Practices, Hearings Before the Committee on Banking and

Currency, United States Senate, 72 Cong., 2 Sess., 1933. Government Printing Office, Washington, 1933.

Yearbook of the United States Department of Agriculture, Government Printing Office, Washington. For the years, 1905, 1906, 1907, 1919, and 1940.

State and Local Records

Annual Report of the South Dakota Commissioner of Insurance to the Governor, n.p., 1929.

Annual Report of the Rural Credit Board for the State of South Dakota. Hipple Printing Company, Pierre, South Dakota, 1922.

Annual Report of the Rural Credit Board for the State of South Dakota, n.p., 1923.

Annual Report of the Rural Credit Board for the State of South Dakota, Hipple Printing Company, Pierre, South Dakota, 1924.

Annual Report of the Rural Credit Board for the State of South Dakota, n.p., 1925.

State of South Dakota, Report of the Rural Credits Board. Mark D. Scott, Printer, Sioux Falls, South Dakota, 1926.

State of South Dakota, Report of the Rural Credits Board. n.p., 1927.

State of South Dakota, Report of the Rural Credits Board. Hipple Printing Company, Pierre, South Dakota, 1928.

State of South Dakota, Report of the Rural Credits Board. n.p., 1929.

State of South Dakota, Report of the Rural Credits Board. n.p., 1930.

Report by W. M. Willy to South Dakota Rural Credits Board. n.p., 1931.

"Special Report of the Rural Credit Department to the Members of the Legislature of the State of South Dakota," January 8, 1945. Mimeographed copy in possession of the author.

Report of an Investigation of the Rural Credit Department. n.p., 1932.

First Biennial Report of the South Dakota Cement Commission. State Publishing Company, Pierre, South Dakota, 1926.

Second Biennial Report of the South Dakota Cement Commission. Hipple Printing Company, Pierre, South Dakota, 1928.

Tenth Biennial Report of the South Dakota Cement Commission. n.p., 1944.

Twenty Years of Progress and Successful Operation. Published by the South Dakota State Cement Commission, 1944.

Fifth Biennial Report of the South Dakota Executive Accountant. The Daily *Leader,* Madison, South Dakota, 1920.

Seventh Biennial Report of the South Dakota Executive Accountant. Hipple Printing Company, Pierre, South Dakota, 1923-24.

Report of the South Dakota Coal Mining Commission to the Governor of South Dakota. Hipple Printing Company, Pierre, South Dakota, 1922.

Fourth Biennial Report of the South Dakota Coal Mining Commission to the Governor of South Dakota. n.p., 1926.

Report of Special Committee Appointed by the Legislature of South Dakota to Investigate the State-Owned Coal Mine. n.p., February 25, 1925.

Message of Governor Peter Norbeck to the Fifteenth Legislative Session, State of South Dakota. n.p., 1917.

Message of Governor Peter Norbeck to the Sixteenth Legislative Session, State of South Dakota. n.p., 1919.

Report of Hail Insurance Department for the Year Ending June 20, 1929. n.p., Pierre, South Dakota.

Sixth Annual Report of the Department of Game and Fish of South Dakota, June 30, 1913 to June 30, 1914. n.p.

Sixteenth Biennial Report of the South Dakota Superintendent of Banks. Hipple Printing Company, Pierre, South Dakota, 1923-24.

South Dakota Senate Journal. n.p., 1913.

South Dakota Senate Journal. State Publishing Company, Pierre, South Dakota, 1917.

South Dakota Journal of the House. State Publishing Company, Pierre, South Dakota, 1917.

South Dakota Journal of the House. n.p., 1919.

South Dakota Legislative Manual. State Publishing Company, Pierre, South Dakota, 1907.

South Dakota Legislative Manual. State Publishing Company, Pierre, South Dakota, 1911.

South Dakota Legislative Manual. State Publishing Company, Pierre, South Dakota, 1915.

South Dakota Legislative Manual. State Publishing Company, Pierre, South Dakota, 1919.

South Dakota Legislative Manual. Mark D. Scott, Sioux Falls, South Dakota, 1921.

South Dakota Legislative Manual. State Publishing Company, Pierre, South Dakota, 1923.

South Dakota Legislative Manual. State Publishing Company, Pierre, South Dakota, 1927.

South Dakota Legislative Manual. State Publishing Company, Pierre, South Dakota, 1937.

South Dakota Session Laws. Hipple Printing Company, Pierre, South Dakota, 1909.

South Dakota Session Laws. Brown and Saenger, Sioux Falls, South Dakota, 1913.

South Dakota Session Laws. Hipple Printing Company, Pierre, South Dakota, 1915.

South Dakota Session Laws. Hipple Printing Company, Pierre, South Dakota, 1916-17.

South Dakota Session Laws. Hipple Printing Company, Pierre, South Dakota, 1919.

South Dakota Session Laws. State Publishing Company, Pierre, South Dakota, 1921.

Twelfth Biennial Report of the South Dakota State Engineer. State Publishing Company, Pierre, South Dakota, 1927-28.

Records of Incorporation. South Dakota Secretary of State, Pierre, South Dakota, 1901.

Records of Incorporation. North Dakota Secretary of State, Bismarck, North Dakota, 1905.

Records of the Redfield City Auditor, Redfield, South Dakota, 1905-09.

Records of the Registrar, University of South Dakota, Vermillion, South Dakota, 1893.

Teacher's Report, Prairie Center School, District 27, Clay County, Vermillion, South Dakota, 1884-85.

Catalogue, Dakota University, 1887 and 1888-89. Published by the University of Dakota, Vermillion.

Huron *Daily Huronite,* Huron, South Dakota, 1912 to 1920. South Dakota Historical Society, Pierre, South Dakota.

NEWSPAPERS

Huron *Evening Huronite,* Huron, South Dakota, 1920 to 1936. South Dakota Historical Society, Pierre, South Dakota.

Mitchell *Daily Republican,* Mitchell, South Dakota, 1912 to 1920. South Dakota Historical Society, Pierre, South Dakota.

Mitchell *Evening Republican,* Mitchell, South Dakota, 1921 to 1935. In 1935 the name was changed to Mitchell *Daily Republic.* South Dakota Historical Society, Pierre, South Dakota.

New York *Times,* 1916 to 1936. University of Missouri Library.

Pierre *Daily Capital Journal,* Pierre, South Dakota, 1912 to 1936. South Dakota Historical Society, Pierre, South Dakota.

Pierre *Daily Dakotan,* Pierre, South Dakota, 1916 to 1932. South Dakota Historical Society, Pierre, South Dakota.

Sioux City *Journal,* Sioux City, Iowa, 1916 to 1934. Sioux City Public Library.

Sioux City *Tribune,* Sioux City, Iowa, 1916 to 1936. Sioux City Public Library.

The author consulted scores of other newspapers, as indicated in the footnotes, on specific state and national issues.

BOOKS AND SPECIAL STUDIES

Baird, Frieda, and Claude L. Benner, *Ten Years of Federal Intermediate Credits.* The Brookings Institution, Washington, D. C., 1933.

Baker, Richard C., *The Tariff Under Roosevelt and Taft.* Democrat Printing Company, Hastings, Nebraska, 1941.

Beard, C. A., and Mary, *The Rise of American Civilization.* 2v. The Macmillan Company, New York, 1940.

Black, John D., *Agricultural Reform in the United States.* McGraw-Hill Book Company, New York, 1929.

Black, John D., *Parity, Parity, Parity.* The Harvard Committee on Research in the Social Sciences, 1942.

Blegen, Theodore C., *Norwegian Migration to America, 1825-60.* The Norwegian-American Historical Association, Northfield, Minnesota, 1931.

Bremer, C. D., *American Bank Failures.* Columbia University Press, New York, 1925.

Capper, Arthur, *The Agricultural Bloc.* Harcourt, Brace and Company, New York, 1922.

Christensen, Alice M., "Agricultural Pressure and Government Response in the United States, 1919-1929," Unpublished Ph.D. Thesis, University of California, Berkeley, 1937.

Davis, Joseph S., *The Farm Export Debenture Plan.* Food Research Institute, Stanford University, Palo Alto, California, 1929.

Dunn, Arthur W., *From Harrison to Harding.* 2v. G. P. Putnam's Sons, New York, 1922.

Eliot, Clara, *The Farmers' Campaign for Credit.* D. Appleton and Company, New York, 1929.

Faulkner, H. U., *The Quest for Social Justice.* The Macmillan Company, New York, 1937.

Filler, Louis, *Crusaders for American Liberalism.* Harcourt, Brace and Company, New York, 1939.

Fite, Gilbert C., "The Farm Bloc in the Early Twenties," Unpublished Master's Thesis, University of South Dakota, Vermillion, 1941.

Fossum, Paul R., *The Agrarian Movement in North Dakota*. Johns Hopkins University Studies, Baltimore, 1925.

Fuess, Claude M., *Calvin Coolidge, the Man from Vermont*. Little, Brown and Company, Boston, 1940.

Gaston, Herbert E., *The Nonpartisan League*. Harcourt, Brace and Howe, New York, 1920.

Haynes, Fred E., *Social Politics in the United States*. Houghton Mifflin Company, New York, 1924.

Johnson, Willis F., *The Life of Warren G. Harding*. The John C. Winston Company, Chicago, 1923.

Kenkel, Joseph B., *The Cooperative Elevator Movement*. Catholic University Press, Washington, 1922.

LaFollette, Robert M., *Autobiography*. The Robert M. LaFollette Company, Madison, 1911.

Norbeck, George and Peter, *The Norbecks of South Dakota*. Privately Printed, Redfield, South Dakota, 1938.

Nourse, Edwin G. and associates, *Three Years of the Agricultural Adjustment Administration*. The Brookings Institute, Washington, 1937.

Official Report of the Proceedings of the Eighteenth Republican National Convention. The Tenny Press, New York, 1924.

Olson, Richard, "The Public Career of Peter Norbeck, 1909-21," Unpublished Master's Thesis, University of South Dakota, Vermillion, 1941.

Pecora, Ferdinand, *Wall Street Under Oath*. Simon and Schuster, New York, 1939.

Peterson, E. Frank, *History of Charles Mix County*. H. C. Tucker and Sons, Geddes, South Dakota, 1906.

Pringle, Henry F., *Theodore Roosevelt*. Harcourt, Brace and Company, New York, 1931.

Qualey, Carlton C., *Norwegian Settlement in the United States*. Norwegian-American Historical Association, Northfield, Minnesota, 1938.

Robinson, Doane, *Encyclopedia of South Dakota*. Will A. Beach Printing Company, Sioux Falls, South Dakota, 1925.

Smith, G. M., *South Dakota, Its History and Its People*. 5v. S. J. Clark Publishing Company, Chicago, 1915.

Speh, Henry L., "The Progressive Movement in South Dakota, 1902-1914," Unpublished Master's Thesis, University of South Dakota, Vermillion, 1936.

Spillman, W. J., *Balancing the Farm Output*. Orange Judd Publishing Company, New York, 1927.

Stokdyk, E. A., and Charles H. West, *The Farm Board*. The Macmillan Company, New York, 1930.

Seligman, E. R. A., *The Economics of Farm Relief*. Columbia University Press, New York, 1929.

Sullivan, Mark, *Our Times*. 6v. Charles Scribner's Sons, New York, 1925-36.

Taussig, F. W., *The Tariff History of the United States*. G. P. Putnam's Sons, New York, 1930.

Visher, Stephen S., *The Geography of South Dakota*. State Geological Survey Bulletin, no. 8, Vermillion, South Dakota, 1918.

Webb, Walter P., *The Great Plains*. Houghton Mifflin Company, New York, 1931.

Wilbur, R. L., and A. M. Hyde, *The Hoover Policies*. Charles Scribner's Sons, New York, 1937.

White, Horace, *Money and Banking*. Ginn and Company, New York, 1935.

Wiley, C. A., *Agriculture and the Business Cycle Since 1920*, University of Wisconsin Studies in the Social Sciences and History, No. 15, Madison, 1930.

Willis, H. Parker, and John M. Chapman, *The Banking Situation*. Columbia University Press, New York, 1934.

ARTICLES

Briggs, Harold E., "The Settlement and Economic Development of the Territory of Dakota," University of Iowa, *Studies in the Social Sciences*, Vol. X (1932), 90-103.

Coolidge, Calvin, "Address by Calvin Coolidge," *The Black Hills Engineer*, Vol. XVIII (November, 1930), 344-45.

Christopherson, Fred C., "A State Goes Into Business and Out Again," *Nation's Business*, Vol. XVII (May, 1929), 48-50.

Flynn, John T., "The Marines Land in Wall Street," *Harper's*, Vol. CLXIX (July, 1934), 149-55.

Hanson, Earl, "Iceland's Millennium," *World's Work*, Vol. LIX (January 30, 1930), 92-96.

Ireton, Robert E., "The Legislatures and the Railroads," *Review of Reviews*, Vol. XXXVI (August, 1907), 217-20.

Kelley, Darwin N., "McNary-Haugen Bills, 1924-28," *Agricultural History*, Vol. XIV (1940), 170-80.

Knittel, Barbara Elrod, "Peter Norbeck, Pioneer and Legislator," *The American Swedish Monthly*, Vol. XXX (October, 1936), 14-15.

Norbeck, Peter, "For the Whole Family," *The Country Gentleman*, Vol. LXXXV (February 14, 1920), 4.

Norbeck, Peter, "The Voluntary Allotment," *The Farm Journal*, Vol. LVI (October, 1932), 5-6.

Ravndal, B. Bie, "The Scandinavian Pioneers of South Dakota," *South Dakota Historical Collections*, Vol. XII (1924), 297-330.

Robinson, Doane, "Inception and Development of the Rushmore Idea," *The Black Hills Engineer*, Vol. XVIII (November, 1930), 334.

Ronald, Malcolm B., "The Dakota Twins," *The Atlantic Monthly*, Vol. CLVIII (September, 1936), 36.

Ronald, William R., "Farmers' Troubles and a Remedy," *Current History*, Vol. XXXVIII (April, 1933), 35-40.

Ronald, William R., "The Origin of the Domestic Allotment Plan," *Congressional Digest*, Vol. XII (February, 1933), 37-38.

Tiffany, Burton E., "The Initiative and Referendum in South Dakota," *South Dakota Historical Collections*, Vol. XII (1924), 331-66.

Tucker, Ray T., "Those Sons of Wild Jackasses," *North American Review*, Vol. CCXXIX (February, 1930), 231-39.

Walker, Lewis, "Abuses in the Grain Trade of the Northwest," *Annals of the American Academy*, Vol. XVIII (November, 1901), 488-90.

Wilson, M. L., "The Domestic Allotment Plan," *Day and Hour Series*, University of Minnesota (1933).

Unsigned:

"A Big Tariff Twister on the Horizon," *Literary Digest*, Vol. XC (July 3, 1926), 5-7.

"Game Refuge Bill Becomes Law," *American Game*, Vol. XVIII (March, 1929), 27-30.

"The Migratory Bird Conservation Act," *Bird-Lore*, Vol. XXXI (March-April, 1929), 152-59.

R. Alton Lee

When asked about the origins of his interest in history, Gilbert C. Fite cited Clifford Roloff, his teacher at Wessington Springs Academy and Junior College, as his first inspiration. To complete his bachelor's work, Fite then enrolled at the University of South Dakota where Herbert S. Schell further refined and directed his budding enthusiasm in the specific direction of agricultural history. Fite wrote his master's thesis on the farm bloc of the Roaring Twenties under Schell's tutelage. This success encouraged him to write his doctoral dissertation at the University of Missouri on Peter Norbeck, who was South Dakota's first native-born governor and United States senator and a major proponent of federal farm relief. This book, first published in 1948, is a revision of that dissertation.[1]

Not only has Fite's account of Norbeck's life withstood the test of time, but comparatively little else has been written about the South Dakotan since this book first appeared. In 2002, filmmaker Mark Zwonitzer produced "Mount Rushmore" on the making of the great monument. The film echoes Fite's analysis of Norbeck's relationship with temperamental sculptor Gutzon Borglum, documenting that Norbeck endured the artist's "eccentricities, rude behavior, and fiscal irresponsibilities." Without the South Dakota senator's patience and faith in the project, it would have died aborning in the absence of the vital assistance of federal funding, which Norbeck succeeded in obtaining despite the sculptor's annoying actions.[2]

New works based on new resources have been few through the years. Lydia Norbeck's lengthy memoir, "Recollections of the Years," appeared in *South Dakota Historical Collections* in 1978, offering the perspective of Norbeck's supportive wife.[3] The memoir reveals Lydia Norbeck to be a woman of her times, a loyal wife whose work with family and home was essential to her husband's success. Although she viewed her role as that of helpmate, she realized that women's roles were changing and encouraged her children to make their own choices.

In an engrossing essay in 2002, Suzanne Barta Julin used new sources to trace Norbeck's role in the Sylvan Lake Hotel controversy, adding significantly to his later story. By attempting to influence the location of the hotel and acquire the services of Frank Lloyd Wright as its planner, the senator pursued his long-time interest in promoting tourism. By 1935, however, his health was deteriorating, his political clout was waning, and he was the sole Republican on the Custer State Park commission that made these decisions. Tom Berry, reelected governor in the Democratic landslide in 1934, appointed two members of his own party to join Norbeck on the park board, and they eventually named a native South Dakotan as architect.

During the negotiations, Norbeck's fears that Wright might be an even more temperamental artist than Borglum proved to be true. Even so, the senator believed Wright's artistic theories would better serve South Dakota's interests than the contemporary local "peeled-log-and-boulder" style that eventually won out. By declining to submit proposed sketches without compensation, Wright refused to compromise his professional standards as the park-board majority demanded. Norbeck and the state lost the services of the great designer when the Democratic members voted for Sioux Falls architect Harold Spitznagel to plan the hotel and to locate it in a spot Norbeck believed to be inferior. As Julin concludes, "When art met politics in the Black Hills, art lost."[4]

Several other authors since 1948 have addressed aspects of Norbeck's career. In 1967, Donald W. Grebin traced Norbeck's role in the South Dakota Council of National Defense in World War I in his master's thesis at the University of South Dakota. The following year, Michael A. Turchen analyzed "selected speeches" of Norbeck for his thesis at the same institution. In 1974, the *Water Well Journal* discussed Norbeck's career in producing artesian wells, and in 1980, John N. Olsgaard described his papers in *South Dakota History*. In 1989, Larry Remele's "An Experiment in State-Sponsored Economy" analyzed the Norbeck-sponsored socialistic programs that were inspired by the liberal progressive Republican movement and the agenda of the Nonpartisan League, which had captured the fancy of North Dakota voters. Norbeck feared the league's appeal to South Dakotans and worked to offset it through these programs.[5]

Some essays on Great Plains statesmen in general that mention Norbeck include Paul H. Carlson and Steve Porter, "South Dakota Congressmen and the Hundred Days of the New Deal," in *South Dakota History*; Philip A. Grant, Jr., "Congressional Leaders From the Great Plains, 1921-1932," in *North Dakota History*; Elizabeth Evenson Williams, "The Editor as Politician," in *American Journalism*; and Greg M. Wysk, "The East and West Are One," in *South Dakota History*.[6] David A. Horowitz in *Beyond Left & Right* also includes Norbeck in his analysis of Populist insurgents. None of these works, however, materially affect Fite's presentation and interpretation of Norbeck's political career.[7]

Seen in the broad historical perspective of three-quarters of a century, Norbeck's achievements remain significant today. He doggedly pursued Theodore

Rooseveltian progressivism throughout his political career, even ending it with a ringing endorsement of the Democratic Roosevelt's policies of expansion of governmental powers to help the common people. His liberalism in pursuit of causes for his constituents never faltered. Norbeck himself considered his rural-credits program to assist South Dakota farmers as his greatest achievement, but this experiment in state socialism and other similar projects, such as the state coal mine and cement plant and proposed state construction of hydroelectric dams on the Missouri River, were visionary in scope. Except for the cement plant, which operated successfully for three-quarters of a century, Norbeck's experiments in state socialism failed or, as Larry Remele observed, enjoyed only "qualified success."[8] More lastingly, Norbeck sponsored important railroad legislation, good roads and highways, a grain-marketing act, free textbooks for children, and assistance to veterans of World War I while serving as state senator and governor. His greatest achievements, however, stemmed from his innate love of natural beauty and the outdoors.

Today, Peter Norbeck is best remembered for his contributions to the creation of Custer State Park and of Mount Rushmore. His insistence that the Needles Highway in the Black Hills, a part of the Peter Norbeck Scenic Byway, be constructed without damaging the area's natural beauty proved crucial to its aesthetic success. It is difficult to conceive of the carving of America's "Shrine to Democracy" without Norbeck's political support and personal mediation between the artistic Borglum and the insistent donors and bureaucrats who wanted rules and proper procedures to be followed. "As long as the imperishable granite of Mount Rushmore remains," Fite concludes, "the names of Borglum and Norbeck will be remembered" (p. 207).

Norbeck's name must also be associated with his promotion of the Migratory Bird Act of 1929, which provided sanctuaries and other safeguards to protect wild fowl from probable extinction (pp. 144-48). Likewise, he cooperated with Jay N. Darling, Pulitzer Prize-winning political cartoonist to support the Migratory Bird Stamp Act in 1934. This program of competition in designing the annual hunting stamp continues today. Darling and Norbeck joined forces after Franklin D. Roosevelt appointed Darling to head the Bureau of Biological Survey, later known as the Fish and Wildlife Service.[9]

As chairman of the Senate Banking and Currency Committee following the Great Crash of 1929, Norbeck also deserves great credit for doggedly pursuing the investigation of Wall Street activities despite scathing denunciations that he was retarding economic recovery. These activities took a decidedly positive turn when he secured the services of Ferdinand Pecora as committee counsel, and the probe subsequently became known popularly as the Pecora Committee. These efforts resulted in significant regulations to protect stock-market investors over the next seven decades (pp. 168-83).

The South Dakota senator devoted his public career to helping agricultural interests and to bringing economic equality to his major constituents. While the term "family farm" is not used here, Norbeck's basic goal was to preserve this venerable institution. He won a third term for his Senate seat in 1932 and quickly became one of those progressive Republicans who enthusiastically supported Roosevelt's New Deal programs, especially the agricultural policies designed to preserve the family farm. His support of the Democratic president's efforts bitterly alienated the reactionary leadership of his own party when he endorsed the reelection of Franklin D. Roosevelt in 1936 over opponent Alf Landon of Kansas, the Republican leadership's choice (pp. 202–4).

It is tempting to speculate on Norbeck's probable attitude on agricultural policy had he served in the Senate following World War II. During this later period, agricultural practices underwent sea changes. Mechanization (especially the application of tractor power), use of electricity, insecticides and herbicides, biotechnology, and the increased role of computers truly revolutionized the industry and made it a highly capitalized one, ensuring the extinction of the family farm.[10] Commercialized farmers ruthlessly exploited the federal programs subsidizing agriculture over that half-century. As a result, those rugged agriculturalists for whom Norbeck fought so gallantly have almost disappeared. One can be certain that the South Dakotan would have both disapproved and yet insisted that the enormous expansion of federal powers be focused on serving his favorite constituents, the small farmers of the Land of Infinite Variety.

Gilbert Fite concludes, "The estimate placed on Norbeck and his work will be gauged by the same yardstick that future historians will apply to the New Deal in general" (p. 206). The New Deal and the philosophy of the policies Peter Norbeck pursued have survived a number of schools of revisionist historical interpretations over the decades. No major New Deal program has yet been repealed, and even modern conservative presidents such as Ronald Reagan have adopted Franklin Roosevelt as their patron saint. In retrospect, Norbeck can truly be judged as one of the most prominent South Dakota statesmen of the twentieth century for his outstanding contributions to both state and nation.

Notes

1. "Agricultural History Talks to Gilbert Fite," *Agricultural History* 78 (Spring 2004): 222-23. *See also* Introduction to *Agricultural Legacies*, ed. R. Alton Lee (Vermillion: University of South Dakota Press, 1986), pp. ix–x.

2. Bill Corbett, review of film "Mount Rushmore," *Journal of American History* 89 (Dec. 2002): 1165–66.

3. Nancy Tystad Koupal, ed., "Lydia Norbeck's 'Recollections of the Years,'" *South Dakota Historical Collections* 39 (1978): 1-147.

4. Julin, "Art Meets Politics: Peter Norbeck, Frank Lloyd Wright, and the Sylvan Lake Hotel Commission," *South Dakota History* 32 (Summer 2002): 117-48; quotation on p. 148.

5. Grebin, "The South Dakota Council of Defense, 1917–1919" (M.A. thesis, University of South Dakota, 1967); Turchen, "An Analysis of Selected Speeches of Peter Norbeck" (M.A. thesis, University of South Dakota, 1968); "Peter Norbeck: Well Driller, Statesman," *Water Well Journal* 28 (Oct. 1974): 35–37; Olsgaard, "Dakota Resources: The Peter Norbeck Papers at the University of South Dakota," *South Dakota History* 10 (Spring 1980): 147-51; Remele, "An Experiment in State-Sponsored Economy: Peter Norbeck and William Henry McMaster," in *South Dakota Leaders: From Pierre Chouteau, Jr., to Oscar Howe*, ed. Herbert T. Hoover and Larry J. Zimmerman (Vermillion: University of South Dakota Press, 1989), pp. 207–19.

6. Carlson and Porter, "South Dakota Congressmen and the Hundred Days of the New Deal," *South Dakota History* 8 (Fall 1978): 327–39; Grant, "*Congressional Leaders from the Great Plains, 1921-1932*," *North Dakota History* 46 (Winter 1979): 19–23; Williams, "The Editor as Politician: W. R. Ronald and the Agricultural Adjustment Act of 1933," *American Journalism* 13 (Winter 1996): 48–59; Wysk, "'The East and West Are One': The Missouri River Bridge at Mobridge," *South Dakota History* 29 (Spring 1999): 23–43.

7. Horowitz, *Beyond Left & Right: Insurgency and the Establishment* (Urbana: University of Illinois Press, 1997).

8. Remele, "Experiment in State-Sponsored Economy," p. 214.

9. James B. Trefethen, *An American Crusade for Wildlife* (New York: Winchester Press, 1975), pp. 219-22.

10. Based on interviews with contemporary Kansas farmers, I have detailed many of these changes in *T-Town on the Plains* (Manhattan, Kans.: Sunflower University Press, 1999).

INDEX